DENIS DIDEROT

RAMEAU'S NEPHEW
—
LE NEVEU DE RAMEAU

Open Book Classics

Denis Diderot

Rameau's Nephew
—
Le Neveu de Rameau

A Multi-Media Bilingual Edition

Edited by Marian Hobson

Translated by Kate E. Tunstall and Caroline Warman

Music researched and played by the
Conservatoire national supérieur de musique et de danse de Paris
under the direction of Pascal Duc

http://www.openbookpublishers.com

All external links were active on 14/6/2016 unless otherwise stated and have been archived via the Internet Archive Wayback Machine at https://archive.org/web

Digital material and resources associated with this volume are available at http://www.openbookpublishers.com/isbn/9781909254909#resources

This is the fourth volume of our Open Book Classics series:

ISSN (Print): 2054-216X
ISSN (Online): 2054-2178

ISBN Paperback: 978-1-909254-90–9
ISBN Hardback: 978-1-909254-91-6
ISBN Digital (PDF): 978-1-909254-92-3
ISBN Digital ebook (epub): 978-1-909254-93-0
ISBN Digital ebook (mobi): 978-1-909254-94-7
DOI: 10.11647/OBP.0098

All paper used by Open Book Publishers is SFI (Sustainable Forestry Initiative), and PEFC (Programme for the Endorsement of Forest Certification Schemes) Certified.

Printed in the United Kingdom, United States and Australia by Lightning Source for Open Book Publishers.

Contents

List of Musical Pieces

The music mentioned by Diderot in *Rameau's Nephew* is French and Italian, although Diderot was also well aware of the work of other foreign composers, such as C.P.E. Bach. The pieces specially performed and recorded for this multi-media edition were chosen to provide samples of music or composers that are less well known today, or to give examples of transcription, one of the principal ways that pieces came to be known and played in a private setting at the time.

Throughout this book the musical note symbol identifies when a recording is available. To access these musical pieces either click on the symbol or refer to the relevant endnote. If your device supports MP3 files you will be able to listen to the music directly. Alternatively, you can access the music online by following the links or scanning the QR codes provided.

The musical extracts recorded for this edition are available to download at https://www.openbookpublishers.com/isbn/9781783740079#resources.

Clémentine Frémont, traverso
Josef Žák, violin
Tatsuya Hatano, violin
Rémy Petit, cello
Felipe Guerra, harpsichord

Recording available at http://dx.doi.org/10.11647/OBP.0044.04

Score available at http://gallica.bnf.fr/ark:/12148/btv1b9057234b/f2.image.r=l'art de la modulation.langEN

Fig. 1 The 'real' Rameau's Nephew? Reproduction of a drawing by J.G. Wille, at present not traced. The reproduction was first published by G. Isambert in his edition of Diderot, *Le Neveu de Rameau*, with notices, notes and bibliography (Paris: A. Quantin, 1883).

Preface to the Second Edition

In a famous Parisian chess café, a down-and-out, HIM, accosts a former acquaintance, ME, who has made good, more or less. They talk about chess, about genius, about good and evil, about music, they gossip about the society in which they move, one of extreme inequality, of corruption, of envy, and about the circle of hangers-on in which the down-and-out abides. The down-and-out from time to time is possessed with movements almost like spasms, in which he imitates, he gestures, he rants. And towards half past five, when the warning bell of the Opera sounds, they part, going their separate ways. This is the plot of *Rameau's Nephew*.

Why present another translation of such a well-known work?

Translations need to adapt the work being translated to the language into which it is being put; so much is obvious. Less so is that language creates a context that changes constantly, sometimes at great speed. There is a need for renewal in the reception of a work in translation. A new *Rameau's Nephew*, we felt, was called for.

Why an interactive, online, Open Access edition?

Such an edition opens possibilities not available to earlier translations — techniques move on, as well as languages. An interactive, online edition is particularly suited to Diderot, who wrote mostly in dialogue, though sometimes the dialogue was asymmetric (as in *Rameau's Nephew*, between HIM and ME). In fact, he loved talking. As if in conversation, his writings change their relation to the reader constantly, forcing her to laugh, to argue, to wonder. He usually doesn't write in discursive form but in fragmentary, often teasing fashion. He would like an audience, clearly, he tacks around to force one into being and into action — but he is dead, he is words on a page (and dust in the Church of Saint Roch, Paris). We may come closer to discussing with him through an interactive edition than in any other way.

 http://dx.doi.org/10.11647/OBP.0098.01

Diderot and the Web

'Diderot' is a site under construction. The energetic, the brilliant, the sometimes overbearing, sometimes timid man, or what remains of him, lies unpantheonized somewhere in the Église Saint Roch, in the rue Saint Honoré. An atheist, his friends had to find a sympathetic priest who would allow church burial, and then, gravely ill, he had been moved to the rue de Richelieu to die, so as to be within the parish, his bones were then disturbed in a search for lead from coffins, to make bullets, during the Revolution. Likewise, his manuscripts lie even now lacking a definitive edition (how unlike his friend/enemy Rousseau). Yet in an online memorial[1] 'amorifera', the bearer of love, saying she shares his birthday, October 5th, gaily invites Diderot to dance — he himself had said he was never very good at dancing, much as he would have liked to dance well (one can imagine him repeating this even as he accepts the invitation across death and dust).[2] And he would surely have been convulsed with laughter at one of the adverts funding this memorial site, lady 'singles' seeking partners.

By telescoping time, we can imagine that he would have published his great *Encyclopédie* online.[3] Not merely for the geographical reach it makes possible, much as this would have enthused him: this translator from the English, this critic of colonialism, this satirist of tax manipulators and banking activities, this anxious consciousness of where authoritarian government might lead, would have welcomed no doubt the fluidity and the ability to disappear from notice that the web provides, however imperfectly. Yet, once more, not merely: he wanted what he wrote to produce change. His mind was mobile, but his principles were not, or not

1 See http://www.findagrave.com/cgi-bin/fg.cgi?page=gr&GRid=6239031

2 See the great love poem in which the body-molecules of lovers mix after death, part of a letter to his lover Sophie Volland, 15th October 1759, written 'au Grandval', that is, from the country house of the materialist philosopher, the Baron d'Holbach, in Diderot, *Lettres à Sophie Volland*, édition présentée et annotée par Marc Buffat et Odile Richard-Pauchet (Paris: Non Lieu, 2010), Non Lieu, collection 'lettres ouvertes', pp. 77–79: 'if it were given to us to make up a being in common; if in the sequence of centuries I were again to make a whole with you; if your dissolved lover's molecules were to start to shake, to move around and to seek for yours, scattered abroad in nature...' (grateful thanks to Odile R-P for this reference; translation MH).

3 As has been done now, from Chicago, *Encyclopédie, ou dictionnaire raisonné des sciences, des arts et des métiers, etc.*, eds. Denis Diderot and Jean le Rond d'Alembert. University of Chicago: ARTFL Encyclopédie Project (Spring 2016 edition), ed. by Robert Morrissey and Glenn Roe, http://encyclopedie.uchicago.edu/.

too much. He might dodge and duck and dive to get out of prison or to help a friend who had insulted some great ladies (thereby hurting perhaps even endangering, others);[4] the atheism, the materialism that are the load bearers of his writings did not change: less Church, less intolerance, more toleration of other sexualities, other nations, other opinions. Above all, he sought more freedom to speculate. In his great writing, this surfaces mostly in quizzical, satirical or paradoxical works, often in dialogue. First among which is *Rameau's Nephew*. Would he, Denis Diderot, have published this work online had it been possible?

Well: he didn't publish it in any form, but rather seems to have left it in manuscript and probably in the care of others, several others, without clear instructions that we know of as to what destiny he designed for it. This may have been hesitation, or perhaps mobility of intention — he liked to 'wind others up' like clocks, as English slang so forcefully says, yet he was fearful of giving pain. And if it seems from his autograph manuscript (though less from other copies of the text)[5] that he deliberately arranged the beginning and the end of his *Rameau's Nephew* in terms of precise place and time, one can wonder whether the naming of names that marks out this satire doesn't also include a kind of reserving of final meaning, a speculative swinging, so that the reader cannot always be sure exactly what the aim is. One example: our no. 76 — a note only possible since 2012 and Colin Jones' fine work on the Saint-Aubin manuscript held at the National Trust, Waddesdon Manor, UK,[6] where appears the magnificent caricature of the naked Deschamps, a famous actress and prostitute, being escorted from the house of a tax-collector, Villemorien. This may fill in detail for the reader who wonders why the very next satirized name to be mentioned, in apparently unrelated way, is precisely that of Villemorien.[7] So the cultural effect of the web is to accelerate; in the case of an edition, it quickly coordinates items which might otherwise have taken years to connect. A

4 See M. Hobson's French edition, Denis Diderot, *Seconde Satyre: le Neveu de Rameau* (Geneva: Droz, 2013), pp. 205–13.

5 See the end of this Preface, and also material round the posting of Goethe's translation, at http://www.openbookpublishers.com/9781909254909#resources

6 Colin Jones, 'French Crossings IV: Vagaries of Passion and Power in Enlightenment Paris', *Transactions of the Royal Historical Society*, 23 (December 2013): 3–35. A truly wonderful story, a scatological companion to Rameau the Nephew's account of Bertin and Mlle Hus having sex.

7 Yet another example of how the web can change our view of Diderot's writing, if as do many still, we see it as lacking connection and hopping from subject to subject.

further example: in a chess match played blindfold in London in April 1793 by the great chess-player, composer, and acquaintance of Diderot, Philidor, the pieces, so a contemporary London newspaper tells us, were placed by a nephew of Rameau.[8] This can hardly be our Nephew, dead in great poverty in 1777, but presumably another of the numerous progeny of Rameau the composer's brother. The anecdote allows the surmise that there were connections maintained between the two families which very likely went beyond the mere possibility that Philidor and this Rameau both happened to be keeping a safe distance from Paris during the Revolution.

There is, then, a great deal more that might be found out about the people alluded to in the satire, and why Diderot picks them out. The digital resources associated with this edition are therefore also a site under construction, open to addition and correction. And to speculation. For there exists a kind of connection between Rameau the Nephew and Rousseau, Jean-Jacques, a faint link, but present. A self-description of Rousseau, only known by a passage in a Rousseau manuscript unpublished in his lifetime is actually quoted about Rameau the Nephew: 'Nothing is more unlike the man than he is himself' ('rien ne dissemble plus de lui que lui-même'). This passage, describing HIM, appears here at the very beginning of the dialogue. It had, however, already been used by Rousseau to describe himself in *Le Persifleur* [*The Debunker*], a manuscript newspaper which he and Diderot briefly worked on in the late 1740s, and which wouldn't be published until 1781.[9] Indeed, some of the discussion between ME and HIM might seem like shadowy versions of the debates between those two 'enemy brothers', in Jean Fabre's fine phrase, which we may imagine to have taken place in the period of their close friendship, the 1740s. And it is hard to imagine Diderot writing about Rameau, uncle or nephew, without having Jean-Jacques in mind, he whose bad relations with the great composer had been one cause of trouble to the *Encyclopédie* as an undertaking.

8 *Sporting Magazine*, 2(1) (April 1793): 8, 'Chess Club at Mr. Parsloe's St. James's street, *Sporting Magazine*, 3(5) (February 1794): 282; Paul Metzner, who found this reference, believed it to refer to our Rameau's nephew, which is not possible, as he had been dead nearly twenty years (see *Crescendo of the Virtuoso: Spectacle, Skill and Self-Promotion in Paris during the Age of Revolution* (Berkeley, Los Angeles and London: University of California Press, 1968)).

9 There is no other evidence that Diderot knew the remark, seemingly made about himself by Rousseau. See M. Hobson, 'From Diderot to Rousseau via Rameau' ['Diderot et Rousseau par Rameau interposé'], in *Diderot and Rousseau: Networks of Enlightenment*, ed. and trans. by Kate E. Tunstall and Caroline Warman (Oxford: Voltaire Foundation, 2011), pp. 15–29.

Music in *Rameau's Nephew*

That Diderot admired Rameau's music is clear, even when through the mouth of the Nephew he sends up some of the formulaic quality of its component parts in music or in libretto. It has been recognized at least since the crucial work of Daniel Heartz,[10] how important music is in Diderot's dialogue. But since then, Diderot criticism has tended to see the dialogue as enacting the cusp of an important change in eighteenth-century music, from Rameau to the 'nouveaux chants' as ME and the Nephew call the music of the opera comique and of its associated composers. The music embedded in our edition offers a development of this, for the selection deliberately shows how much Diderot also refers to music which is not that of the opera comique, and which moreover is not likely to be at all familiar to non-specialist modern readers, even those who are lovers of eighteenth-century music: Hasse, Porpora, and a composer whose name Diderot added in the margin, Traetta, for instance. Our publication, with embedded music, has thus hinted that a rebalancing of ideas about the musical background to the text may be needed.

Much of this music is not well known to a general readership, as we have said. But beyond this, it is not always exactly clear from the text which piece of music HIM or ME are referring to. In introducing music into our edition, we hope that gradually through future work it may become clearer whether Diderot refers in every case to precise pieces or passages of music. A better grasp of this dilemma would throw light on the much more general question of how allusively (or not) Diderot writes, a question whose importance the first part of this preface began to suggest. We have offered suggestions about the music, which can now be discussed and endorsed or corrected.

We could have been content with references to online excerpts. To have done so would have meant to rely on excerpts not always or by any means of the best quality.[11] But the most important innovation for readers is more adventurous: to introduce music, specially recorded for this interactive

10 Daniel Heartz, *Music in European Capitals: The Galant Style 1720–1780* (New York and London: WW. Norton & Co., 2003); Heartz, *From Garrick to Gluck: Essays on Opera in the Age of Enlightenment*, ed. John Rice (New York: Pendragon Press, 2004), Opera series no. 1.

11 Our notes nonetheless supply links for the interested reader.

book, which is embedded in the digital editions and can also be listened to on smart-phones or online. This obviated major problems that we would otherwise have faced: that of the cost of rights, if music recorded on DVD had been used; that of hiring an orchestra, which would have involved huge expense, quite beyond our research budget so generously provided by a grant from the Leverhulme Trust. Even so, our examples are often necessarily limited to excerpts, not whole pieces. Our solution, only possible through the kind cooperation of the *Conservatoire national de musique et de danse de Paris*, is dual: the pieces specially selected, performed and recorded for this multi-media book were chosen, as our first edition indicated, 'to provide samples of music or composers that are less well known today', or 'to give examples of transcription, one of the principal ways that pieces came to be known and played in a private setting at the time',[12] for music circulated in the eighteenth century as much by transcription and private performance as by public performance and publication. Pascal Duc directed its performance by students of the Department of Early Music. For this collaborative work, of translation, edition, performance and commentary, we (PD, MH, KT, CW) renew here the expression of our great gratitude to all the students involved, whether in performance or in recording and in postproduction techniques, as to all the staff of the *Conservatoire* who supported the project.

On some editions of *Le Neveu de Rameau*

In this second edition, in addition to the English translation, we have posted a French version, the one Kate E. Tunstall and Caroline Warman translated. It is that presented in the Droz edition (see note 4 above) and is based on the transcription of Diderot's autograph published by Georges Monval in 1891, but collated against the editions by Jean Fabre and by Henri Coulet,[13] and against a microfilm supplied by the Pierpont Morgan Library, New York, who hold the autograph manuscript. We have also posted, in 'Additional Resources' (at http://www.openbookpublishers.

12 M. Hobson (ed.), *Denis Diderot's 'Rameau's Nephew': A Multi-Media Edition*, translated by K.E. Tunstall and C. Warman. Music researched and played by the Conservatoire National Supérieur de Musique de Paris under the direction of P. Duc (Cambridge: Open Book Publishers, 2014), p. xix, http://dx.doi.org/10.11647/OBP.0044

13 Jean Fabre, edition of Diderot, *Le Neveu de Rameau* (Geneva: Droz, 1950); Henri Coulet, *Le Neveu de Rameau*, vol. XII, Œuvres *completes de Denis Diderot* (édition *DPV*), ed. H. Dieckmann, J. Proust, J. Varloot (Paris: Hermann, 1975–).

com/9781909254909#resources) Goethe's translation into German, 1805, which was the first printed published text of the work *in any language*. Goethe translated from a copy that has disappeared. The first authentic version in French was published by Diderot's daughter in 1823, with the publisher Brière, as volume XXI of Œuvres *inédites de Diderot*. Neither the Brière version nor what can be surmised from Goethe's translation of the original French it used, was that of the autograph from which they differ in slight but interesting ways. For instance, there is one passage in the Goethe version which is not in the autograph and which yet appears in Brière (1823, p. 31); there is a note in the great nineteenth-century edition of Diderot's complete works, by Jules Assézat and Maurice Tourneux (vol. V, p. 408 no. 1) saying that the same passage was in the copy they were using. It is a kind of metacommentary, not attributed to the speaker in the dialogue ME, but to an Editor. In Goethe's version it runs:

> 'Hier findet sich im Manuskript eine Lücke. Die Szene ist verändert und die Sprechenden sind in eins der Häuser bei dem Palais Royal gegangen'.
>
> ['Here there is a gap in the manuscript. The scene has changed, and the speakers have gone into one of the houses near the Palais Royal'.][14]

This passage is lacking in the autograph manuscript.[15] Fabre in his introduction describes this as clearly an intervention in the margin of folio 42 of Tourneux' copy, brought back from Russia, which he attributes to 'an early reader making up by his activity for his lack of intelligence' ('un lecteur précoce aussi zélé que peu intelligent', Fabre, p. xix). There are other jumps in the text which might have attracted a similar comment from Fabre's 'early reader', but have not. The first publisher of the text of Diderot's autograph manuscript (1891), Georges Monval, pointed this out in a note. He quoted the first more or less authentic text, Brière, here:

> *Nota* de l'édition Brière (1823): 'There is here a lacuna in the manuscript and we must suppose that the speakers have gone into the café, where there was a clavichord'.
>
> ['Il y a dans le manuscrit une lacune, et on doit supposer que les interlocuteurs sont entrés dans le café où il y avait un clavecin'.]

14 'Denis Diderot's Rameaus Neffe', with notes by Joanna Raisbeck, additional online resource available at https://www.openbookpublishers.com/shopimages/resources/2.Rameaus-Neffe.pdf, p. 12.

15 See p. 23 of the translation into English by Tunstall and Warman (Open Book Publishers, 2014), p. 39; edition by Hobson (Droz, 2013), p. 25; edition by Fabre (Droz, 1950).

And continued firmly (we are in 1891):

> 'The autograph original shows that there is no lacuna: the speakers have not gone out of the café, where there is no clavichord'.
>
> ['l'original autographe montre qu'il n'y a aucune lacune: les interlocuteurs ne sont pas sortis du café, où il n'y a pas de clavecin'.]

Coulet, in his edition of the text,[16] which is at present by far the most complete as a critical edition, has suggested that this marginal edition comes from alterations made in other copies (those in Leningrad/St. Petersburg, Vandeul I) which suppress mention of the café *la Régence* in which the conversation is taking place, because, as Monval and before him, Asselineau, had pointed out, the 'correctors' haven't understood that the harpsichord on which the Nephew plays is imaginary.[17]

However, following a suggestion from the musicologist David Charlton,[18] it seems possible that we have with this problem an almost effaced sign of a slightly different version. He relates this to 'pp. 77-78 [...] where the text apparently refers to an earlier version of the scene, imagined taking place outdoors in the street instead of the café interior, when 'the neighbours came to their windows'. Charlton believes that the later part of the dialogue, in particular the passages round the nature of song, may incorporate patches of developments out of Diderot's earlier dialogue, *Entretiens sur le 'Fils naturel'*, published in 1757.

Our interactive edition

So we must recognize the still incomplete state of our knowledge about the actual way in which Diderot developed his dialogue. *Rameau's Nephew*, is entitled 'Satyre seconde' and nothing else on the title page of the autograph manuscript. The spelling reminds us of the licentious mythical beast, the goat-man; the work itself has some very funny dirty stories. Yet it is a satire in a different sense, it is stuffed with personal allusions, it names and shames a whole roll of minor actresses and big stars, Grub Street

16 Diderot, *Le Neveu de Rameau*, ed. Henri Coulet (Paris: Hermann, 1989), p. 96 (vol. XII of *DPV*).

17 *Le Neveu de Rameau*, ed. Charles Asselineau (Paris: Poulet-Malassis, 1862).

18 Kindly made in private communication.

inhabitants, dodgy newspapers and especially the then version of bankers, the 'farmers' of taxes or of offices. It takes them off, it takes them down, several or every peg they ever climbed. This kind of edition makes it much easier to understand who these people are, why Diderot may be getting at them. At a click, the reader can cause their portrait and their biography to appear.

The click is worth making — the similarity to our post-financial crisis world is hard to miss: bankers, celebrities, *paparazzi*, rise from the pages, with little sense of shame and often little talent, except for pushing themselves ahead. The dialogue's very lack of conclusion, where the talkers just separate at the sound of the opera bell announcing the performance, leaves us looking at what may be coming towards us, in somewhat shaky or indistinct fashion. The instability of attitude, the changes of scale and weight in what HIM and ME talk of, makes me wonder about what is only a couple of decades down the time-line: 1789, and ask whether its shadow is perceptible in Diderot's dialogue.

Likewise, Diderot seems to foretell a transformation outside politics, one of sensibility, of our relation to our own feeling for music. We hope to have made an understanding of this possible in this edition — the digital form has enabled us to embed into the text pieces of music specially selected and directed by Pascal Duc. This engenders, we hope, an awareness of the musical context of the dialogue, enlarging it well beyond its relation to opera comique.

This bringing forward of Neapolitan comic opera, with its often physical comedy, connects implicitly with Diderot's dazzling descriptions of the Nephew's pantomimes. The foolery performed with musical instruments by the great Swiss clown, Grock (http://www.youtube.com/watch?v=-JUgPO2VF-k, one of many clips), and the telling movements of the great violinist Gidon Kremer when playing (for an extreme and breathtaking version, performed with others and developed into dance, see http://www.youtube.com/watch?v=UAM2y1SOsIs) are both inheritors of the tradition into which Diderot places his dialogue: the near-dancing, the use of the body as an instrument. But the clowning, the spilling-over of expression moves with Rameau the nephew from the active and the liberating into almost painful movements, into bows and scrapes which are as if extorted. He is, but he is also made to be.

So gesture and pantomime as well as utterances explore the self-awareness of HIM, his consciousness of his lack of freedom, subject as a musician both to his instrument and to his audience. HIM has exploited this lack of freedom — he bows, he scrapes with artistic flair. By perfecting his flattery through self-consciousness, by not being identical to what he is made to be by his patrons, he has contrived to turn his very servitude into a kind of liberty, a liberty raised to the second power, arrived at through an awareness of his bonds. His ironic exploitation of his own turpitude brings it to the level of an art. The strange form of the dialogue reinforces this, for it allows a sideways take on what is said, a striking but puzzling contrast between an objectivized persona, HIM, and first person experience — the narrative by ME. The form, a dialogue not as face to face but as if skewed, seems to have been invented by Diderot and it is puzzling that, to my knowledge, this form is only found in German authors who actually met Diderot or who were interested in him: Lessing, Wieland, Herder, F.H. Jacobi.

Indeed, the first interest in *Rameau's Nephew* came from Germany. It was Goethe who at the promptings of Schiller engineered in 1805 its first appearance on the stage of 'world literature' — to use a term first coined by the great German poet himself. It was thus not in French but in Goethe's German translation that the work was first read. One of the reasons why Goethe produced the term '*Weltliteratur*' was to escape the divisions of the Napoleonic wars and to seal the claims of his national literature to an attention equal to that accorded to classical French literature or the works of Shakespeare. It is for this reason that we have posted Goethe's translation in the additional resources available at http://www.openbookpublishers.com/9781909254909#resources, *Weltliteratur* fits the work of Diderot like a glove, if only by the roster of major thinkers who have commented on it: Hegel, Engels, Freud, Bernard Williams.

Each found there a link to his own work. To take the closest to Diderot in time: Hegel probably had personal reasons to draw attention to *Rameau's Nephew* in his *Phenomenology* (1807), for earlier he had asked Goethe for help in obtaining a post. But there are intellectual reasons also. With exemplary insight, through careful quotation, he picks out two main threads in Diderot's dialogue: first, the question of '*species*', *espèce*, translated, for the most part, in the present version as *specimen*. One of the philosophical problems that Hegel embeds in the very structure of his major work is the '*besondere*', the particular. As he moves through the experience of humanity, like a weaver's shuttle between the universal and the singular, all and one, summarizing and linking, he picks out what lies between them, the particular, what can form a 'species', what catches different possible groupings of experience, of moments of thought. And Diderot throughout this work plays with lists, with different ways of collecting together actions and professions and characteristics. The second area on which Hegel insists is music. What appears to interest him most is the way in which Diderot has, through music, sketched out a kind of movement of history, whereby consciousness and hence sensibility make each moment unique, differentiated from the past by what has been in our past. Our ears carry our experience, and we cannot have innocent ears, or innocent experience either. Having listened to the music of the Italian comic opera, Diderot suggests through the mouth of HIM, we cannot go back unchanged and listen to the French composers, to Rameau, as before.

There is another attraction for Hegel. The 'hero' of *Rameau's Nephew* twists and turns in his argument, moving from assertion to negation and back through negation to assertion. Hegel places his discussion of Diderot's work in the moment before the great cataclysm that was the French Revolution, in an historical space where complex historical forces vie against each other, *acting and reacting against each other*. Jean Starobinski, examining in detail the texture of Diderot's writing has pointed out the use of a rhetorical form which is not one of true Hegelian dialectic (where we might move from a thesis which is negated to a new thesis developed from negating the negation) but is that of *chiasmus*. In this figure of rhetoric, a position negated leads us back to the starting point; we do not move on, but stay as it were blocked by a contradiction.[19] Yet Diderot ends his dialogue by letting it swing into an open future, one of generality and indistinctness conveyed by the proverbial saying — 'he who laughs last laughs longest', says HIM.

How then does Diderot structure his dialogue, if it is left wide open? He makes the beginning and end definite in time and place: as said, it begins after lunch, at the café de la Régence; it comes to a stop shortly before five-thirty, when the opera is about to commence — it was close by. Diderot,

19 Jean Starobinski, 'L'emploi du chiasme dans le *Neveu de Rameau*' ['The use of the figure of the chiasme in *Le Neveu de Rameau*'], *Revue de métaphysique et de morale*, 89(2) (1984): 182–96.

then, seems to place different sections of the composition, one after the other, with no discernible linear order. Indeed, one wonders if some sections do not recur as variations on a theme. For example, Voltaire's play, *Mahomet,* occurs twice in relation to Voltaire's public actions, one criticized — his writing *In Praise of Maupéou,* the other praised — his rehabilitation of the judicially murdered Protestant, Jean Calas. The reader in fact wanders and wonders. We move through a hailstorm of allusions, a multitude of moods. We hope that the appreciation of this strange work, the route we take as we read, will be made clearer and livelier by this new translation, and the resources of music and images it brings with it.

What these comments on editions, including our own, show is how little what Diderot was up to was understood by his very early readers and perhaps by his modern ones. The line between studying different editions of a Diderot text and following his game-play may be very hard, even impossible to draw. In the case discussed above at p. 7, Jean Fabre, to whom so much is owed, pointed out how the commentary from a puzzled editor was very early incorporated into the flow of Diderot's text. One can understand why this might have been done if one thinks of his novel *Jacques le fataliste,* where exactly this sort of remark is part of the game played by the writing, and which Schiller and Goethe so much admired.[20]

List of French editions consulted

J.L.J. Brière, *Œuvres inédites de Diderot: le Neveu de Rameau Le Voyage en Hollande, à Paris,* MDCCCXXI [in fact, 1823].

Charles Asselineau, ed. Diderot, *Le Neveu de Rameau* (Paris, 1862).

Jules Assézat and Maurice_Tourneux, *Œuvres complètes de Diderot,* vol. V, *Le Neveu de Rameau* (Paris, 1875).

20 We list here some modern writings which seem to us to endorse the vividness and power of Diderot's dialogue, without necessarily mentioning it: Jérôme David, *Spectres de Goethe: les métamorphoses de la 'littérature mondiale* [*Ghosts of Goethe, Metamorphoses of World Literature*] (Paris: Les Belles Lettres, coll. 'Les prairies ordinaires', 2012), a dialogue for the most part between LUI and MOI [HIM and ME]. Stéphane Audeguy, *Fils unique* [*Only Son*] (Paris: Gallimard, 2010) — an 'autobiography' of Rousseau's elder brother (who disappeared without trace in Rousseau's childhood). Thomas Bernhard, *Wittgenstein's Nephew,* translated Ewald Osers (London: Quartet Books, 1986) [original German, 1983]. Saul Bellow, *Dangling Man* (New York: Vanguard Press, 1944).

Georges Monval, Diderot: *le Neveu de Rameau, Satyre publiée pour la première fois sur le manuscrit original* [...] (Paris, 1891).

Jean Fabre, *Diderot: le Neveu de Rameau,* édition critique avec notes et lexique, (Genève: Droz, 1950).

Henri Coulet, *Le Neveu de Rameau,* vol. XII, Œuvres *completes de Denis Diderot* (édition *DPV*), ed. H. Dieckmann, J. Proust, J. Varloot, vol. XII (Paris: Hermann, 1989).

Denis Diderot, *Contes et romans,* Édition publiée sous la direction de Michel Delon avec la collaboration de Jean-Christophe Abramovici, Henri Lafon et Stéphane Pujol (Paris: Gallimard — Collection Bibliothèque de la Pléiade, no. 25, 2014).

Michel Delon, Denis Diderot, *Le Neveu de Rameau,* Édition de Michel Delon Collection Folio classique (no. 4464) (Paris: Gallimard, 2006).

Denis Diderot, *Satyre Seconde: Le Neveu de Rameau,* ed. Marian Hobson (Droz: Geneva, 2013).

Fig. 2a *Portrait of Denis Diderot* (1766), by Jean-Baptiste Greuze.

Rameau's Nephew

Second Satyre[1]

Vertumnis, quotquot sunt, natus iniquis
['Vertumnus scowled on his birth, and made him a versatile failure']

Horace, Book II, 7th Satire.[2]

It is a habit of mine to go for a walk in the Palais Royal[3] pleasure gardens every afternoon at five, whatever the weather. That's me you see there, always by myself, daydreaming on d'Argenson's bench.[4] I have conversations with myself about politics, love, taste or philosophy. I give in to my mind's every fancy. I let it be master and allow it to pursue the first idea that comes to it, good or mad, and to behave just like those young libertines of ours we see chasing some flighty, pretty courtesan with bright eyes and a snub nose along Foy Walk, leaving her for another one, stalking them all and sticking to none. In my case, my thoughts are my sluts. If it's too cold or too rainy, I like to take shelter in the Café de la Régence and watch chess being played. Paris is the place in all the world, and the Café de la Régence the place in all of Paris, where it is played the best. Rey's café is where
Legal the Unfathomable,[5] Philidor the Cunning,[6] and Competent Mayot 1
do battle, and where you can see the most surprising moves and hear the most vulgar things, for if you can be a clever man and a great chess-player like Legal, you can also be a great chess-player and a dunce, like Foubert and Mayot.[7] One afternoon, when I was there, doing a lot of watching, not much speaking, and listening as little as I could, I was approached by one of the most bizarre characters in a country which, thanks to God's bounty, isn't short of them. He's a mixture of the lofty and the sordid, of good sense and unreason. The notions of what's decent and what's indecent

 http://dx.doi.org/10.11647/OBP.0044.02

must be strangely mixed up in his head since he displays the good qualities that nature has given him unostentatiously and the bad ones shamelessly. Moreover, he is possessed of a strong constitution, a singularly heated imagination, and an exceptionally vigorous set of lungs. If ever you meet him and his originality doesn't stop you in your tracks, either you'll put your fingers in your ears or you'll turn on your heels and run. Heavens, what a terrifying pair of lungs! Nothing is more unlike the man than he himself. Sometimes, he is as thin and pale as someone in the last stages of consumption and you can count his teeth through his cheeks — you'd think he'd not eaten for days or that he'd just come out of a Trappist monastery. A month later, he is as fleshy and replete as if he'd been at a banker's dinner table the whole time or been comfortably cloistered with the Bernardins.[8] Today, skulking in dirty linen, with torn breeches, his coat in tatters, his shoes hanging off his feet, and his head held low, you'd be tempted to call him over and slip him a coin. Tomorrow, hair powdered and curled, well shod and well dressed, he goes about in public, his head held high, and you would almost take him for a respectable man. He lives from one day to the next. Sad or cheery, depending on the circumstances. His first concern when he gets up in the morning is where he'll have dinner; after dinner, he wonders where he'll go for supper. Nightfall brings its own anxiety. Either he makes his way back, on foot, to his tiny attic, unless his landlady has got fed up with waiting for the rent and asked him to return the key, or he falls back on a tavern on the outskirts of town where he waits for dawn with a bit of bread and a mug of beer. When he hasn't even got sixpence in his pocket, which does happen to him sometimes, he has a word with either a cab driver or the coachman of some great lord to see if they'll let him bed down in the straw next to the horses. In the morning, he still has half his mattress in his hair. If the season is mild, he spends the night walking up and down the Cours-la-Reine or the Champs-Elysées.[9] He reappears in town along with the daylight, still wearing the clothes he had on yesterday, which, moreover, sometimes stay on him for the rest of the week. I have no respect for such oddballs. Other people make close acquaintances out of them, even friends. But they do stop me in my tracks once a year when I meet them because their character is so unlike other people's: they disrupt that annoying uniformity which our education, social conventions, and codes of conduct have inculcated in us. If such a man is present in a group, he acts like a pinch of yeast, fermenting and giving a portion of each person's natural individuality back to them. He stirs things up, shakes them about, provokes approval or blame; he makes the truth come out; he reveals who's genuinely good, he unmasks villains; and that's when a man of good sense pricks up his ears and sees the world for what it is.

I had known this one for a long time. He frequented a household that had opened its doors to him because of his talent. They had an only daughter. He kept on swearing to both mother and father that he would marry their daughter. They would shrug their shoulders, laugh in his face, tell him he was mad — but I actually saw him do it. He used to borrow money, which I gave him. He had somehow gained entry to some honest households where a place would always be set for him on the condition he not speak without permission. He would keep silent and eat with rage. Muzzled in this way, he was a magnificent sight. If ever he got it into his head to break the agreement and open his mouth, no sooner had he uttered a word than everyone round the table would shout: Oh Rameau! And then his eyes would burn with rage, and he would go back to eating even more furiously. You were curious to know the man's name, and now you do. He's the nephew of that famous musician[10] who delivered us from Lulli[11] and his plain chant which we had been intoning for more than a hundred years, and who set down all those unintelligible visions and apocalyptic truths about the theory of music which neither he nor anyone else ever really understood, and who left us with a certain number of operas which have some harmony, some snatches of song, some disconnected ideas, some banging and crashing, some flights, some triumphs, some spears, some glories,[12] some murmurings, some breathless victories, along with a few dance tunes which will last forever and which, having killed off the Florentine, will in turn be killed off by the Italian virtuosi — something he foresaw and which made him sombre, unhappy and aggrieved, for there is no one as bad-tempered, not even a pretty woman who wakes up in the morning with a spot on her nose, as an author threatened with outliving his own reputation, as we are reminded by the examples of Marivaux[13] and Crébillon the Younger.[14]

He comes up to me. Aha! There you are, Mister Philosopher, and what are you doing hanging around here with this bunch of layabouts? Don't tell me you too are wasting your time pushing pawns about a board? That's what people mockingly call playing chess or draughts.

ME — No, but when I've got nothing better to do, I enjoy spending a few moments watching other people doing a good job of it.

HIM — In that case, you don't enjoy yourself very often; apart from Legal and Philidor, the rest of them don't have a clue.

ME — And what about Monsieur de Bissy then?[15]

HIM — Monsieur de Bissy is to chess-playing what Mademoiselle Clairon is to acting. What each of them knows is everything that can be taught.[16]

ME — You're very hard on them. I see that only men of sublime genius escape your judgement.

HIM — Yes: at chess, draughts, poetry, eloquence, music, and other nonsense like that. What's the point of mediocrity in such genres?

ME — Not much, I agree. But the thing is that you need a lot of people working really hard at something for one man of genius to emerge. He is one in a multitude. But let's move on. It's been an age since I saw you last. You know, when I don't see you, I barely think about you — but I'm always pleased to see you when I do. What have you been up to?

HIM — What you, me, and everyone else have been doing: some good things, some bad things, and a great deal of nothing. And sometimes I've been hungry and I've had something to eat when I could; and having eaten, I got thirsty and sometimes I got a drink. Meanwhile, my beard kept growing, and when it did, I had it shaved off.

ME — You shouldn't have. That was the only thing missing for you to be a sage.

HIM — I agree. My forehead is large and furrowed, my eyes blaze, my nose is prominent, my cheeks are broad, my eyebrows are black and bushy, my mouth is wide, my lips are full, and my jaw is square. If this great chin were only adorned with a long beard, don't you think that it would look rather good modelled in bronze or marble?

ME — Right up there with a Caesar, a Marcus Aurelius, a Socrates.

HIM — No. I'd be better off somewhere down between Diogenes[17] and Phryne.[18] I'm as impudent as the one, and I do enjoy a visit to the others.

ME — Are you still keeping well?

HIM — Yes, mostly, but today, I'm not quite in the pink.

ME — What? Look at you with your belly hanging out like Silenus's[19] and a face...

HIM — A face you'd think was at odds with the belly. The problem is that the spleen shrivelling up my dear uncle appears to be having the opposite effect on his dear nephew.

ME — Talking of said uncle, do you see much of him?

HIM — Oh, you know, to pass in the street.

ME — Is he really never kind to you?

HIM — If he's ever kind to anyone, it's entirely without realizing it. He's the philosopher of his species. He thinks of no one but himself; he couldn't give a damn about the rest of the universe. His wife and daughter can drop dead whenever they feel like it, just so long as when the parish bells ring for them, they resonate at the twelfth and seventeenth intervals[20] — then everything will be fine. It's lucky for him he's like that, and it's what I particularly value in geniuses. They're only good for one thing. Apart from that, nothing at all. They don't have the least idea what it is to be a citizen, father, mother, brother, relation, friend. Between you and me, we should aspire to be like them in every way, but shouldn't want the spark to be too widespread. We need men, but, as for men of genius, no thanks. Good God, no, we don't need them at all. They're the ones who change the face of the planet, but when it comes down to the smallest things, stupidity is so widespread and so dominant that no one can do anything about it without kicking up a huge fuss. Some of what they dreamt up gets done, and some stays just as it was, and that's why there are two versions of the gospel, like a Harlequin costume. The wisdom of Rabelais's monk is best for his own peace of mind and for everyone else's: do one's duty as far as possible, always have a good word for the Reverend Prior, and let the world follow its fancy. The world is fine as it is, because the multitude is happy with it. If I knew any history, I'd show you that here on earth, evil is always caused by some man of genius. But I don't know any history because I don't know a thing. I'll be damned if ever I learnt a thing, and if, having never learnt a thing, I was any the worse for it. One day I was seated at the table of one of the King of France's ministers who's as clever as they come;[21] well, he showed us as clear as two and two make four that nothing was more useful to all peoples of the world than lies, and nothing more dangerous than the truth. I can't remember now exactly how he proved it, but the obvious conclusion was that geniuses are an odious lot, and that if any child should come into the world bearing the mark of this dangerous gift of nature on its forehead, it should either be suffocated or thrown in the gutter forthwith.

ME — And yet the type of person you're talking about always claims to possess it, however hostile to genius they say they are.

HIM — I do believe that's what they think inside themselves, but I don't believe they'd ever dare admit it.

ME — That's just because they're being modest. And it must be what made you conceive such a deadly hatred for genius.

HIM — An undying one.

ME — But I remember a time when you were despairing of ever being anything other than an ordinary man yourself. You'll never be happy if the pros and the cons upset you equally. You have to choose your side and stick to it. I agree with you that men of genius are usually unusual — as the saying goes, There is no great mind without a touch of madness — and there's nothing we can do about that, but centuries which do not produce them will be scorned. Nations which do, will be honoured on their account; sooner or later, statues will be put up to them, and they will be viewed as the benefactors of the human race. With all due respect to that sublime minister you were talking about, I believe that even if lies can be useful in the short term, they are necessarily harmful in the long term, whereas on the contrary, the truth is necessarily useful in the long term, although it can turn out to be harmful in the short term. All of which leads me to conclude that the man of genius who denounces some widely held view as false, or who helps demonstrate some great truth, will always be worthy of our veneration.[22] This person may fall victim to prejudice and to the prevailing law of the land, but there are always two sorts of laws, those that are universally applicable and just, and those that are bizarre and owe their authority only to wilful blindness or to necessity born of circumstance. Infringing this second sort only temporarily sentences the guilty man to an ignominious fate; it is one that time reverses, sentencing judges and nations in their turn to eternal ignominy. Of Socrates and the judge who made him drink the hemlock, who is dishonoured today?

HIM — That'll be a whole lot of use to him now! They still condemned him, didn't they? He was still executed, wasn't he? In any case, wasn't he a thoroughly troublesome citizen? Didn't his disrespect for one bad law encourage madmen to disobey the good ones? Was he not a most brazen and bizarre individual? What you've been saying is hardly helpful for the cause of men of genius.

ME — Now listen, my dear fellow. A society should not have bad laws, and were it only to have good ones, it would never be in a position to persecute a man of genius. I never said genius was inextricably linked to wickedness, nor wickedness to genius. A fool is more likely to be wicked than a clever man is. If a man of genius were hard-hearted, prickly, unbearable, and generally difficult to get on with, even truly wicked, what would you say?

HIM — That the bottom of the river's the best place for him.

ME — Calm down, dear fellow. Let's not use your uncle as an example. He may be hard-hearted, violent, inhumane, and grasping. He may be a bad father, a bad husband, and a bad uncle; but it is not yet clear that he really is a man of genius, that he truly has taken his art very far forward, and that anyone will still be talking about his works in ten years' time. But what about Racine? He was a genius, no doubt about it, and he's not supposed to have been a particularly nice man. And what about De Voltaire?[23]

HIM — Don't press me about him because I will follow through.

ME — What would you rather? That he were a good man, forever at his shop counter, like Briasson,[24] or never without his tape measure, like Barbier,[25] regularly giving his wife one legitimate child a year, busy being a good husband, a good father, a good uncle, a good neighbour, an honest tradesman, but nothing more; or that he were scheming, cheating, only out for himself, envious, and wicked, but also the author of *Andromaque, Britannicus, Iphigénie, Phèdre*, and *Athalie*?

HIM — Good grief, in his case, of the two, perhaps it would've been better to be the first.

ME — That's infinitely more true than you could ever realise.

HIM — Oh there you go again, you lot! If ever we say anything worthwhile, it's got to be by accident, like madmen or fantasists. You think you're the only ones to understand yourselves. Actually, Mister Philosopher, I do understand myself, and I understand myself just like you understand yourself.

ME — We'll see about that! Why would it be better for him then?

HIM — Because all those fine things he did didn't earn him twenty thousand francs, and if he'd been a good silk merchant on the rue Saint-Denis or the rue Saint-Honoré, a good wholesale grocer, or an apothecary with plenty of customers, he'd have amassed a great fortune, and while amassing it, there wouldn't have been a single pleasure he couldn't have enjoyed: he could have tossed a coin from time to time to some poor devil of a clown like me who'd have made him laugh, procured him a girl, as required, to relieve the endless boredom of being with his wife; we'd have had excellent meals at his house, gambled large sums, drunk excellent wines, excellent liqueurs, excellent coffees, and had country parties; and so you see, I understood myself perfectly all along. You laugh, but let me speak. That would've been a great deal better for the people around him.

ME — I don't disagree, so long as he didn't do anything indecent with the wealth he'd legitimately built up, and kept his house clear of all those gamblers, parasites, tedious hangers-on, layabouts and useless degenerates, and got his shop boys to beat up the man who arranges for husbands to have a bit of variety, relieving them of the familiar tedium of their wives.

HIM — Beat up, Sir, beat up! No one gets beaten up in a well governed city. This is an honest profession we're talking about. Many people, some of them titled, are involved in it. What the devil do you want people to spend their money on, if not on good food, good company, good wine, beautiful women, every pleasure on the spectrum, every species of amusement? I'd rather be a beggar than have a great fortune and deny myself those pleasures. But let's get back to Racine. That man only did any good to people he didn't know or once he was no longer around.

ME — Granted. But you have to weigh up both sides. In a thousand years from now, he'll still be moving people to tears; he'll be admired in every country in the world. He will inspire them with feelings of humanity, compassion, tenderness, they will want to know who he was, where he came from, and on account of him, France will be the envy of the world. He inflicted suffering on some people who are no more, people in whom we have almost no interest. We have nothing to fear either from his vices or his defects. Doubtless, it would have been better if nature had endowed him with the virtues of a good man and the talents of a great one. He is a mighty tree who starved some other trees growing nearby and stifled the plants at his feet, but his own crown reached the sky; his branches stretched out wide; he provided welcome shade for those who came, still come and always will come in search of rest by his majestic trunk; the fruits he gave were exquisite, and they keep growing back.[26] Of course, it would be desirable for De Voltaire to have Duclos's[27] kindness, the Abbé Trublet's[28] simplicity, and the Abbé d'Olivet's[29] integrity; but as that can never be, let's view the matter from the only truly interesting perspective, and disregard for a moment our position in time and space, and look beyond to the centuries to come, to the furthest lands and the peoples yet to be born. Let's consider the good of our species. If we can't be open-minded, at least let's not blame nature for being wiser than we are. If you pour cold water over Greuze's[30] head, you might extinguish his talent along with his vanity. If you make De Voltaire less sensitive to criticism, he may no longer be able to fathom the depths of Mérope's[31] soul. He will no longer move you.

HIM — But if nature were as powerful as it is wise, why did it not make them good as well as great?

ME — But don't you see that with an argument of that sort, you overturn the general order of things, and that if everything here on earth were excellent, nothing would be excellent?[32]

HIM — You're right. The important thing is that we should exist, you and me, and that we should exist as you and me. In any case, let everything find its way in the world. The best order of things, in my opinion, is the one that has me in it, and I couldn't care less about the best possible world, if I'm not in it. I'd rather be alive and offend everyone by speaking out of turn than not be alive at all.

ME — There isn't a single person who doesn't think like you, and who doesn't criticize the way things are, without thereby wishing himself out of existence.

HIM — True.

ME — So let's accept things as they are. Let's see what we lose and what we gain in doing so, and let's leave aside the big picture which, in any case, we don't have a clear enough view of to be able to apportion praise or blame, and which may in itself be neither good nor bad, but simply necessary, which is what many respectable people think.[33]

HIM — I don't really understand what you're going on about. It sounds like philosophy to me, and I'm warning you now, I never get involved in that. All I know is, I'd rather be someone else, even if it meant being a man of genius, a great man. In fact, there's something inside me telling me so. I've never been able to listen to anyone else being praised without becoming secretly furious. I am an envious person. Whenever I hear some degrading detail about their private lives, I prick up my ears in delight. It makes us more alike. It allows me to bear my own mediocrity more easily. I tell myself: sure, you never wrote *Mahomet*, but at least you didn't write in praise of Maupeou.[34] I have always been and I still am angry about being mediocre. Yes, yes, I admit it, I am mediocre and angry. I have never heard the overture to *Les Indes galantes*[35] [*The Galant Indies*] being played, never heard *Profonds abîmes du Ténare*[36] [Deep Chasms of Tainaron], *Nuit, éternelle nuit* [Night, Eternal Night] sung, without feeling pain and sighing: 'That's something I'll never be able to do'. The thing is, I was jealous of my uncle, and if, at his death, there'd been a few fine harpsichord pieces among his papers, I wouldn't have hesitated a moment to stay myself and also be him.

ME — If that's all that's upsetting you, it's hardly worth the worry.

HIM — It's nothing, these things pass.

(Then he went back to singing the overture to *Les Indes galantes* and the air, *Profonds abîmes*, adding:)

HIM — That something inside me, speaking to me and saying: 'Rameau, you'd really have liked to have composed those two pieces… If you had composed those two pieces, you'd be able to do two more; and once you'd done a certain number of them, everyone would be playing and singing you, and when you walked anywhere, you'd hold your head up high, you'd be conscious of your own merit, and people would point you out. They would say: He's the one who did those pretty gavottes'. Then he sang the gavottes, and he looked touched like someone overflowing with joy, a tear in his eye, and added, rubbing his hands together: You would have a fine house – and he showed how big it was, putting out his arms; a fine bed – and he casually stretched out on it; fine wines – and he tasted them, smacking his tongue against his palate; a fine carriage – and he lifted his foot to climb in; pretty women – and already he was feeling their bosoms and leering at them; a hundred spongers would come and worship at my feet – and now he saw them all around him; he could see Palissot,[37] Poinsinet,[38] the Frérons, father and son,[39] La Porte;[40] he could hear them, he puffed himself up, endorsed their words, smiled, brushed them off, looked down on them, sent them packing, summoned them back again; and then he went on: and this is what it would be like: you'd wake up to hear you were a great man; you'd open the *Trois Siècles* [*Three Centuries*][41] and read you were a great man; you'd go home in the evening convinced you were a great man; and the great man, Rameau the Nephew, would fall asleep to the sweet sounds of praise, singing in his ears; even asleep, he would have a satisfied air; he would breathe easily, his chest filling out, rising and falling majestically; he would snore like a great man; – and saying all this, he lay down on a long cushioned seat; he closed his eyes, and mimed the contented sleep he was imagining. After a few sweet moments of this repose, he woke up suddenly, stretched his arms, yawned, rubbed his eyes, and started looking around for his witless sycophants.

ME – So you think a happy man does sleep?

HIM – Sure I do! As for me, poor wretch that I am, when I get back to my garret and my miserable bed at the end of the day, I huddle under the cover, my chest feels tight; my breathing is difficult; it's a strained little whimper which you can barely hear, whereas any banker will make his apartment shake and the entire street vibrate with his snores. But what's upsetting me today isn't whether or not I snore or sleep badly like miserable wretches do.

ME – Although that is still sad.

HIM – What's happened to me is much sadder than that.

ME – What is it then?

HIM – You have always shown some interest in me, have you not, because I'm a poor devil whom you basically despise but who amuses you?

ME – Yes, that's right.

HIM — And now I'm going to tell you what it is.

Before he begins, he lets out a deep sigh and clutches his head in both hands. Then, he regains his calm and says:

You know that I am an ignoramus, a fool, a madman, an upstart, a hanger-on, what the Burgundians[42] call a dirty scally, a cheat, a greedy pig...

ME — What an encomium!

HIM — Don't argue, please. Every word is true. No one could deny it. Nobody knows me better than I know myself, and I'm not telling you the half of it.

ME — I have no wish to make you angry, and so I'm happy to go along with it all.

HIM — So, at the time, I was living with some people who took to me precisely because I was exceptionally gifted at being all those things.

ME — That's peculiar. Until now, I had always supposed that one would either hide such things from oneself or forgive oneself for them, and that one despised them in others.

HIM — Hide them from oneself — is that possible? You can be sure that when Palissot is alone and takes a good look at himself, he doesn't hold back. You can be sure that when it's just him and his colleague, they openly admit that they are a right pair of low-lifes. Despise them in others? Well, my lot were fairer than that, and they had the sort of character that meant I was a great hit with them. I was like a pig in clover. They made a great fuss of me. I couldn't be out of their sight for a single moment without their missing me. I was their little Rameau, their pretty Rameau, their Rameau who was such a madman, such an upstart, such an ignoramus, a hanger-on, a greedy-guts, a clown, such a great beast of a Rameau. Not one of these familiar epithets came without a smile, a caress, a little pat on the shoulder, a slap, a kick, or without, at dinner, a lump of meat being flung onto my plate, and after dinner, the permission to take liberties without there being any consequences, because I am of no consequence. People can do to me, with me, and in front of me whatever they like without me taking offence; and what about those little presents they showered me with? Stupid great ass that I am, I lost it all! I lost it all because I succumbed to a moment of common sense, just once in my life. Argh! That never happens to me!

ME — So what was it all about then?

HIM — A foolishness beyond compare, beyond comprehension, beyond forgiveness.

ME — What foolishness then?

HIM — Rameau, Rameau, is that what they took you on for? Oh the foolishness of having shown a bit of taste, a bit of wit, a bit of sense. Rameau, my friend, that'll teach you to stay as God made you and as your protectors wanted you to be. So they grabbed you by the shoulders, showed you the door and said: Scum, get out and don't come back; I do believe it thinks it can have sense and reason! Out! We've got quite enough of those things ourselves. And off you went biting your lip when it was your tongue you should have bitten. And just because you didn't, here you are now, out on the street, penniless, wondering what to do next. They fed you like a king, and now you'll go back to living off scraps; you had a nice place to live, and now you'd be only too happy to get your garret back; you had a comfy bed, and now all you can hope for is a place in the straw with Monsieur de Soubise's coachman[43] on one side and our friend Robbé[44] on the other. Instead of the sweet and peaceful sleep you used to enjoy, you'll have horses whinnying and shuffling in one ear, and the scratching sound of harsh, barbaric verse in the other, which is a thousand times worse. Bad luck, bad judgement, I must have been possessed — by a million devils!

ME — But is there no way of going back? Is the sin you committed so unpardonable? If I were you, I'd try and get back in with them. They need you more than you think.

HIM — Ha! I'm sure that now I'm not there to make them laugh, they'll be bored to death.

ME — So I'd go back if I were you. I wouldn't give them the chance to get along without me and start seeking out some more honest amusement; for who knows what might happen then?

HIM — That's not what I'm afraid of; that'll never happen.

ME — However sublimely talented you might be, someone else can always take your place.

HIM — Only with difficulty.

ME — True. All the same, I'd go to them looking pale and wan, eyes rolling, shirt undone, hair in a mess, in the same tragic state I see you in now. I'd hurl myself at the goddess's[45] feet. I'd press my face to the ground, and without looking up, I'd say in a deep sob: I am sorry, Madame! I am so sorry! I am not worthy, I'm a disgrace. It was a mishap: as you know, I don't usually display even an ounce of common sense, and I promise never to display any ever again as long as I live.

What is funny is that while I was saying this, he was miming along. He had prostrated himself, pressed his face to the ground, he seemed to have his hands round the toe of a slipper, he was weeping, he was sobbing, he was saying: Yes, my little queen, yes, I promise, I will never show any ever again, ever. Then abruptly getting up, he added in a serious and thoughtful tone:

HIM — Yes, you are right. I think that's the best thing to do. She is a good person. Monsieur Viellard[46] is always saying what a good person she is. It's true she has been quite good to me too. Nevertheless, to have to bow down to that ape-woman! To beg for mercy at the feet of a wretched little diva who is booed by audiences everywhere! Me, Rameau, son of Rameau, apothecary of Dijon, a worthy man, who never knelt down to anyone in his

life! Me, Rameau, nephew of the man who calls himself the great Rameau,[47]

and who is to be seen in the Palais Royal walking upright, waving his arms in the air, ever since Carmontelle drew him bent over with his hands

behind his back under his coat-tails![48] Me, composer of harpsichord pieces that nobody plays, but which may one day be the only ones to pass into posterity, when they'll be played by everyone; me! Has it come to this? To have to go... Honestly, Sir, that cannot be. And putting his right hand on his chest, he added: I sense something here rising up and telling me: Rameau, you'll do nothing of the sort. There should always be a certain dignity bound up with the nature of man, which nothing can stifle. It awakens at the drop of a hat, yes, at the drop of a hat, for there are other days when it wouldn't cost my dignity a thing to go as low as they wanted me to; on those days, give me a farthing, and I'll kiss that little Hus's arse.[45]

ME — Ahem! But, my friend, she is pretty, young, fair-skinned, soft, plump; and it would be an act of humility that a man of yet more delicate taste than you might sometimes stoop to.

HIM — Let's be clear about this: there's literal arse-kissing and there's metaphorical arse-kissing. Ask that fat Bergier who kisses Mme de La Marck's[49] arse both literally and metaphorically; and good God, how I would dislike that, literally or metaphorically.

ME — Well then, if the expedient I'm suggesting doesn't suit, have the courage of your convictions and be a beggar.

HIM — It's hard to be a beggar when there are so many wealthy fools to live off. And then there's the self-hatred; it's unbearable.

ME — You mean you've had that feeling?

HIM — Haven't I just! How many times have I said to myself: Come on, Rameau, how is it that there are ten thousand dinner tables in Paris, and room for fifteen to twenty at each, and no seat for you! There are purses full of gold, showering in every direction, and not a single coin comes your way! A thousand little men of wit with no talent or merit; a thousand little beauties, with no charm; a thousand dullards scheming for fine clothes, and yet you'd go out without a stitch on? Would you be that stupid? Can't you be as sycophantic as the next man? Can't you lie, swear an oath and then break it, make a promise, pledge allegiance and then break it? Can't you get down on all fours like everyone else? Can't you facilitate Madame's little intrigue and deliver Monsieur's love notes? Can't you encourage that young man to talk to Mademoiselle and persuade Mademoiselle to listen like everyone else? Can't you make the daughter of one of our shopkeepers see that she looks dowdy, and that a pretty pair of earrings, a dab of rouge, a nice bit of lace, and one of those Polish-style dresses with big ruched-up skirts[50] would make her look ravishing? That those dainty feet aren't made for walking outside? That there is a handsome and wealthy young man, in a suit trimmed with gold, who has a magnificent carriage and six tall footmen, and who, having caught a glimpse of her, has fallen for her charms, been unable to eat or drink ever since, and is now lying awake every night thinking of her, and generally dying of love? But what will my Papa say? — Yes, yes, your Papa! He'll be a little bit cross to begin with. — And Mama who so wants me to be a good girl? And who tells me that the only thing that matters in this world is being a good girl? — Old-fashioned stuff and nonsense. — And my confessor? — You won't have to see him any more; or if you will persist in your fanciful desire to go and tell him all about your amusements, then it'll cost you a few pounds in sugar and coffee. — But he's a very strict man who's already refused to grant me absolution for singing *Viens dans ma cellule* [*Come into My Cell*].[51] — That's because you didn't have anything to give him... But once you go and see him in your lace... — You mean I'll have lace? — Of course, you will, and lots of it... and in your diamond earrings... — You mean I'll have beautiful diamond earrings? — Yes. — Like the ones that Marquise wears who sometimes comes to buy gloves from our shop? — Exactly; in a fine carriage drawn by dapple-grey horses, two tall footmen, a negro pageboy, and a linkboy; rouge, beauty spots, someone to carry your train... — And shall I go to the ball? — Yes, to the ball... and to the Opera and the Theatre[52] too... Her heart was already a-flutter with excitement. What's that piece of paper you've got in your hand? — It's nothing. — But it must be something. — It's a note. — Who for? — For you, if you're at all curious. — Curious? Yes, very. Let's see. (She reads.) A meeting, I can't. — On the way to mass. — Mama always comes with me; but if he came a bit early perhaps; I always get up first and I'm at the counter before anyone else is up. So along he comes; she likes what she sees; and one fine day, at dusk, the girl vanishes, and I am paid my two thousand ecus... What! You are capable of doing all that and yet you go hungry? Aren't you ashamed of yourself, you miserable wretch? It makes me think of a pack of rogues who weren't half as talented as me, but who were up to their eyes in gold. I'd be in my goatskin overcoat, and they'd be all decked out in velvet; they'd be leaning on their canes with gold knobs on or fancy beak-shaped handles, their fingers decked out with cameo rings of Aristotle or Plato. And what were this lot anyway? For the most part, miserable scribblers; but now they're all some species of lord. So I took heart, felt my soul rise up and my mind soar, and I knew I could do anything. But it appears these happy feelings were not to last, for, to date, I've not got very far. Be that as it may, this is exactly how I often address myself, and you can rearrange the words of my soliloquy however you fancy, so long as you always conclude from it that I am a man acquainted with self-hatred, that I know that tormented conscience which comes from not having been able to use the talents bestowed upon us by heaven above. It would almost have been better if such a man had never been born.

I was listening to him, and as he was acting out the scene between the pimp and the young girl he was seducing, I felt my soul pulled in two opposite directions; I didn't know whether I'd end up giving in to the urge to laugh or puffing up in furious indignation. It was painful. Twenty times, I burst out laughing and every time this stopped me from exploding in anger; twenty times, the anger that was bubbling up inside me erupted into laughter. I was dumbfounded by how insightful and at once how sordid what he said was, by how right and then how wrong his ideas were, by how totally perverse his sentiments were, by the spectacle of such utter depravity, and by how uncommonly open about it he was. He noticed the conflict going on in me: What's the matter? he asked.

ME — Nothing.

HIM — You look troubled to me.

ME — That's because I am.

HIM — But what would you advise me to do then?

ME — To change the subject. Oh, unhappy man! What a state of utter abjection you were born in, or have fallen into!

HIM — I accept that. But don't let my state get you down too much. My plan, in speaking openly to you in this way, was not to cause you any distress. I did manage to put a bit aside when I was with those people. Don't forget that I was in need of nothing, nothing at all, and that I even had a small amount of pocket money.

And then he started punching himself again on the forehead, biting his lip, rolling his eyes and staring up at the ceiling, adding: But it's over and done with now. I've set something aside. Time has passed, and it's been piling up.

ME — You mean slipping away.

HIM — No, no, piling up. We grow a little richer with every day that passes. One less day alive or one ecu more, it's all the same. The important thing is to go easily, freely, pleasurably, copiously and daily each evening on the chamber pot. *O stercus pretiosum* [O Precious Turd]![53] That's the grand outcome of life whatever the rank. In their last moments, everyone is equally rich, be they Samuel Bernard,[54] that man who, with all his thieving, pillaging, and bankrupting, is leaving twenty-seven million in gold, or Rameau, who won't be leaving anything at all, Rameau whose winding sheet will be paid for by the parish. The dead man doesn't hear the bell toll for him. It's all very well for hundreds of priests to chant themselves hoarse and for mourners, bearing flaming torches, to process ahead and follow on behind, his soul isn't there to process beside the Master of Ceremonies. Whether you rot beneath marble or under the ground, you still rot. Whether you have the Boys in Red or the Boys in Blue[55] to sing at your funeral, or no one at all, what does it matter? See this wrist, it was as stiff as the devil. These ten fingers were like sticks stuck in a wooden wrist-bone, and these tendons were like old gut strings, only drier, stiffer and with less give in them than the old ropes off a carpenter's wheel. But I really have tortured, smashed and broken your strings, haven't I, dear fingers? And you, dear hand, you don't want to move anymore. But by God, I say you will; and so it shall be.

And while he was speaking, he had grabbed his left hand in his right and was pulling his fingers and wrist backwards and forwards so that he made the very tips of his fingers touch his arm; his joints cracked with the effort, and I was worried his bones would be permanently dislocated.

ME — Watch out, I told him, you'll do yourself an injury!

HIM — Don't worry, they're used to it; I've been doing a lot worse than that to them for the last ten years. However much they complained, the poor buggers just had to get used to it and learn to land on the right keys and fly up and down the strings. So now they're fine. Yes, they're fine.

At this point, he is striking the pose of a violin-player; he is humming an
5 allegro by Locatelli;[56] his right arm is miming the action of the bow, his left hand and fingers look as though they are skipping all the way up the fingerboard; if the tuning goes out, he stops to tighten or lower the string; he plucks it with his nail to check it's right; he picks up the piece where he left off; he beats time with his foot, he throws himself into it completely, head, feet, hands, arms, body. Which is what you will sometimes have seen Ferrari or Chiabran or some other virtuoso do at the *Concert spirituel*[57] when they go into the same convulsions and present me with the same scenes of torture and make me feel more or less the same pain; for is it not

painful to see someone tormenting himself in an effort to paint me a scene of pleasure? Screen that man off from me, if he must act the part of a man being tortured. In the midst of his writhing and howling, when there was a pause — one of those harmonious moments when the bow moves slowly across many strings at once — an expression of bliss would come across his face, his voice would soften, he would be in ecstasy just listening to himself. His ears could truly hear the chords resonating, and so could mine. Then tucking the instrument under his left arm with the hand he'd been holding it in, and letting his right hand drop with the bow, he said: So, what do you think of that?

ME — Amazing!

HIM — Pretty good, I'd say; it sounds much the same as everyone else.

And straightaway, he squatted like a musician seating himself at the harpsichord. Mercy, I implore you, for both our sakes, I said.

HIM — No, no; now that I've got you here, you have to listen to me. I don't want you singing my praises without knowing why. Your praises will ring truer, and I'll get a student out of it.

ME — I know hardly anybody, and you'll tire yourself out in vain.

HIM — I never get tired.

Since there was no point me pitying my man who was still drenched in sweat following his violin sonata, I decided to let him get on with it. So here he is, sitting at the harpsichord, legs bent, head looking up at the ceiling, which you would have thought had the music written on it, singing, warming up, playing a piece by Alberti[58] or Galuppi,[59] I'm not sure 
which. His voice swooped up and down and his fingers tripped along the keys, sometimes skipping from the upper keys to the lower, sometimes moving from the accompaniment back to the tune. His face expressed each of the passions in turn, tenderness, anger, pleasure, pain; you could hear the *pianos* and the *fortes*, and I'm sure that someone more attuned than me would have recognised the piece by its movement, its character, the expressions of his face, and by the snatches of song that escaped him every so often. But, what was bizarre was that from time to time, he faltered, then he corrected himself as if he'd missed a note, and looked crestfallen that his fingers no longer knew the piece.

So you see, he said, standing back up, and wiping away the drops of sweat that were rolling down his cheeks, we are just as good at augmented fourths and fifths, and we know all about the sequencing of dominants. These enharmonic passages, which one's dear uncle made such a fuss about, aren't that difficult; we'll manage.[60]

ME — You have gone to a lot of trouble to show me how extremely skilled you are; I was ready to take your word for it.

HIM — Extremely skilled? Ha! No; I know my trade more or less, and that's more than I need to get by. After all, in this land of ours, do we have to understand the things we teach?

ME — No more than we have to understand what we learn.

HIM — How true, damn it! How very true! Now, Mister Philosopher, hand on heart, tell me straight. There was a time when you weren't quite so well off as you are today.[61]

ME — I'm still not that well off.

HIM — But you don't go to the Luxembourg Gardens[62] in summertime any more, like you used to, remember...

ME — Can we not talk about that, I do remember, yes.

HIM — In a shaggy grey overcoat...

ME — Yes, yes.

HIM — Worn thin down one side; in a shirt with torn cuffs, and black woollen stockings darned at the back with white thread.

ME — Yes, yes, and all the rest.

HIM — What were you doing there, in the Walk of Sighs?

ME — Being pretty pathetic.

HIM — And you'd come out onto the street and go trotting off.

ME — I would.

HIM — You were giving lessons in mathematics.

ME — Without knowing the first thing about it: isn't that what you were getting at?

HIM — Precisely.

ME — I learnt by teaching others, and I produced some good students.

HIM — That may well be; but it doesn't work the same way with music as it does with algebra or geometry. Now that you're such a big man...

ME — Less of the big.

HIM — And so well-heeled.

ME — Not that well.

HIM — And get tutors for your daughter.

ME — Steady on, not yet. It's her mother who's in charge of her education — anything for a bit of peace and quiet at home.

HIM — Peace and quiet? Damn it! You'll only get that if you're either the master or the servant, and I'll tell you for free, the master's the one to be. I did have a wife. God rest her soul; but sometimes she used to talk back, so I'd bridle, I'd thunder, I'd proclaim like God: Let there be light; and there was light. And do you know, in four years, we didn't raise our voices at each other more than ten times. How old is your child?

ME — That's irrelevant.

HIM — How old is your child?

ME — Damn it! Leave my child and how old she is out of it, and let's get back to the tutors she'll be having.

HIM — Good Lord! I have never come across anything as pig-headed as a philosopher. Might one be permitted to make a most humble request of Your Worship the Philosopher, that he kindly convey to one the approximate age that her little ladyship his daughter might be?

ME — Let us say she's eight years old.[63]

HIM — Eight! Then it should have already been fingering the keys for four years.

ME — But maybe I wasn't particularly concerned about ensuring that the plans for her education included the study of something which takes up so much time and is of so little use.

HIM — And so, pray tell, what will you be teaching her then?

ME — To think logically, if I can, which is such a rare thing among men, let alone women.

HIM — Let her think as illogically as she likes, as long as she's pretty, funny, and flirty.

ME — Since nature has been so unkind as to give her delicate health and a sensitive soul, and to expose her to the same difficulties in life as someone with robust health and a heart of steel, I shall teach her, if I can, to endure them with fortitude.

HIM — So let her weep, suffer, sulk, have irritable nerves like everyone else, as long as she's pretty, funny and flirty. What! No dance lessons?[64]

ME — No more than are necessary to learn to curtsey, have good posture, hold herself well and walk with grace.

HIM — No singing lessons?

ME — No more than are necessary to speak well.

HIM — No music lessons?

ME — If I could find a good musical harmony tutor, I'd have him teach her two hours a day for one or two years, but not more than that.

HIM — And what are you putting in the place of the essential things you're doing away with?

ME — Grammar, mythology, history, geography, a bit of drawing and a lot of ethics.

HIM — I could easily prove to you how useless all those subjects are in a world like ours. What am I saying, useless? They may well be dangerous. But I'll just ask one question for the time being: is she not in need of one or two tutors?

ME — I'm sure she is.

HIM — Well, there you are then! And these tutors of yours, you expect them to know the grammar, mythology, history, geography, ethics that they'll be giving her lessons in? Pipe dreams, my dear sir, pipe dreams; if they knew these subjects well enough to teach them, they wouldn't be teachers.

ME — Why's that then?

HIM — Because they'd have spent their whole lives studying them. You need a profound understanding of any art or science to have a real grasp of the basics. Textbooks can only be done properly by men who have grown old and white-haired on the job. It's the middle and the end that illuminate the darkness of the beginning. Ask your friend, Monsieur d'Alembert,[65] the leading light of mathematical science, whether he's too good to write a textbook. It was only after thirty to forty years' work that my uncle first caught sight of the first glimmers of musical theory.

ME — You are mad, stark raving mad! I exclaimed. How can there be so many good ideas jumbled up with so many outrageous ones in that wicked head of yours?

HIM — Who the devil knows? Chance throws them at you, and they stick. There are so many of them that if you don't have the whole lot, you might as well not have any. We don't know where one thing is going, where another has come from, nor where one or the other thinks it should go, which one should go first, or which would be better off in second place. Can you be a good teacher if you lack method? And method, where does that come from? Listen, my dear philosopher, in my head, physics will always be a poor science, a droplet of water lifted out of the vast ocean on the point of a needle, a speck of earth removed from the Alpine range. And the reasons behind natural phenomena? In truth, we might as well know nothing at all as know as little as we do, and know it so inadequately; and that's where

I'd got to when I decided to become a tutor in musical composition and accompaniment. What are you thinking about?

ME — I'm thinking that everything you've just been saying is more specious than solid. But let's move on. You say you've taught accompaniment and composition?

HIM — Yes.

ME — And you didn't know the first thing about them?

HIM — No, believe me, and that's why I wasn't as bad as some, the ones who thought they knew something. At least I wasn't spoiling the children's judgement or their hands. When they went from me to a good teacher, since they hadn't learnt anything, at least they didn't have anything to unlearn, and that's a great saving of time and money.

ME — So what did you do?

HIM — What they all do, these teachers. I would turn up, throw myself into a chair, and say: What dreadful weather we're having! The streets are so exhausting! I would tell them some gossip: Mademoiselle Lemierre[66] was due to play a vestal virgin in the new opera, but she's pregnant for the second time, and no one knows who'll be replacing her. Mademoiselle Arnould[67] has just left her little count, and they say she's entering into negotiations with Bertin.[45] Meanwhile the little count has happened upon Monsieur de Montamy's treatise on porcelain.[68] At the last Amateurs' Concert, there was an Italian girl who sang like an angel. That Préville's an amazing actor, you should see him in *Le Mercure galant* [*Mercury, the Galant Messenger*];[69] the bit with the puzzle is priceless. That poor actress, Dumesnil,[70] hasn't got a clue what she's saying or doing anymore. Well now, Mademoiselle, do you want to get your music out? While Mademoiselle, who is in no hurry, is hunting about for her music and can't find it, and the housemaid is called in, and words are had, I carry on: La Clairon is making no sense at the moment. There's talk of an utterly extraordinary marriage: it's Mademoiselle — what's her name? That little woman he's been keeping, who's had two or three children by him, and who had previously been kept by all those other men. — Come on, Rameau, that's not possible; you're talking nonsense. — I am not. Apparently, the marriage has actually taken place. Rumour has it that De Voltaire is dead; that's good news. — Why should it be good news? — Because it must mean he's about to come out with some hilarious new joke. He always dies a fortnight before he does that. What else have I got to tell you? Then I would tell some filthy new anecdotes that I'd picked up from the other households I'd been in, because we're all great gossip-mongers. I was playing the fool. They listened to me. They laughed. They exclaimed: He's always so charming. Meanwhile Mademoiselle's music had finally turned up under an armchair where it had been dragged, chewed, and torn up by some puppydog or kitten. Mademoiselle sits down at the harpsichord. To begin with she would clatter about all by herself. Then I would go over, having signalled to the mother how pleased I was. The mother: Not bad at all; if only we were willing to practice a little more, but we appear not to be. We prefer to waste our time chatting, messing about with our dresses, running about, doing goodness knows what. No sooner do you leave than the music gets put away again not to be opened until your next visit. And yet you never tell her off... So, as I did have to do something, I took her hands and placed them for her. I winced, I yelled: G, G, G; Mademoiselle, it's a G! — The mother: Mademoiselle, do you not have ears? I'm not at the harpsichord, I can't see the music, and even I can tell it should be a G. This is so painful for Monsieur. I can't believe how patient he's being. You never listen to what he tells you. You're making absolutely no progress... — So then I would tone things down a bit, and gently nodding, I would say: If I may, dear Madame, if I may. Things could be better if Mademoiselle wanted, if she were willing to practice a bit; but it's not going badly. — The mother: In your position, I'd have her working on the same piece for a year. — Well now! We could do that, and not let her off until she can do all the difficult bits, but it wouldn't take as long as Madame supposes. — The mother: Monsieur Rameau, you flatter her. You are too good. This is the only thing she'll retain from the entire lesson, and she'll be reciting it back at me at every opportunity. And so the hour would pass. My pupil would hand me my fee with a graceful flourish and the curtsey she'd been taught by her dancing master. I would be putting it in my pocket while the mother was saying: Very good, Mademoiselle. If Javillier[71] were here, he'd be impressed. I would stay to chat a little longer out of politeness; and then off I'd go — and that's what used to be known as a music lesson.

ME — And is it any different these days?

HIM — Good gracious! I should say so. I arrive. I am serious. I quickly remove my jacket; I open the lid of the harpsichord; I try the keys. I am always in a hurry: if I am made to wait even for a moment, I scream as though I'm being robbed. In one hour's time, I need to be somewhere else; in two hours, at the Duchess of XYZ's house. I am invited to dine with a beautiful Marquise; from there, I'm due to go straight to a concert that the Baron de Bacq[72] is holding in his residence on the rue Neuve-des-Petits-Champs.

ME — And in fact you've got nowhere to go at all?

HIM — True.

ME — So why do you have to play these paltry little games?

HIM — Paltry! And why do you call them that, if you don't mind my asking? It's what everyone does in my position; I am hardly demeaning myself if I'm doing exactly what everyone else goes around doing all the time. I didn't make the rules, and it would be bizarre and hapless of me not to abide by them. I'm very well aware that if you apply certain general principles, belonging to some morality or other — which everyone preaches and no one practises — you can prove that white is black and black is white. But, Mister Philosopher, there is such a thing as a general conscience, just as there is a general grammar, and exceptions to it in every language, which you, you and your learned friends, refer to, I believe, as... what is it again, as...

ME — Peculiarities.[73]

HIM — Exactly. Similarly, every walk of life has its own particular exceptions to the general conscience that I think we might call its peculiarity.

ME — I see. Fontenelle[74] is a good speaker and a good writer, although his style teems with French peculiarities.

HIM — And the sovereign, the minister, the banker, the magistrate, the soldier, the man of letters, the lawyer, the prosecutor, the merchant, the banker, the artisan, the singing master, the dancing master, are all very honourable people, although their behaviour deviates in many ways from the general conscience, and is full of moral peculiarities. The longer something has been instituted, the more peculiarities it will have; the unhappier the times, the more the peculiarities will multiply. A man is only as good as his profession; and vice versa — in the end, a profession is only as good as the people in it. And so we talk up our profession as much as we can.

ME — The only thing that's clear to me in all your convoluted rambling is that there are precious few professions with honourable standards, or precious few honourable men of professional standing.

HIM — Quite! There are none at all; although, that said, they're not so bad when they're not at work; and everything would be fine if it weren't for a certain number of people who get called hard-working, careful, and conscientious in the way they carry out their duties, and are high-minded, or who, and this amounts to the same thing, are always at work, doing their job from morning to night, and not doing anything else. And so they're the only ones who grow plump and become respected members of the community.

ME — All because of peculiarities.

HIM — Exactly; I see you've got my point. And so there is one peculiarity that we find in almost all walks of life, because there are some which are actually common to all countries and all times, just as there are common idiocies, and that common peculiarity is to secure as many jobs as possible, and the common idiocy is to believe that the best man is the one with the most jobs. And these are two exceptions to the general conscience and we should go along with them. It's about getting some sort of credit — it has no intrinsic worth; its value comes instead from what people say. They say *A good reputation is worth its weight in gold*. And yet the person with a good reputation is never the one with the gold, and I have noticed that these days the person with the gold is never without a reputation. What you have to have, if you can, is both the lustre and the lucre. And that's my aim when I boost my credit by resorting to what you call devious tricks and nasty little ruses. I give my lesson, and I give it well — that's the general rule. I make it look as if I've got more lessons to give than there are hours in the day, and that's the peculiarity.

ME — And so, your lesson, is it any good?

HIM — Yes, not bad, it'll pass. Dear uncle's fundamental bass has made all that much simpler. Before, I was robbing every student, yes, I was, that's for sure. These days, I earn my fee, that is, as much as anyone does.

ME — And didn't you feel any remorse?

HIM — Oh, none whatsoever! They say that when *a robber is robbed, the devil steals a smile*. The parents were up to their necks in wealth, acquired God knows how; there were courtiers, bankers, wholesalers, accountants, businessmen. I helped them redistribute their wealth, me and a load of other people they also employed. In nature, all species prey on each other; in society, people of all stations prey on each other too. We're forever passing sentence on each other without the law being involved. These days it's La Guimard,[75] like La Deschamps[76] before her, punishing the banker on behalf of the prince, and it's the dressmaker, the jeweller, the decorator, the laundrymaid, the conman, the chambermaid, the cook, the saddler, punishing La Deschamps on behalf of the banker. In the midst of all this, only the imbecile or the idler get hurt without having offended anyone, and quite right too. Which just goes to show that these exceptions to the general conscience, or these moral peculiarities, which people have been up in arms about and calling *perks of the job*, are nothing to get worked up about at all, and when it comes right down to it, the only thing you really need is a good eye.

ME — I admire yours.

HIM — And then there's the abject poverty. The voice of conscience and honour can barely be heard over the sound of hunger gnawing at the guts. Suffice it to say, if ever I get rich, I'll have to redistribute, and I am completely determined to do my redistribution in every possible way, by eating, gambling, drinking, and womanizing.

ME — But I'm worried you may never be rich.

HIM — I suspect as much myself.

ME — But if it doesn't turn out like that, what would you do?

HIM — What any beggar made good would do; I'd be the most outrageous shit ever; I'd think back to every little thing those upstarts had done, and get them back for all the times they'd humiliated me. I like being in control, and I will be. I like being praised, and I will be. I'll have the whole Villemorien[77] gang in my pay, and I will say to them what was said to me: Come on, scum, entertain me, and I'll be entertained; I'll order them to bad-mouth decent people, and they'll be bad-mouthed, if there are decent people left; and then we'll get some girls in, and get all familiar once we're drunk; we'll get drunk and tell each other stories, we'll indulge all sorts of whims and vices. It'll be fabulous. We will prove that De Voltaire has no genius; that Buffon[78] is just stuck up and nothing more than a sermonizing old windbag; that Montesquieu[79] is merely a wit; we'll send d'Alembert back to his sums;[80] we'll give all you little Catos a good thrashing for looking down on us when really all you are is envious, your modesty merely a mask for pride, and your sobriety simply the dictate of necessity. And will there be music? Absolutely, and we'll be the ones making it.

ME — Given the noble use you'd put your wealth to, I can see what a great pity it is you should be poor. Living that way, you'd do great credit to the human race, be of great use to your fellow citizens and earn great glory for yourself.

HIM — But I sense you are mocking me. Mister Philosopher, you appear not to know who you're pitting yourself against; you appear unaware that at this moment I represent the majority in town and at court. Our wealthy fellow men in every walk of life have either said to themselves what I have just confided to you, or they haven't, but the fact is that the life I'd lead if I were them, is exactly the life they do lead. Now you know where you stand, you and your friends. You believe happiness is made the same for everyone. What a strange vision! Your happiness presupposes a certain romantic turn of mind that we do not have, a singular soul, a peculiar taste. You confer the title of virtue on this weirdness; you call it philosophy. But are virtue and philosophy made for everyone? Enjoy them if you can, hold onto them if you can. Imagine what a wise and philosophical universe would be like; you must agree it'd be miserable as hell. Come on, long live philosophy, long live the wisdom of Solomon: let's drink good wine, gorge ourselves silly on delicate morsels, roll around with pretty women, and go to sleep in lovely soft beds. What else is there? The rest is vanity.

ME — What! What about defending one's country?

HIM — Vanity![81] There is no country anymore; all I can see from one end of the earth to the other is tyrants and slaves.

ME — And serving one's friends?

HIM — Vanity! Do any of us have any friends? And if we did, why would we want to make them ungrateful? Take a good look around and you'll see that's almost always what you get for doing anyone a service. Gratitude is a burden, and all burdens are made to be shaken off.

ME — Having a position in society and fulfilling its duties?

HIM — Vanity! What does having a position matter, as long as you're rich, since you only take them on for the money. Fulfilling your duties, what does that get you? Jealousy, trouble, persecution. Is that how to get ahead? Pay court, damn it! Pay court, observe the great and powerful, study their tastes, indulge their fancies, serve their vices, approve their acts of injustice: that's the secret.

ME — Attending to the education of one's children?

HIM — Vanity! That's the tutor's business.

ME — But if the tutor is imbued with your principles and neglects his duties, who will suffer for it?

HIM — God knows it won't be me, but one day it might be my daughter's husband or my son's wife.

ME — But what happens if they both rush headlong into debauchery and vice?

HIM — That's what anyone in their position would do.

ME — But what if they are dishonoured?

HIM — Whatever you do, you can't be dishonoured if you are rich.

ME — And what if they're ruined?

HIM — Tough luck for them.

ME — I can see that if you decide you don't have to attend to the conduct of your wife, your children, your servants, you might easily end up neglecting your affairs.

HIM — Excuse me; sometimes it is difficult to put together enough money, and it is prudent to plan ahead.

ME — Won't you take any care of your wife?

HIM — No, I won't, thank you very much. The best strategy to adopt with one's better half is, I believe, to do whatever suits her best. Don't you think society would be entertaining if everyone just got on with their own thing?

ME — Why not? I never enjoy an evening more than when I am pleased with my morning.

HIM — Me too.

ME — What makes fashionable people so refined when it comes to their amusements is their profound idleness.

HIM — Don't you believe it; they're always rushing around.

ME — Since they never tire, they never need to rest.

HIM — Don't you believe it; they are constantly exhausted.

ME — Pleasure is always business to them and never a need.

HIM — Just as well — a need is always a pain.

ME — They wear everything out. Their souls stagnate. Boredom takes hold of them. Hemmed in as they are by an overwhelming abundance of riches, anyone who does away with them would be doing them a service. The only aspect of happiness they recognize is the bit that froths up quickest. I don't look down on sensory pleasures. I too have a palate, and it is tempted by a delicate morsel or a delicious wine. I too have a heart and eyes, and I love to see a pretty woman, I love to feel the firm round flesh of her bosom in my hands, to press my lips on hers, to feel aroused when I look deep into her eyes, and to expire with pleasure in her arms. Every so often, I am not averse to an evening of debauchery amongst friends, even quite a riotous one. But I will not conceal from you that I find it infinitely more delightful to come to the aid of someone in need, to bring a fraught situation to an end, to give a salutary piece of advice, to read something pleasant, go for a walk with a man or woman dear to my heart, spend a couple of instructive hours with my children, write a good page, fulfil the duties of my position, say some tender loving words to the one I love and receive her embrace in return. There are some things I would give anything to have done. *Mahomet* is a sublime piece of work,[82] but I would rather have cleared the Calas[83] name. A man I know of fled to Carthagena.[84] He was a younger son, in a country where the custom is for the oldest son to inherit everything. One day, he learns that his older brother, ever the spoilt child, having stripped his over-indulgent father and mother of everything they possessed, had evicted them from their château, and that they were now languishing in poverty in a small country town. So what does he do now, this younger son, who had been so harshly treated by his parents, and had gone to seek his fortune far away? He sends them help; he hurriedly winds up his affairs. He comes back wealthy. He restores his father and mother to their home. He arranges for his sisters to be married. Oh! My dear Rameau, this man looked upon this as the happiest period of his life. He told me about it with tears in his eyes; and as I tell you this story, I can feel my heart fill with joy, and it gives me such pleasure I can hardly speak.

HIM — What a strange lot you are!

ME — What a pitiful lot you are, if you can't see that we have risen above our fate, and that no one need be unhappy ever again if only they did a couple of good deeds like this one.

HIM — Well that's a sort of felicity I'm unlikely ever to be familiar with, since one encounters it so rarely. But the way you see it, then, is that we ought to be decent and honourable?

ME — If we want to be happy? Certainly.

HIM — And yet I see infinite numbers of honourable people who are not happy, and infinite numbers of people who are happy without being honourable.

ME — That's what you think.

HIM — And isn't it because I had a moment's common sense and told the truth for once that I don't know where tonight's meal is coming from?

ME — No it isn't! It's because you haven't always shown common sense and been truthful, and because you didn't realize soon enough that the first thing you'd need to do would be to find a way of being independent and free from servitude.

HIM — Independent or not — at least, my way is the easiest.

ME — And the least secure and the least honourable.

HIM — But the most suited to my character since I'm a layabout, a fool, and an all-round waste of space.

ME — Granted.

HIM — And since I can make my own happiness through vices that are natural to me, which I have done no work to acquire and make no effort to maintain, which suit the morals of my nation, are to the taste of my patrons, and are better tailored to their particular little needs than those virtues which would simply embarrass them by showing them up from morning to night, it would be very odd of me to go and torture myself like a soul in hell, castrate myself, and turn myself into someone I'm not, to go and adopt a character and qualities that are alien to me, though I accept they are highly admirable because I don't want to get into an argument, and which would cost me an awful lot of effort to acquire and put into practice, and would get me nowhere or worse than nowhere, given that I'd be showing up the rich people that beggars like me have to try and live off. We praise virtue but in fact we hate it and run away from it because it's freezing cold, and in this world you need to keep your feet warm. On top of that, it would put me in a foul mood, inevitably — why else do we so often see the pious being so harsh, irritable, and unsociable? It's because they have inflicted on themselves a task which isn't natural to them. They are suffering, and when you suffer, you make other people suffer too. That's not my way and it's not my patrons' way either; I need to be cheery, versatile, amusing, foolish, funny. Virtue commands respect, and respect is uncomfortable. Virtue commands admiration, and admiration is no fun. My business is people who get bored, and I need to make them laugh. And ridicule and madness are what make people laugh, so I need to be ridiculous and mad; and even if nature hadn't already made me that way, the easiest thing would be to pretend to be. Luckily, I don't need to be a hypocrite; there are already so many hypocrites, of every stripe, and that's not including the ones who are downright hypocritical with themselves. That Chevalier de La Morlière,[85] with his hat cocked over one ear and his head held high, looking down his nose at you as you go by, with his great long sword smacking against his thigh as he strides about and an insult ready for anyone not carrying one, who looks ready to jump down everyone's throat, what's he actually doing? Everything he can to convince himself that he's a man of courage — but he's a coward. Go over and flick him on the nose, and he'll take it lying down. How do you make him lower his voice? Raise your own. Show him the end of your stick or apply your foot to his backside, and he'll be so astonished to discover that he's a coward that he'll ask you who told you so and how you found him out. He himself was unaware of it till the moment before; he'd spent so long aping heroics that he'd ended up convincing himself. He'd played the part so often, he thought he was the real thing. And as for that woman who mortifies herself, does prison visits, is involved in every parish act of charity, who walks along with her eyes downcast, wouldn't dare look a man in the face, and is forever on guard against the temptation of her senses: does all this prevent her heart from burning, hold back her sighs, keep her true nature from flickering into life, does it stop her being haunted by her desires or replaying in her imagination, all night and all day, scenes from *Le Portier des Chartreux*[86] [*The Charterhouse Porter*] and Aretino's *Positions*?[87] What becomes of her? What does her maid think when she wakes up in the night and goes running in her nightdress to the aid of her mistress who sounds as though she's at death's door? Justine, go back to bed, it wasn't you your mistress was calling out for in her delirium. And if good old Rameau were, one day, to start looking as if he despised money, women, feasting, idleness, and start behaving like a little Cato[88] instead, what would that make him? A hypocrite. Rameau has to be who he is: a happy thief in the company of wealthy thieves, and not someone who trumpets his virtue or who is actually virtuous, chewing his crust of bread on his own or with other beggars. And to be perfectly blunt with you, your felicity doesn't suit me in the slightest, nor does the happiness of a handful of visionaries like you.

ME — I see, my dear man, that you have no idea what it is, and that you haven't even got it in you to find out.

HIM — Just as well, damn it! Just as well. I'd end up dying of hunger, of boredom, and of remorse, perhaps.

ME — In that case, the only advice I have for you is to get straight back into that household you so carelessly got yourself kicked out of.

HIM — And do what you don't disapprove of when it's literal, and what I'm slightly disgusted by when it's metaphorical.

ME — That's what I think.

HIM — Quite apart from this metaphor, which I am finding unpleasant right now, but which I won't mind another time.

ME — How odd!

HIM — There's nothing odd about it. I'm happy to be abject, but I don't want there to be any constraints on it.[89] I'm happy to give up my dignity... Are you laughing?

ME — Yes, your dignity makes me laugh.

HIM — Everyone has their own; I'm happy to forego mine, but at my discretion and not at someone else's command. Should people be able to say to me: Crawl, and then I have to crawl? It's what worms do, it's what I do; and that's what we both do when left to our own devices, but we rear up when people step on our tails. I have had my tail stepped on, and I shall rear up. And besides, you've got no idea what a madhouse it is. Imagine a melancholic and surly personage, consumed by the vapours, all wrapped up in his great big dressing gown, who dislikes himself and everything else, whom you can hardly get a smile out of whatever contortions you push your mind or body into, who sits in stony silence, unmoved by the funny faces I pull, and the even funnier sentences I pronounce; because, between you and me, that wretched Benedictine, Father Noël,[90] for all his famous funny faces and success at court, is, in comparison with me — and I'm not saying this to flatter myself, let alone him — no better than a wooden doll. It's all very well my torturing myself to reach the sublime heights of Bedlam, there's nothing doing. Will he laugh? Won't he laugh? That's what I'm reduced to wondering in the midst of my contortions, and you can imagine how such uncertainty undermines my talent. My lord hypochondriac, his head stuffed up inside a nightcap which comes right down over his eyes, looks like some kind of paralyzed puppet[91] sitting in an armchair with a string attached to its chin dangling down all the way to the floor. You wait for the string to be pulled, but no one pulls it, or, if the jaw does happen to open, it's to utter some distressing remark that reveals that your best efforts have gone unnoticed, and all your mimicry and monkeying around have been in vain. The remark is a reply to a question you asked him four days before; and once it's been uttered, the mastoid spring releases, and the jaw closes back up.

Then he began to do an impression of his man; he'd sat himself in a chair, head perfectly still, hat pulled down low, eyes half-closed, arms dangling, moving his jaw like an automaton, and saying: Yes, you are quite right, Mademoiselle, it needs a little refining there. The thing is, it gets to decide, it's always doing the deciding, and its decisions are always final, in the evening, in the morning, as it gets dressed, at dinner, at the café, at cards, at the theatre, at supper, in bed, and, I do believe, God forgive me, in the arms of its mistress. I'm not party to the latter decisions, but I'm damn tired of the rest of them. Miserable, indecipherable, and immovable, like destiny, that's what our boss is.

His opposite number is a stuck-up prude, with looks you could just about bring yourself to compliment as she's still got them, although she does have a few sores on her face here and there, and is gaining fast on Madame Bouvillon[92] for sheer size. I love a nice bit of flesh myself, but there is such a thing as too much, and motion is an essential quality of matter, after all.[93] And another thing, she is nastier, prouder and sillier than a goose. And another thing, she thinks she's witty. And another thing, you have to convince her all the time that you think she's wittier than anyone else. And another thing, it has no idea about anything, and it also gets to decide things. And another thing, you have to applaud these decisions with your feet, as well as your hands, you have to jump for joy, be struck dumb with admiration: That's so wonderful, so exquisite, so beautifully expressed, so subtly observed, it shows such original feeling! How do women learn all that? Untutored, by sheer force of instinct, by natural insight alone: it seems miraculous. And then people come and sob to us about the beauties of experience, study, thought, education, and a whole load of other nonsense. Bowing ten times a day, one knee bent in front of the other, the other leg stuck out behind, arms outstretched towards the goddess, trying to read her every look, hanging on her every word, awaiting her command, and shooting off in a flash. What sort of a person is it who can subject themselves to such a role, if not the wretch who has no other way of appeasing the torment of his intestines two or three times a week? What are we to make of the others, people like Palissot, Fréron, the Poinsinets, Baculard,[94] who aren't even in need, and whose abject behaviour can't be excused by the rumblings of a suffering stomach?

ME — I'd never have taken you for such a stickler.

HIM — I'm not. When I was starting out, I would watch what the others were doing, and I would do the same, but better, because I am more openly brazen, a better actor, hungrier, and possessed of a better pair of lungs. Apparently, I am directly descended from the famous Stentor.[95]

And to give me a proper idea of the strength of this organ, he began to clear his throat so violently that the café windows rattled and all the chess-players looked up.

ME — But what's the use of being able to do that?

HIM — Can't you guess?

ME — No, I'm a bit limited.

HIM — Imagine an argument in full swing and the outcome as yet undecided: up I get, and unleashing my thunder, I say: Mademoiselle is quite right. Now that's what I call good judgement. That really gives our pretty little wits something to think about. A genius couldn't put it any better. But you mustn't always show your approval in the same way. It'd be monotonous. You'd seem false. You'd become insipid. That can only be avoided with good judgement and constant inventiveness; you have to know how to pave the way for the major chords so that you can suddenly bring them in, grasping the opportunity at the right moment;[96] when, for instance, there is a difference of opinion, and the argument has reached its highest pitch, when you can't hear the sound of your own voice and everyone's talking at once, you've taken up a position on the side-lines, in the corner of the room the furthest away from the battlefield, you've kept quiet for a good long time so as to create maximum impact and suddenly you drop like a mortar bomb into the midst of the combatants. Nobody is more skilful at this than I am. But my most surprising skills are at the other end of the scale; I can produce tiny sounds which I accompany with a smile, an infinite variety of approving expressions; my nose, my mouth, my forehead, my eyes can all come into play; I can bend my back with ease, I have a way of twisting my spine, of raising and lowering my shoulders, extending my fingers, inclining my head, closing my eyes and being awestruck as if I had just heard an angelic and divine voice coming down from heaven. That's what really flatters them. I am not sure you entirely appreciate the impact of this last pose. I am far from having invented it, but nobody has surpassed me in its execution. Look, look...

ME — It is true that that is unique.

HIM — Do you think there's a female brain alive with even the slightest touch of vanity that could hold out against it?

ME — No. I have to agree that you have taken the art of playing the fool and abasing yourself as far as it can go.

HIM — They can try as hard as they like for as long as they like but they'll never get as far. Even the best of them, Palissot, for instance, will never be more than a good apprentice. If the role can be fun at first, provided you can enjoy laughing at the stupidity of the people you're diverting, in the long run, the joke wears off; and besides, after you've invented a certain number of things, you end up having to repeat yourself. Thought and skill have their limits. Only God and a few rare geniuses can have careers that keep stretching out before them as they advance. Bouret[97] may be one such genius: some of the things he does seem to me — yes, even me — to be sublime strokes of genius. The little dog, the Book of Felicity, the torches lighting the way to Versailles are amongst those things which confound and humiliate me; it's enough to make me think there's no point carrying on with the profession.

ME — What do you mean, the little dog?

HIM — Where have you been all this time? What, seriously, you really don't know what this extraordinary man did to persuade his little dog to leave him for the Keeper of the Seals,[98] who'd taken a fancy to the creature?

ME — No I really don't, I admit.

HIM — Oh good. It's one of the most brilliant things anyone ever came up with; the whole of Europe marvelled at it, and there wasn't a courtier alive who wasn't green with envy. You're not short of ideas, let's see what you'd have done in his place. Remember Bouret was adored by his dog; remember that the bizarre clothes the minister wore terrified the little animal; remember that Bouret only had a week to overcome these obstacles. You need to understand all the background to really appreciate how ingenious the solution was. So come on then!

ME — Oh I give up! I must confess that even the slightest thing of this kind is too much for me.

HIM — Listen then, he said, giving me a little slap on the shoulder, because he's familiar that way, listen and be amazed. He has a mask made that looks just like the Keeper of the Seals; he borrows the voluminous robe[99] from a valet. He covers his face with the mask. He puts on the robe. He calls his dog, he strokes him. He gives him a little biscuit.[100] Then all of a sudden, changing costume, he's no longer the Keeper of the Seals, he's Bouret calling his dog and whipping him. In under two or three days of doing this morning to night, the dog knows to run away from Bouret the Tax Farmer and run towards Bouret the Keeper of the Seals. But I'm being too kind, you don't believe in this sort of thing and so you don't deserve to be initiated into the mysteries of the miracles happening around you.

ME — Even so, I beg you, please, what about the book, the flaming torches?

HIM — No, no. Even the cobblestones know about them, so go and ask them; you should take advantage of happening to find yourself in my company to discover things that nobody knows apart from me.

ME — You're right.

HIM — Borrowing the Keeper of the Seals's robe and wig — I had forgotten the wig! Having a mask made to look like him! It's the mask I find so staggering. What's more, this man is held in the highest esteem; what's more, he has millions. There are people with the Cross of Saint-Louis[101] who've got nothing to eat; so what's the point of going all out for a cross and risking a broken back, when you can choose a walk of life that doesn't put you in danger and is never without its recompense? Now that's what I call aiming high. But role models like these are depressing. You feel sorry for yourself, and you get discouraged. The mask! The mask! I'd give my little finger to have come up with the mask.

ME — But with such enthusiasm for brilliant things and such a fertile genius, haven't you invented anything yourself?

HIM — I beg your pardon; what about the way of doing an admiring bow which I told you about; I consider it to be mine, although my claim may be contested by the envious. I believe it may well have been in use before me; but who ever realized how well-suited it would be for having a secret laugh while bowing down before some upstart? I have over a hundred ways of setting up the seduction of a young girl, while in her mother's presence, without the latter realizing, and sometimes even turning her into an accomplice. I'd hardly started out in this career when I realized that all the common ways of slipping someone a love-letter were beneath me. I have ten different ways of forcing people to snatch them from me, and among those ways, I flatter myself that some of them are novel. I have a particular talent for encouraging shy young men; guided by me, even men as thick as two short planks and as ugly as sin have been successful. If it were ever written down, I believe people would acknowledge I had some genius.

ME — Doing you a singular honour.

HIM — I don't doubt it.

ME — If I were you, I'd get it all down on paper. It would be a pity if it were lost.

HIM — True; but you have no idea how unimportant I think method and instructions are. If you need a manual, you won't get very far. Geniuses read little, do a lot, and are their own creators. Look at Caesar, Turenne,[102] Vauban,[103] the Marquise de Tencin, her brother the Cardinal and his secretary, the Abbé Trublet.[104] And what about Bouret? Who ever gave

Bouret any lessons? No one. It's nature that forms these rare men. Do you think the dog and the mask is written down anywhere?

ME — But what about those wasted hours in the middle of the night when you can't sleep because your empty stomach is bothering you or your bloated stomach is troubling you so badly it keeps you awake...

HIM — I'll think about it. It's certainly better to write great things than perform small ones. That's when your soul takes wing, your imagination heats up, catches fire and blazes forth, whereas it shrivels up when it has to express astonishment to the little Hus about the applause the stupid audience insists on lavishing on that simpering little Dangeville[105] whose acting is so flat, who walks about on stage practically bent double, whose particular affectation is to always look the person she's speaking to in the eye, but still underact, who thinks the way she grimaces is terribly subtle and the way she trots about is graceful; applause which it also lavishes on that booming Clairon who is more scrawny, affected, studied, and stilted than you could possibly imagine. That idiotic audience claps until it hurts[106] and does not realize what a mass of charms we are; it is true that the mass is increasing a bit, but what does that matter? We have the most beautiful skin, the most beautiful eyes, the prettiest little pouty mouth, not very tender, it's true, we're a little heavy on our feet, but not quite as clumsy as people say. When it comes to feeling, on the other hand, we're a cut above the rest.

ME — What do you mean? Are you being ironic or are you telling the truth?

HIM — The problem is that this wretched feeling is all inside, and not one glimmer gets out. But let me tell you because I know, I really do, that she has lots of feeling. Or if that's not precisely what it is, it's something like that. When we're in a bad mood, you should see how we treat the valets, how the chambermaids get slapped about, how we stick the boot in Old Casual Parts, whenever he fails to show us the respect we are due. She's a little fiend, I tell you, full of feeling and dignity... Look at you, you still can't make head or tail of it, can you?

ME — I admit I am completely unable to tell whether you're speaking in good faith or spreading wicked lies. I am a decent man; kindly have the decency to be more straightforward with me, and leave out the clever stuff.

HIM — That's the sort of thing we wheel out for the little Hus, about La Dangeville and La Clairon, along with a few words here and there that would tip you the wink. I'm happy for you to think I'm a waster but not a fool, for only a fool or a man madly in love could come out with such absurdities in all seriousness.

ME — But how can anyone bear to say such things?

HIM — It doesn't come easily at first, but bit by bit, you get there. *Ingenii largitor venter* [That teacher of art, that donor of talent — the belly].[107]

ME — Your belly would really have to be grumbling to go that far.

HIM — That may well be. But, however egregious such things seem to you, believe you me, the people to whom they are addressed are far more used to hearing them than we are to venturing them.

ME — Is there anyone amongst you brave enough to agree with you?

HIM — What do you mean, anyone? It's what the whole of society says and feels.

ME — In which case those of you who aren't terrible wasters must be terrible fools.

HIM — Fools, us? I swear there's only one, and it's the man who rewards us for deceiving him.

ME — But how can anyone allow themselves to be taken in by such a cheap trick? Because it's not as if we don't know that La Dangeville and La Clairon are far more talented.

HIM — People can swallow whole any flattering lie, but the bitter truth only goes down in tiny drops. And besides, we look so convinced, so sincere!

ME — But surely you must have sinned against the principles of your art, and just once, by mistake, let slip one of those bitter and wounding truths, because I do believe, in spite of the wretched, abject, vile, abominable role you play, that, deep down, you possess a delicate soul.

HIM — Me? Not at all. I'll be damned if I know what I am, deep down. In general, my mind is as straight as a rule, and my character as honest as the day; never false when it's in my interest to be true, never true when it's in my interest to be false. I say whatever comes into my head: if there's any sense in it, so much the better; if it's absurd, nobody takes any notice. I take every opportunity to speak my mind. Never in my life have I reflected, before, during or after speaking. So I never give offence.

ME — But nonetheless that must have been what happened with those honest people you used to live with, and who were so kind to you.

HIM — What do you mean? It was bad luck, a bad moment — they happen in life. There's no such thing as uninterrupted felicity; I was having too much of a good time; it couldn't go on. We have, as you know, more friends than anyone else and ours are the best. We are a school for humanity, we revive the hospitality of the Ancients. All those failed poets, we give them a home. We took in Palissot in the wake of his *Zara*,[108] Bret following *Le Faux Généreux* [*The False Benefactor*],[109] all the musicians who've been jeered at, all the authors no one reads, all the actresses who've been booed, all the actors who've been hissed at, a load of miserable rejects, dull parasites led by yours truly, brave chieftain of a faint-hearted flock. I'm the one who encourages them to eat the first time they come; I'm the one who gets them a drink. They hardly take up any space! Some of them are young men in tatters who don't know where to turn, but have a certain something; others are old letches who fawn over their host and lull him into a stupor so that once he's finished, they can get at the hostess. We appear cheerful; but deep down, we are resentful and voracious. Wolves are not as hungry, nor tigers as cruel. We are as ravenous as wolves after the long winter snows; we rip to pieces anyone or anything that is at all successful. Sometimes the Bertin, Monsauge and Villemorien[110] gangs get together, and that's when it gets really noisy in the zoo. You've never seen so many miserable, embittered, spiteful and ferocious beasts all in one place. You hear nothing but the names Buffon, Duclos, Montesquieu, Rousseau,[111] Voltaire, d'Alembert, Diderot, along with God knows what epithets. None shall have wit unless he be as foolish as thee and me.[112] That's where the play *Les Philosophes*[113] was born; the scene with the man hawking books, that was mine, based on *La Théologie en quenouille* [*Theology Fallen into Female Hands*].[114] You come in for just as much as the others.

ME — Good! Perhaps I'm being done a greater honour than I deserve. I'd be mortified if those people who say bad things about so many clever and honourable men took it upon themselves to say good things about me.

HIM — There are a lot of us, and we each have to pay our way. Once we've sacrificed the great beasts, we slaughter the rest of them.

ME — To attack knowledge and virtue for your living — that's pretty expensive bread.

HIM — I've already told you, we are people of no consequence. We insult everybody and upset nobody. Sometimes we are joined by that ponderous Abbé d'Olivet, that fat Abbé Leblanc,[115] and Batteux,[116] that hypocrite. The fat Abbé only starts to get nasty after dinner. Once he's had his coffee, he collapses into an armchair, puts his feet up against the fireplace, and falls asleep like an old parrot on its perch. If things get too riotous, he yawns, stretches his arms, rubs his eyes and says: Well, now! What's happening, what's happening? — We're arguing about whether Piron[117] is wittier than De Voltaire. — Let's be clear. You're talking about wit? Not taste, because where taste is concerned, Piron hasn't got a clue. — Hasn't got a clue? — No. And then we're off on a discussion about taste. And that's when the boss raises his finger to get our attention, because taste is what he really prides himself on. — Taste, says he... taste is something which... Good grief, I don't know what the something was, and neither did he.

Sometimes our friend Robbé joins us. He entertains us with his cynical stories, his eye-witness accounts of the Convulsionaries and their miracles,[118] and a few cantos from the poem he's writing on a subject he knows all too well. I can't stand his verses, but I like hearing him recite them: he looks like a man possessed. Everyone around him exclaims: There's a real poet for you! Between you and me, that sort of poetry is nothing but a hullabaloo, a whole load of noises jumbled up, like the barbaric squawking coming from the Tower of Babel.

There's also this fellow who comes to visit: he looks dull and stupid, but he's got the devil of a wit and is sneakier than an old monkey.[119] He's got one of those faces that's just asking to be made fun of and that you want to stick your tongue out at, and which God created in order to teach those who judge on appearances something they should already have realized from looking at themselves in the mirror, that is, that it is as easy to be a witty man and look like a fool as it is to conceal a fool beneath a witty physiognomy. There's nothing so common or so lazy as attacking a good man for the amusement of others. And this fellow is always on the receiving end. In fact, we set him as a trap for newcomers, and I've practically never seen anyone fail to fall into it.

I have on occasion been surprised at the accuracy of this madman's observations about men and characters, and I told him so.

The reason is, he replied, that there are rewards to be had from keeping bad company just as there are from following your fancies. You lose your innocence but the compensation is that you also lose your prejudices. If you live alongside wicked people, they show you their true face, and you learn what they're really like. Besides, I've done a bit of reading.

ME — What have you read?

HIM — I have read and am reading and forever re-reading Theophrastus, La Bruyère, and Molière.

ME — Those are indeed excellent books.

HIM — They're even better than people think; but who is capable of reading them?

ME — Everyone, according to their level of intelligence.

HIM — Hardly anybody then. Would you mind telling me what it is they're reading them for?

ME — Amusement and instruction.

HIM — But what sort of instruction? Because that's the point.

ME — Knowing what your duty is, loving virtue, hating vice.

HIM — What I take from them is what to do and what not to say. So when I read *L'Avare* [Molière's *The Miser*], I tell myself: be a miser if you like, but make sure you don't speak like one. When I read *Tartuffe*, I tell myself: be a hypocrite if you like, but make sure you don't speak like one. Hold onto any vices that you find useful, but don't sound or look as if you have these failings because they'd make you seem ridiculous. To protect yourself from sounding or looking as if you do, you have to know what they're really like, and these authors have portrayed them extremely well. I am myself and I remain myself, but I act and I speak according to the rules. I am not one of those people who despises the moralists; they've got a lot to offer, particularly the ones who show morality in action. Vice itself only occasionally causes harm, but a character displaying obvious signs of it causes permanent offence. Perhaps it would be better to be contemptuous than to have a contemptuous physiognomy; the contemptuous character is only insulting from time to time, whereas the contemptuous physiognomy is continuously insulting. And don't go thinking I'm the only one of my species who reads like this. The only merit I can claim for myself is that I have a system, based on clear thinking and rational, true observation, for doing what most people do instinctively. And that's why when they read, they are not improved any more than I am; on the contrary, they carry on looking ridiculous; whereas I only look ridiculous when I want to, and then, I leave them far behind, because the skill which has taught me to escape ridicule when I need to, is the same skill which enables me to attract it to a remarkable degree. At such times, I draw on everything people have said, everything I've read, and add in everything I can call up from my inner fund which, when it comes to this sort of thing, is surprisingly fertile.

ME — I am glad you revealed these mysteries to me; otherwise, I would have thought you were being inconsistent.

HIM — No, I'm not; because if there are times when I have to avoid ridicule, fortunately there are hundreds more when I have to make sure I don't. There's no better role to play in the company of great men than the fool. The title of King's Fool was in existence for a long time, you know, whereas the title King's Wise Man never was. I myself am Bertin's fool, and lots of other people's fool too, maybe yours at the moment, or perhaps you're mine: a wise man wouldn't have a fool; a man with a fool is therefore not wise; if he's not wise, he is a fool; and perhaps, if he were king, he'd be his fool's fool. Besides, remember that when it comes to a subject as variable as morals, there are no absolute, essential or general rights or wrongs except the law of self-interest, according to which we must always be what it wants us to be, good or bad, wise or foolish, decent or ridiculous, honest or wicked. If virtue had happened to offer a route to fortune, I would have been virtuous or pretended to be, like everyone else. Ridiculous is what they wanted me to be, and so that's what I became; as for wicked, nature did that all by herself. When I say wicked, I'm speaking your language, for if we were ever to have it out, we might discover that what you call vice, I call virtue, and what you call virtue, I call vice.

We are also joined for dinner by the dramatists from the Opéra-Comique, their actors and actresses, and more often their managers, Corbi, Moette[120]... all resourceful people of great merit.

And I was forgetting the great literary critics, *L'Avant-Coureur* [*The Herald*],[121] *Les Petites Affiches* [*What's On*],[122] *L'Année littéraire* [*The Literary Year*],[123] *L'Observateur littéraire* [*The Literary Observer*],[124] *Le Censeur hebdomadaire* [*The Weekly Critic*],[125] the whole clique of hacks.

ME — *L'Année littéraire*! *L'Observateur littéraire*! That's impossible; they hate each other.

HIM — True, but beggars can't be choosers. Damn that *Observateur littéraire*, him and his paper can go to hell! That stupid little dog of a priest,[126] with his penny-pinching, stinking, grasping ways, he's the one who caused my downfall. He appeared over our horizon yesterday for the first time; he arrived at the moment when we all come out of our dens: dinnertime. When it's raining, you're a lucky man if you've got the cab fare in your pocket. One of our number made fun of another for having arrived in the morning all spattered in mud and completely wet through, but when he went home in the evening, exactly the same thing happened to him. Someone else, I can't remember who it was now, got into a fight, a few months ago, with the shoe-cleaner from Savoy who'd set himself up outside our front door. They had set up a running account; the creditor wanted the debtor to settle up, and the latter was not in funds. Dinner is served,[127] the Abbé is guest of honour and is seated at the head. I come in, I see him. What's all this, Abbé, I said, are you presiding at this table? That's all very well for today, but tomorrow, you'll come down by one place, if you please, and the next day, by another one, and so on, from one place to the next, either down the left side or the right, until you reach the place I sat in once, where Fréron once sat after me, Dorat[128] once after Fréron, Palissot once after Dorat, until you come to a halt next to me, a poor useless bugger just like yourself, who *siedo sempre come un maestoso cazzo fra duoi coglioni.*[129] The Abbé, who's a genial old rogue, and who can take anything, started laughing. Mademoiselle, penetrated by the truth of my observation and the accuracy of my comparison, started laughing too; everyone sitting to the left and right of the Abbé and who'd been bumped down a notch by him, started laughing; by this time, everyone is laughing, except for Monsieur, who gets angry, and starts saying things to me which wouldn't have meant a thing if we'd been on our own: Rameau, you are an impertinent upstart. — I'm well aware of that, and it was on that basis that you took me on. — Scum. — No more than the next man. — A beggar. — Would I be here otherwise? — I'll have you kicked out. — After dinner, I'll go of my own accord. — I suggest you do. So we ate dinner; I ate up every last bit. Having eaten a lot and drunk more, after all that's what I'd have done anyway, Maestro Gastro[130] being someone I've never resisted, I made up my mind, and prepared to leave. I had given my word in front of so many people that I had no choice but to keep it. I spent quite some time wandering around the room looking for my hat and cane in places where they couldn't possibly be, still hoping that the boss would come out with a fresh torrent of invective, that someone would step in, and we would finally be able to argue ourselves back together again. I walked round and round for an age, for I bore no grudge myself, but the boss was looking darker and more brooding than Homer's Apollo shooting his arrows at the Greek army;[131] his cap even lower than usual, he paced up and down with his chin sunk on his fist.[132] Mademoiselle comes up to me: But, Mademoiselle, what's so extraordinary about what I did today? Was I any different from how I normally am? — I want him out. — I will go; I didn't let him down. — I beg your pardon; Monsieur l'Abbé was our guest, and... — He brought it on himself by inviting the Abbé, and by letting me in, along with a whole load of spongers like me. — Come on, my little Rameau, go and ask Monsieur l'Abbé for his forgiveness. — I don't care about his forgiveness. — Come on now, come on, it'll all calm down... She takes me by the hand and drags me over to where the Abbé is sitting; I stretch out my arms, I gaze at the Abbé with a sort of admiration, for has anyone ever asked the Abbé for forgiveness before? Abbé, say I, Abbé, this is all quite ridiculous, is it not? And then I start laughing, and so does the Abbé. So that's me forgiven on that front, but now I've got the other one to deal with, and what I had to say to him was a whole other kettle of fish. I can't quite recall how I phrased my apology... Sir, here's our fool come to see you. — I've been finding him a bloody nuisance for too long now; I don't want to hear another word about him. — He's angry. — Yes, I am very angry. — He'll never do it again. — Until the next time. I don't know whether it was one of those days when he was in a bad mood and Mademoiselle is afraid to go near him, or has to treat him with kid gloves, or whether he didn't hear what I said properly, or whether I just didn't say it properly, but it was worse than before. Damn it! Doesn't he know me by now? Doesn't he know I'm like a child, and that sometimes I can't hold it in? And in any case, I don't believe I'd ever get a moment to myself, God forgive me, to let it out in private. Even a puppet made of steel would get worn out if its strings got pulled all day and all night. My job is to keep them from getting bored; that's the deal; but I've got to have some fun myself sometimes too. In the midst of all this hoohah, a dangerous thought flashed through my mind, a thought which puffed me up with pride and insolence: the thought that they couldn't do without me, that I was indispensable.

ME — Yes, I believe you are very useful to them, but they're even more useful to you. You wouldn't be able to find another situation in such a good household, even if you wanted to, because for every vacancy they've got for a fool, a hundred will come knocking.

HIM — A hundred fools like me! I can assure you, Mister Philosopher, they're not that common. Sure, there are plenty of basic fools. But stupidity is more demanding than talent or virtue. I am uncommon in my species, yes, very uncommon. Now they haven't got me anymore, what do you think they're doing with themselves? They'll be bored to death. I am an endless source of rude remarks. I was always ready with a quip that would make them weep with laughter, I was their own personal little Bedlam.

ME — And besides, you had bed and board, jacket and breeches, coat and shoes, and a monthly allowance.

HIM — Well, that's the upside and those are the advantages; but what you're not mentioning are the costs. For starters, if there was the slightest rumour of a new play, whatever the weather, I'd have to ferret around in all the garrets of Paris until I found the author, got hold of a copy, and gently hinted that one of the parts might be exactly right for someone I happened to know... And who might that be, if you don't mind saying? — Who might that be? You're so right to ask! She's the embodiment of grace, sweetness, and delicacy. — Do you mean Mademoiselle Dangeville? Do you know her, by any chance? — I do, a little, but it's not her. — Then who? I'd whisper her name. — Her! — Yes, her, I'd repeat, a little ashamed, for I do sometimes feel shame, and you should have seen how the poet's face fell at her name, and at other times how they laughed in my face. But whatever his reaction was, I'd have to bring my man along to dinner, and watch him trying to avoid making a commitment he'd regret, baulking at the idea, and thanking me all at once. You should've seen how they treated me when my negotiations didn't come off: I was an idiot, a fool, an oaf, I was completely useless; I wasn't even worth the water they gave me to drink. It was much worse when she was on stage, and I had to be brave and stand right in the middle of an audience that was booing loudly — and they are good judges, whatever anybody says — and clap loudly enough to be heard; have people stare at me, sometimes attract the catcalls instead of her, and hear people around me whispering: It's only because he's in the pay of the man she's sleeping with. Won't that lout ever shut up?... They don't realize what drives a man to it; they suppose it's sheer ineptitude, but in fact, the reason behind it excuses everything.

ME — To the extent of disturbing the peace.

HIM — After a while, they knew who I was anyway, and they'd say: Oh! It's just Rameau. What I used to do was make a few snide remarks to stop them ridiculing my solitary applause, which they then interpreted as the opposite. You will accept that you'd need a powerful motive to brave such an assembled audience, and that every single one of these tasks was worth more than the pittance I was paid.

ME — Why didn't you call in reinforcements?

HIM — Sometimes I did, and I made a bit extra out of it. Before turning up at the scene of torment, I'd have to memorize where all the best speeches fell so as to make sure the others knew when to clap. If ever I forgot and came in at the wrong bit, I'd come home a nervous wreck; you've never heard such a rumpus. And then back at the house, there'd be the pack of dogs to look after; it's true that I'd stupidly taken this task upon myself; and then there were the cats I had to supervise, and I was only too pleased if *Kitty* deigned to use her claws on my cuffs or my hand. *Fluffy* is prone to colic; it's my job to rub her tummy. Mademoiselle used to have the vapours; these days, it's nerves. I won't even go into the other slight indispositions that they talk about quite freely in front of me. I let it go; I've never been one to censor. I read somewhere, I can't remember where, that a prince known as The Great, sometimes used to lean over the back of his mistress's privy. We make our familiars privy to our every movement, and back then, I can tell you, I was more familiar than anyone. I am the apostle of familiarity and of privy movements. I used to practice what I preached, without anyone taking offence; the only thing they could do was to let me get on with it. I've already sketched out the boss for you. Mademoiselle is beginning to get a bit heavy, and you should hear the funny stories they're telling about her.

ME — You're not one of those people, are you?

HIM — Why shouldn't I be?

ME — Because it's indecent, to say the least, to ridicule your benefactors.

HIM — But isn't it even worse to use your benefactions as a means of giving yourself the authority to humiliate your protégé?

ME — But if the protégé hadn't degraded himself all on his own, there'd be no way the protector could acquire that authority.

HIM — But if these characters hadn't made themselves ridiculous all on their own, there'd be no funny stories to tell. And anyway, is it my fault if they degrade themselves? And is it my fault, if, once they have degraded themselves, they get betrayed and cast aside? Once you resign yourself to living with the likes of us, if you've got any common sense, you'd better be prepared to be endlessly stabbed in the back. When they take us on, do they not see us for the self-interested, low-down, treacherous souls that we are? If they do, all's well with the world. There is a tacit agreement[133] that they will be good to us, and that sooner or later, we will repay them for it by doing them harm. Is this not the same agreement that exists between a man and his monkey or a man and his parrot? Brun[134] is going around screeching that Palissot, his companion and friend, has written some verses attacking him. Palissot had no choice but to write those verses, and it's Brun who's at fault. Poinsinet is going around screeching that Palissot is blaming him for the verses Palissot wrote attacking Brun. Palissot had to blame Poinsinet for the verses he wrote attacking Brun, and it's Poinsinet who's at fault. Little Abbé Rey[135] is going around screeching that his friend Palissot has snatched his mistress from under him, when it was thanks to him that Palissot was even allowed through the front door in the first place. The point is that you should never allow a Palissot anywhere near your mistress, unless you're prepared to lose her; Palissot did what he had to do, and it's Abbé Rey who is at fault. David,[136] the bookseller, is going around screeching that his associate Palissot has been sleeping with his wife, or that he wanted to; and the wife of David the bookseller is going around screeching that Palissot is hinting to anyone who's interested that Palissot did sleep with her, whether Palissot had slept with her or not, which is difficult to be sure about, since the wife had no choice but to deny it, and it was quite within Palissot's power to hint at something which wasn't true.

Whatever the truth of the matter, Palissot did what his role required of him, and it's David and his wife who are at fault. The same goes for Helvétius who's currently going around screeching that Palissot has represented him on stage as a dishonest man, when Palissot still owes him the money he lent him to pay his doctor's bills, and to buy food and clothes.[137] What else should he have expected from a man who'd taken depravity to new depths, who'd make his friend renounce his religion for the hell of it,[138] who'd steal his associates' possessions, who lacks all faith, principles, and feeling, who's only after the money and will do whatever it takes to get it *per fas et nefas* [by hook and by crook] who measures his life in wicked deeds; and who has even represented himself on stage as a most dangerous scoundrel,[139] the outrageous cheek of which I don't think has ever been seen before or will ever be seen again. No. No, it is not Palissot, but Helvétius who's at fault. If you take a young man from the provinces to the zoo at Versailles, and he is stupid enough to stick his hand through the bars of the tiger or the leopard cage; and if he doesn't pull his arm away when the wild animal opens its jaws, whose fault is that? All of this is written down in the tacit agreement. Tough luck on anyone who didn't realise that that was how it worked, or had forgotten. With the help of this universal and sacred pact, I can defend anyone accused of wickedness, when in fact it's ourselves we should be accusing of stupidity. Yes, you, you fat Countess,[140] you're the one who's at fault when you surround yourself with what is known amongst people of your sort as specimens,[141] just as you are when these same specimens play nasty tricks on you, make you play nasty tricks on others and lay you open to the indignant resentment of honourable people. Honourable people do what they must, and so do specimens, and you're the one who's at fault for welcoming them in. If Bertinhus[142] had lived quietly and peacefully with his mistress; if they had been of honourable character and had therefore known honourable people; if they had surrounded themselves with men of talent, people well known for their virtue; if they spent time in each other's company, loving each other, and saying so in silence and seclusion, and then set aside a few of those precious hours for a small and select company of enlightened people; do you think we'd have told any stories about them at all, good or bad? So what did they get? What they deserved. They were punished for their carelessness; and we're just the ones appointed by Providence to stand in eternal judgement on the Bertins of the day,[143] us and people like us; our nephews in generations to come will stand in judgement on the Montsauges and the Bertins of the future. And yet while we are busy passing Providence's rightful judgement on stupidity, you are busy painting us as we are, and passing Providence's rightful judgement on us. What would you think of us if, with our filthy morals, we claimed we were in good standing with the public? That we were out of our minds. And as for those who expect to have honest dealings with people who were born wicked and whose characters are vile and abject, are they being wise? Everything has to be paid for in this world. There are two public prosecutors, and one of them is at your door, punishing crimes against society; the other is nature herself. She is familiar with all those vices that escape the law. If you go in for debauchery and women, you'll get dropsy. If you're venal, you'll get consumption. If you invite rogues into your house and surround yourself with them, you'll be betrayed, made a fool of, and despised. The easiest thing to do is to resign yourself to the fairness of these judgements, say to yourself, fair enough; shake yourself down and mend your ways, or stay as you are, albeit in accordance with the aforementioned conditions.

ME — You're right.

HIM — And moreover, all those awful stories, they're not mine, I don't make them up; I just hawk them around. What I've heard is that a few days ago, at about five in the morning, there was a massive racket; all the bell-pulls were going; what you could hear was the strangulated and stifled cries of a man who was suffocating: Help, help, I'm suffocating! I'm dying! These cries came from the boss's room. Everyone rushes in to help. Our fat creature who had lost her head, didn't know where she was and couldn't see straight, as does happen in such moments, continued with her pounding motion, raising herself on both hands as high as she could and letting the entire weight of her two to three hundred pounds come crashing down on top of his casual parts, at a speed of furious pleasure. We had a lot of trouble getting him out from underneath. What possessed such a little hammer to place itself beneath such a heavy anvil?

ME — You just can't resist a dirty joke. Let's change the subject. All the time we've been talking, there's been something I've been wanting to ask you.

HIM — What's been stopping you?

ME — I was afraid it might be indiscreet.

HIM — After what I've just told you, I can't imagine what secrets I could possibly have left.

ME — You are not in any doubt as to my judgement of your character, are you?

HIM — Not at all. In your eyes, I am an utterly abject, thoroughly despicable being, and that's what I am in my own eyes too sometimes, but not very often. I more usually congratulate myself on my vices than blame myself for them. You are more consistent in your contempt.

ME — True; but why would you reveal the depths of your moral turpitude to me?

HIM — You already knew most of it anyway, and I thought I stood to gain more than I'd lose if I told you the rest.

ME — How could that be, may I ask?

HIM — If there's one genre it's worth being sublime in, it's evil.[144] We'll spit in the face of a petty thief, but can't help admiring a great criminal — his courage astounds us and his atrocities make us shudder. We value unity of character in all things.

ME — But this admirable unity of character, you don't yet have it. I think you yourself waver from time to time with respect to your principles. It is unclear whether you were born naturally wicked or whether you learnt it, and indeed, whether your learning has taken you as far as it might.

HIM — I agree, but I've done my level best. Have I not had the modesty to acknowledge that there are beings more perfect than myself? Have I not sung Bouret's praises? Bouret is, to my mind, the most admirable man in the world.

ME — But just beneath him, it's you?

HIM — No.

ME — So it's Palissot?

HIM — It is Palissot, but not Palissot alone.

ME — And who is worthy of sharing second place?

HIM — The Renegade of Avignon.[145]

ME — I've never heard of this Renegade of Avignon, but he must be a very remarkable man.

HIM — Indeed he is.

ME — I have always been fascinated by the lives of great men.

HIM — I can well believe it. This one lived with a good and honest man, one of the descendants of Abraham, father of the faithful, whose seed was promised to him numberless as the stars.

ME — You mean, with a Jew?

HIM — Yes, with a Jew. The Renegade had initially managed to inspire him with compassion, then with kindness, and finally with complete confidence; for that's the way it always goes: we value our good deeds so highly that we rarely keep a secret from those to whom we give generously. How can you possibly expect there not to be lots of ungrateful scroungers when the temptation is there and they can get away with it? This is an important consideration which didn't occur to our Jew. He confided in the Renegade that his conscience would not let him eat pork. You will soon see what an inventive mind did with a confession like this. A few months went by in which our Renegade became increasingly affectionate. Once he believed his attentions had so thoroughly moved, ensnared, and convinced his Jew that he had no better friend in all the tribes of Israel, then... Admire the lengths the man went to. He doesn't rush it. He lets the pear ripen before shaking the branch. If he'd been too keen, the whole plan could have fallen through. The point is that, ordinarily, greatness of character is the natural result of two or more opposing qualities balancing each other out.[146]

ME — Leave out the musings, and get on with the story.

HIM — That's just not possible. There are some days when I have to muse. It's a disease which has to be allowed to run its course. Where was I?

ME — The Jew and the Renegade were already intimate friends.

HIM — So the pear was ripe... But you're not listening, what are you thinking about?

ME — I'm thinking about how unequal your tone is, sometimes lofty, sometimes low.

HIM — Can a wicked man keep to a single tone? The Renegade turns up one evening at his friend's house, looking terrified, hardly able to speak, shaking all over, looking like death. — What's wrong? — We are done for. — Done for, how? — Done for, I tell you; there's no way out. — Tell me what you're talking about. — Give me a moment to recover. — Of course, take your time, said the Jew instead of saying: You are a liar and a crook, I don't know what you've got to tell me, but you're a liar and a crook; and all this terror is an act.

ME — And why should he have said that to him?

HIM — Because he was false and because he'd overdone it.[147] It's perfectly clear to me, and don't interrupt me anymore. — We are done for, done for, there's no way out! Can't you hear how affected all this repetition of 'done for' is? A traitor has reported us to the Holy Inquisition, you as a Jew and me as a renegade, a vile renegade. See how the traitor doesn't blush to use the most odious expressions. It takes more courage than you might think to say out loud what you really are. You have no idea how hard it is to do that.

ME — No, I don't. But what about this vile Renegade?...

HIM — He's duplicitous, but his duplicity is extremely clever. The Jew takes fright, tears his beard, flings himself to the ground, sees the guards already at the door and himself in a sanbenito[148] with his sacrificial pyre[149] ready and waiting. — My friend, my dear friend, my only friend, what shall we do? — Do? Go out in public, pretend not to have a care in the world, behave as if nothing was wrong. The tribunal works in secret, but at least it's slow. We must make use of this time to sell up. I'll go and hire a ship or get someone else to do it for us; yes, a third party, that would be best. We'll stow your wealth on it, because it's your wealth they're really after; and we shall sail away, you and I, to a far-off land where we will be free to serve our God and follow the law of Abraham and our conscience. The crucial thing, given our perilous situation, is not to do anything rash. — It was no sooner said than done. The ship is hired and stocked with provisions and sailors. The Jew's wealth is on board. Tomorrow at the break of day, they'll set sail. They'll be able to have their meals in peace and sleep soundly.

Tomorrow, they escape their persecutors. During the night, the Renegade gets up, relieves the Jew of his wallet, purse, and jewels, boards the ship, and off he goes. And if you think that's the end of it, well, just you wait and see. When I first heard this story, I worked out what was really going on, but I've kept it from you to see how sharp you are. You were right to be an honourable man because you'd have been a lousy crook. So far, the Renegade is nothing more than that. He's a contemptible little cheat whom nobody would want to resemble. What's truly sublime about his wickedness is that his good friend, the Israelite, really had been denounced, and it was the Renegade who had done it. The Holy Inquisition came for the Jew the next morning, and put him on a nice, big bonfire a few days later. And that's the story of how the Renegade came to enjoy the fortune of this accursed descendant of those who crucified Our Lord.

ME — I don't know what I find more horrific, the wickedness of your Renegade, or the way you talk about it.

HIM — But that's the point: the atrocity of his actions takes you beyond contempt, and that's why I am perfectly sincere in my admiration. I wanted you to know how brilliant I am at my art, to compel you to admit that at least I have an original way of degrading myself, to make you think of me as the latest in a long line of glorious good-for-nothings, and proclaim: *Vivat Mascarillus, fourbum imperator* [*Long live Mascarillus, Master Trickster*]. Come on, Mister Philosopher, make it joyful, all together now: *Vivat Mascarillus, fourbum imperator*.

And at that, he began to sing a fugue, a thoroughly singular one. At times, the melody was serious and full of majesty, at others, light and playful; one moment, he was imitating the bass, the next, the top parts; he would stretch out his arm and neck to show when to hold a note, performing and composing his own triumphal march, and showing he knew more about good music than good morals.[150]

I wasn't sure, for my part, whether I should stay or run away, laugh or get angry. I stayed, with the aim of bringing the conversation round to some subject that would clear my soul of the horror that was overwhelming it. I was beginning to find it hard to bear the presence of a man who could talk about a horrendous deed, a hideous crime in the same way as a connoisseur of painting or poetry would examine the beauties of a work of art, or as a moralist or a historian would bring out and highlight the details of a heroic deed. I became sombre despite myself. He noticed, and said:

HIM — What's the matter? Are you feeling ill?

ME — A bit, but it'll pass.

HIM — You have the worried air of a man tormented by some distressing idea.

ME — Exactly.

We were both silent for a while, during which time he walked up and down, whistling and singing. To get him to talk about his talent again, I said: What are you working on at the moment?

HIM — Nothing.

ME — That must be very tiring.

HIM — As if I wasn't already feeling low enough, I went to hear that music by Duni[151] and our other young tunesters, and it really finished me off.

ME — So you approve of this genre, do you?

HIM — Certainly.

ME — And you can hear beauty in these new kinds of song?[152]

HIM — Can't I just! By God, I can, I swear. You should hear how they sing the words! How true it feels! How expressive!

ME — All imitative arts have their model in nature. What model does the musician choose when he writes a song?

HIM — Why don't we start with a more fundamental question? What is song?

ME — I confess this question is beyond me. And so it is for all of us. We have nothing in our memory but words, which we think we understand because we use them frequently and sometimes even accurately; and nothing in our minds but vague notions.[153] When I say the word 'song', I don't have any clearer notion than people like you do when they say reputation, guilt, honour, vice, virtue, modesty, decency, shame, ridicule.

HIM — Song is the imitation of a scale, either invented by art or inspired by nature, whichever you prefer, using either vocal or instrumental sound to imitate either physical noises or emotional accents; and you'll see that if you just replace a few of the terms in this definition, it would also apply to painting, eloquence, sculpture and poetry.[154] Now, to come to your question, what is it that singing or composing is trying to imitate? Declamation, if the model is living and thinking; noise, if the model is inanimate. We should consider declamation as one line, and song as another line, winding its serpentine way[155] around the first. The more confident and true the declamation, which in itself is a type of song, the more frequently the song line following it will cross back and forth: the truer the song will be, and the more beautiful. And that's what our young musicians have instinctively felt. When we hear: *Je suis un pauvre diable* [I am a poor devil], we recognise a miser's lament; if he weren't singing it, he would entrust his gold to the earth in the very same tones, and say: *O terre, reçois mon trésor* [*O Earth, receive my treasure*].[156] And that young girl, her heart beating fast, blushing, getting flustered, and begging His Lordship to let her go, would she express herself any differently? In these works, there are all sorts of characters, infinite varieties of declamation. This is sublime, I assure you, and I should know. You must go and hear the piece in which the young man feeling his life slipping away, cries out: *Mon cœur s'en va!* [*My heart is departing!*][157] Listen to the singing; listen to the way the parts fit together; and then tell me if there's any difference between the way a man who's really dying speaks, and the shaping of this song.[158] You'll see whether the line of the melody exactly coincides with the line of the declamation or not. I'm not talking about beat or time, which is another necessary component of song, I'm only talking about expression, and there's nothing clearer than the following saying which I've read somewhere:[159] *Musices seminarium accentus*, accent is the seedbed of melody. This tells you how difficult and how important it is to know how to do recitative well. There's no fine aria that can't be turned into a fine piece of recitative, and no fine piece of recitative that a talented man can't draw a fine aria out of.[160] I wouldn't want to claim that someone who can declaim well will also sing well; but I'd be surprised if someone who sings well wasn't able to recite well. And you should believe everything I'm telling you, because it's the truth.

ME — I should like nothing better than to believe you, only there's a slight problem holding me back.

HIM — And that problem is?

ME — That if this sort of music is sublime, then the music of the divine Lulli,[161] of Campra,[162] Destouches,[163] Mouret, and even, between you and me, dear uncle's, must be rather flat.

HIM, coming over and whispering in my ear, said: — I wouldn't want to be overheard, as there are lots of people here who know me, but the thing is, you're right, it really is. It's not that I'm concerned about dear uncle, since we're calling him 'dear'. He's a stone. I could have my tongue hanging down to the ground with thirst, and he still wouldn't give me a glass of water. But it's all very well him doing his octaves and sevenths, with his la, la; fa, fa; tra, tra, tra, tralala,[164] and making a devil of a racket; but those people who know anything about it, and who therefore no longer mistake cacophony for music, will never want to listen to it again. It should be forbidden by order of the police for anyone of any quality or status
7 to arrange a performance of Pergolesi's *Stabat Mater*.[165] This *Stabat* should have been burnt by the public executioner. Good God, these wretched Italians with their opera buffa, their *Servante Maîtresse* [*The Servant Turned Mistress*],[166] their *Tracollo*,[167] have really buggered us up the arse. In the past, pieces like *Tancrède*,[168] *Issé*,[169] *Europe galante*,[170] *Les Indes*,[171] and *Castor*[172] or *Les Talents lyriques*,[173] used to run for four, five, six months. There was no end
8 to the performances of a piece like *Armide*.[174] Now that's all come tumbling down like a house of cards. And so Rebel and Francœur[175] are erupting in
9 flame and fury. They're saying it's all over, that they're ruined, and that if we allow the rabble from the fairground theatres to carry on with their caterwauling, then our national music is doomed, and the Royal Academy down its back passage might as well shut up shop. There's something in this. All the old fogeys who've been coming along every Friday for thirty or forty years, instead of enjoying it like they did in the past, are now yawning in boredom without quite knowing why.[176] They're wondering what's gone wrong, and they haven't got an answer. Why don't they come to me? Duni's prophecy will be fulfilled, and at this rate, I'll bet my life that

four or five years after *Le Peintre amoureux de son modèle* [*The Painter in Love with his Model*],[177] there won't be any bums on any seats down that famous passage.[178] These good people, they've given up their own symphonies to play the Italian symphonies instead. They supposed their ears would get used to listening to them and that it'd have no effect on their vocal music,[179] as if instrumental music weren't to song, depending on how much free play the range of the instrument and the nimbleness of the fingers allow, what song is to actual speech.[180] It's not as though the violin doesn't ape the human voice, although one day, if difficulty takes the place of beauty, the human voice will ape the violin.[181] The first person to play Locatelli was the apostle of the new sort of music. Every age has its own apostle. We'll get used to hearing the accents of passion or the phenomena of nature being imitated in song, voice, and instrument, for that's all music really aims to do, and you're telling me we'll keep our taste for flights, spears, glories, triumphs, victories?[182] *Va-t'en voir s'ils viennent, Jean* [*Pull the other one, John*].[183] They imagined they could laugh or cry at scenes of comedy or tragedy, set to music, that their ears could hear the accents of fury, hatred, jealousy, the true laments of love, the ironies and jokes of Italian and French theatre, and that they'd still admire *Ragonde*[184] and *Platée*.[185] I swear that's what they thought, they'd believe anything, the fools: they even thought they'd be able to experience how easily, how smoothly, how subtly the Italian language, with its harmony, prosody, ellipses, and inversions, lends itself to the art, movement, expression and phrasing of song, as well as to tempo, and that they would remain unaware of how stiff, deaf, hefty, heavy, pedantic, and monotonous their own language is.[186] Oh yes, yes indeed! They were convinced that after having cried along with a mother grieving for her son, and trembled at a tyrant ordering a murder, they would not be bored by all their whimsical fairyland, their insipid mythology, their sickly little madrigals[187] which are as much a mark of the bad taste of the poet as they are of the poverty of the art which finds them acceptable. Oh good people! That didn't happen and it was never going to. The true, the good, and the beautiful will always have their way.[188] We can argue with them all we like, but we end up admiring them. If art doesn't bear their hallmark, we'll admire it for a while, but it'll end up making us yawn. Yawn away, gentlemen, yawn away at your leisure. Don't hold back. Nature and my Trinity are quietly establishing their empire, and the gates of hell will never be strong enough to withstand my Trinity: the True, which is the Father and engenders the Good, which is the Son who creates the Beautiful, which

is the Holy Spirit. The foreign god humbly goes to sit down next to the local idol on the altar; bit by bit, he grows stronger; and one fine day, he gives his companion a little shove, and booboom, down the idol falls.[189] That's how they say the Jesuits planted Christianity in China and the Indies. And the Jansenists can say what they like, but this way of doing politics, which achieves its goal without making a stir, without any bloodletting, without creating martyrs, without so much as a tuft of hair being pulled out, seems the best to me.[190]

ME — There's some sense, more or less, in everything you've just said.

HIM — Sense! Just as well. I'll be damned if that's what I was aiming at. I just say whatever comes to me. I'm like the musicians of the Back Passage, when my uncle turned up. If I hit the mark, it's because the coal boy will always explain his trade better than a whole academy and all the Duhamels[191] in the world.

And off he goes, walking up and down, making guttural humming noises to the tunes of *L'Île des fous* [*The Island of Fools*],[192] *Le Peintre amoureux de son modèle*,[193] *Le Maréchal-ferrant* [*The Blacksmith*], *La Plaideuse* [*The Lady Litigant*],[194] and occasionally he would raise his hands and look up to the skies, and exclaim: Is it beautiful? Good grief! Is it beautiful? How can you have two ears on your head and ask such a question? He started getting all impassioned and singing softly. He got louder the more impassioned he became; next came the gestures, the grimaces, and the bodily contortions; and I said: Here we go, he's lost his head, and we'll be seeing some new scene any minute now, and in fact, he immediately lets rip: *Je suis un pauvre misérable* [*I am a poor wretch*][195]... *Monseigneur, monseigneur, laissez-moi partir* [Your Lordship, Sir, please let me leave]... *O terre, reçois mon or, conserve bien mon trésor* [O Earth, receive my gold, keep my treasure safe]... *Mon âme, mon âme, ma vie! O terre!* [My soul, my soul, my life! O Earth!]... *Le voilà le petit ami, le voilà le petit ami!* [Here he comes, the likely lad, here he comes, the likely lad], *Aspettare e non venire* [Wait and do not come]... *A Zerbina penserete* [Zerbina always on your mind]... *Sempre in contrasti con te si sta* [I never know where I am with you].[196] He piled up and mixed together thirty tunes, Italian, French, tragic, comic, with lots of different characters;[197] at points, he would descend to the depths of the underworld in a low baritone, at others, he would go right up high in a glass-shattering fake falsetto, mimicking the different

singing roles in the way he walked, held himself, and gestured; by turns furious, soothed, imperious, sneering. Now he's a young girl weeping, and he acts out her every simpering move; now he's a priest, he's a king, he's a tyrant, he threatens, he commands, he loses his temper; he's a slave, he obeys. He calms down, he is sorry, he complains, he laughs; never a false note, never out of time, always capturing the meaning of the words and the character of the music. All the pawn-pushers had left their chessboards and gathered round him. The café windows were crammed with passers-by who had stopped to see what the noise was. The laughter was loud enough to bring the ceiling down. He was completely oblivious; he carried on, in the grip of a fit of mental alienation, of enthusiasm so close to madness as to make it uncertain whether he'd ever emerge from it, or whether we oughtn't throw him in a cab and have him taken straight to Bedlam,[198] while singing a passage from Jomelli's *Lamentations*.[199] He performed the most beautiful sections of each piece with extraordinary precision, truth, and intensity; that beautiful passage of accompanied recitative[200] when the prophet describes the devastation of Jerusalem had him and everyone watching in floods of tears. It had everything, exquisite singing, powerful expression, and great sorrow. He emphasised those places where the composer had displayed particular mastery; if he abandoned the sung part, it was so as to pick up the instrumental line, which he would then suddenly drop to go back to the voice, weaving the two together in such a way as to respect the relation between each of the parts as well as the unity of the whole; capturing our souls and keeping them suspended in the strangest state I have ever experienced... Was it admiration? Yes, it was! Was I moved? Yes, I was, but these feelings were tinged with ridicule, and it transformed their nature.[201]

But you would have roared with laughter at the way he impersonated the different instruments. The horns and bassoons, he did puffing his cheeks up like balloons, and making hoarse, low sounds; he made a piercing, nasal noise for the oboes; his voice catapulting up and down at incredible speed, he did as close an imitation of the strings as he could; he whistled the piccolos and cooed the flutes; shouting, singing, charging about like a madman, single-handedly doing the dancers, both male and female, the singers, both male and female, a whole orchestra, a whole opera company, dividing himself between twenty different roles; running around, suddenly stopping and looking like a man possessed, his eyes blazing, foaming at the mouth. It was boiling hot in there, and the sweat running along the furrows in his brow and down his cheeks got some hair powder mixed in with it, and streamed down and streaked the top of his coat. What did I not see him do? He wept, he laughed, he sighed; he gazed tenderly or serenely or intensely; he was a woman, overcome with sorrow; he was an unfortunate man, giving in to despair; he was a temple going up; birds falling silent at sunset; water burbling in a cool and solitary grove, or gushing forth in torrents from the mountain tops; a storm, a tempest, the cries of those about to perish, together with the howling of the wind and the crashing of the thunder; he was night in all its darkness, he was shadow and silence, for even silence can be painted in sound.[202] He had completely lost his head. Worn out with exhaustion, like a man emerging from a long sleep or from deep concentration, he was unable to move, he was stupefied, stunned. He kept on looking around, like a man lost and trying to work out where he was. He waited for his strength and wits to come back; he kept mechanically wiping his face. Like a man who wakes up and sees a large number of people grouped round his bed, and who has completely forgotten or never known what he has been doing, he immediately exclaimed: Oh hello, gentlemen, what's going on? Why are you laughing and looking so surprised? What's going on? And then he added: Now that's what we ought to call music and being a musician! Nevertheless, gentlemen, there's no need to despise all of Lulli. I challenge you to improve on the *Ah! j'attendrai* [Ah! I'll wait for you][203] scene without changing the words. There's not even any need to despise all of Campra, nor my uncle's violin tunes, nor his gavottes, nor the bits where the soldiers, priests, and high priests all come on... *Pâles flambeaux, nuit plus affreuse que les ténèbres* [Pale torches, more hideous than the shadows][204]... *Dieu du Tartare, Dieu de l'oubli* [God of Tartarus, God of oblivion][205]... At this point, his voice swelled; he held the notes; the neighbours came to their windows; we stuck our fingers in our ears. He added: This is when you need really good lungs, proper organs, some serious air capacity. But before you know it, it's goodbye to Assumption Day; Lent and Epiphany are long gone.[206] They don't yet know what to set to music or what will suit composers. Lyric poetry is yet to be born. But they'll get there if they listen  to enough Pergolesi, Hasse the Saxon,[207] Terradellas,[208] Traetta,[209] and the  rest;[210] if they read enough Metastasio,[211] they'll get there in the end.

ME — What! Are you saying that Quinault, La Motte, Fontenelle[212] didn't have a clue?

HIM — Not when it comes to the new style.[213] No six lines together in any of their charming poems could be set to music. They are ingenious maxims, light, tender and delicate madrigals, but if you want to know how unproductive they are for our art, which is the most violent of them all, not excepting Demosthenes's, get someone to recite those passages to you, and you'll see how cold, languishing, monotonous they are. That's because they haven't got anything, which could serve as a model for song. I'd sooner have to set to music La Rochefoucauld's *Maxims* or Pascal's *Pensées*.[214] It's for the animal cry of passion to dictate the line we should take. These expressions need to come thick and fast; the phrasing needs to be tight; the meaning cut off, left hanging; the composer needs to be able to freely arrange the whole and each of the parts, to leave out or repeat it, to add what he feels is missing, to twist it and turn it inside out like a polyp, without destroying it; all of which makes French lyric poetry much harder than languages that use inversion, which do these things all by themselves... *Cruel barbarian, plunge your dagger into my breast. I am ready for the fatal blow. Strike. Don't be afraid... Ah! I am fading, I am dying... A secret fire inflames my senses... Cruel love, what do you want from me?... Do not deprive me of that sweet tranquillity that gave me such delight... Bring me back from madness...*[215] These passions need to be strong; the composer and the lyric poet must be capable of the highest emotional pitch. The tune is almost always the culmination of the scene. We need exclamations, interjections, half-finished or broken-off phrases, affirmations, negations; we appeal, we invoke, we shout, we moan, we weep, we laugh out loud. None of that wit, none of those epigrams, none of those dainty thoughts. That's all too far removed from the simplicity of nature. So don't go thinking that the way actors move and speak on stage could serve as a model. Not at all! It needs to be more energetic, less mannered, more truthful. Simple speeches, the shared voices of passion are all the more important when the language is monotonous and unaccented. The animal or human cry gives it its accent.

While he was telling me all this, the people who had crowded round us, who had either not understood or not been interested in what he was saying, given that children, like adults, and adults, like children, would always rather have fun than learn anything, had moved away; everyone had gone back to their games; and we were back by ourselves in our corner. Sitting on a banquette, his head leaning against the wall, his arms dangling, his eyes half open, he said: I don't know what's the matter with me; when

I got here, I was refreshed and on form, whereas now I'm shattered and broken as if I'd just run ten leagues. It came over me quite unexpectedly.

ME — Would you like something to drink?

HIM — Very much so. I feel completely shattered. All my strength is gone; and I have a bit of a pain in my chest. This happens to me almost every day and I don't know why.

ME — What can I get you?

HIM — Whatever you fancy; I don't mind; beggars can't be choosers.

We order beer and lemonade. He pours himself two or three large glassfuls and downs them one after another. Then, like a man coming back to life, he coughs loudly, stretches, and says: But in your opinion, Milord Philosopher, is it not rather odd that a foreigner, an Italian, one Duni, should be the one to come and teach us how to put accents into our music,[216] how to make our melody obey movement, tempi, interval, declamation, without harming the prosody? It really shouldn't have been all that difficult. Anyone who'd ever heard a beggar in the street asking for money, a man in a rage, a jealous and furious woman, a lover in despair, a flatterer, yes, a flatterer, sweetening his tone, pouring honey on his every syllable, in a word, anyone who'd ever heard the voice of passion, any passion, so long as it had energy enough to serve as a worthy model for the composer, should have noticed two things: firstly, that the syllables, whether they're long or short, have no fixed duration and no predetermined relationship between their durations; secondly, that passion can arrange prosody almost as it wishes; thirdly, that it can jump huge intervals, and that the man who cries out when his pain is at its most intense: Oh! Woe is me!, is taking the exclamatory syllable up to the highest, most acute pitch, and the others down to the lowest and deepest pitch, jumping an octave or an even bigger interval, and giving each sound the quantity that best suits the turn of the melody, without being offensive to the ear, and without either the long or the short syllable retaining the length or brevity they have when calmly uttered. How far we've come since the time we used to hold up the incidental remark in *Armide*: *Le vainqueur de Renaud, Si quelqu'un le peut être* [Renaud's conqueror, If anyone can be];[217] the line in *Les Indes galantes*: *Obéissons sans balancer* [*We should obey without hesitating*],[218] as marvels of musical declamation! Nowadays, such marvels make me shrug they're so pathetic. The rate this art is moving forward, I can't imagine what the final result will be. Meanwhile, let's have a drink.

He downs two, three, without realizing what he was doing. He would have carried on and drowned himself without realizing, he was so exhausted, if I hadn't removed the bottle he was absent-mindedly reaching out for. So then I said:

ME — How can it be that you have such insight, such a delicate sensibility when it comes to the beauties of musical art, and yet be so blind to things of beauty when it comes to morals, so indifferent to the charms of virtue?

HIM — It's because apparently there's this sense I don't have, a fibre I wasn't given, a loose fibre you can pluck all you want, it still won't vibrate; or perhaps it's that I've always lived with good musicians and bad people; with the result that I have developed a very finely tuned ear, but my heart is tone deaf.[219] And then race also has something to do with it. My father's blood and my uncle's blood are the same blood. My blood is the same as my father's. The paternal molecule was hard and obtuse, and that accursed first molecule has absorbed everything else.

ME — Do you love your child?

HIM — Do I, the little savage! I'm mad about him.

ME — Won't you want to do everything you possibly can to impede the progress of the accursed paternal molecule?

HIM — Any effort I'd make, would, I think, be a complete waste of time. If he's meant to become a good man, I won't put anything in his way. But if the molecule wanted him to be a waster like his father, any trouble I might have gone to to turn him into an honourable man would turn out to be very damaging to him: since his education would be forever going against the bent of the molecule, he'd be pulled in two opposing directions at once, and would zigzag his way through life, as I've seen so many do, and they're all as inept as each other in their attempts to be either great men or great criminals; they're what we call specimens, that most daunting of epithets, because it signals mediocrity, and is the ultimate mark of contempt. A great waster is a great waster, and is in no way a specimen.[220] Before the paternal molecule managed to reassert itself and guide him to the same state of consummate abjection that I have attained, he'd need endless amounts of time; and he'd have passed his prime. I'm not doing anything about it at the moment, I'm just letting him get on with it. I'm keeping an eye on him. He is already greedy, duplicitous, thieving, lazy, and a liar. I fear it runs in the family.

ME — And will you make a musician of him as well to complete the resemblance?

HIM — A musician! A musician! Sometimes I look at him and grind my teeth, and say to myself: if you ever learn so much as a single note, I do believe I'll wring your neck.

ME — And why would that be, may I ask?

HIM — Because it gets you nowhere.

ME — It gets you everywhere.

HIM — Yes, if you excel at it; but who can be sure his child will excel? It's ten thousand to one he'll never be any good and will just saw away at the strings, like I do. Do you realise that it might be easier to find a child able to govern a kingdom and be a great king than to find one who could ever become a great violinist!

ME — I would say that a man able to please others with his talents, mediocre though they might be, will go far and fast in a country without morals, sunk in depravity and luxury. Believe you me, I overheard the following conversation between some species of patron and some species of protégé.[221] The latter had been introduced to the former as an obliging man likely to be able to help him: — Monsieur, what can you do? — I'm fairly good at mathematics. — In that case, teach mathematics; and after having pounded the streets of Paris in all weathers for ten or twelve years, you'll be able to command four hundred pounds a year. — I have studied jurisprudence and am well versed in the law. — If Puffendorf and Grotius[222] were to come back to life, they'd die of hunger on the roadside. — I know a lot about history and geography. — Were there any parents truly devoted to their children's education, your fortune would be made; but there aren't. — I'm quite a good musician. — Why didn't you say so in the first place? And to give you some idea of how well you can do out of that talent, I have a daughter. Come along every day from seven-thirty to nine in the evening, give her a lesson, and I will give you twenty-five louis a year. You'll have lunch, dinner, tea, and supper with us. The rest of the day will be yours to do with what you like.

HIM — And this man, what became of him?

ME — If he'd been wise, he'd have made his fortune, which appears to be the only thing you have in view.

HIM — No doubt about it. Gold, gold. Gold is everything; and without it, the rest is nothing. And therefore, instead of stuffing his head with fine maxims, which he'd need to forget for fear of ending up no better than a beggar, if ever I have a louis, which doesn't happen very often, I plant myself squarely in front of the child. I take the louis out of my pocket. I show it to him admiringly. I look up to heaven. I kiss the louis in front of him. And to make him really understand the importance of the sacred coin, I make my voice tremble when I point out all the things you can buy with it, a fancy jerkin, a fancy cap, a tasty cake. Then I put the louis in my pocket, strut around with pride; I lift my coat-tails; I pat my purse; and that's how I make it clear to him that it's only the louis I've got in there that gives me this confidence.

ME — It couldn't be done better. But if one day, his profound conviction of the louis's value were to mean that...

HIM — I see what you're saying. One must turn a blind eye. There's no moral principle that doesn't have its downside. At worst, it'd be a bad fifteen minutes, and then it'd all be over.[223]

ME — Even after having heard such brave and wise views, I persist in believing that it'd be good to make a musician of him. I know of no quicker way of getting close to the great and powerful, of serving their vices and profiting from one's own.

HIM — True; but I have some plans that guarantee rapid results. Oh! If only he were a girl! But you don't always get what you want, you have to take what comes and make the best of it, and not do what most fathers stupidly do, which, if they'd given a moment's thought to how unhappy it would make their children, they would realise was the very worst thing to do, that is, give a Spartan education to a child destined to live in Paris.[224]

If it's wrong, then it's my nation's morals that are to blame, not mine. And who'd be willing to shoulder that? I want my son to be happy, or, what comes to the same thing, I want him to be respected, rich, and powerful. I know a bit about the easiest ways of reaching that goal, and I'll teach them to him early on. You may blame me, you and your wise friends, but the masses will absolve me, and so will success. He'll have gold; believe you me. If he has a lot of it, he'll want for nothing, not even your esteem and respect.

ME — You might be mistaken.

HIM — Or he'll go without, as many have done before him.

In all of this, he said lots of the things we all think, and which guide what we do, but which never get said out loud. And here, in truth, we have the most significant difference between my man and most of the people around us. He admitted to the vices he had and which everybody else has, but he wasn't a hypocrite. He was neither more nor less horrendous than anyone else, he was simply more open, and more logical; and occasionally, he was profound in his depravity. I trembled to think what his child would become with such a master. There can be no doubt that, by modelling ideas of education so strictly on our morals, he would go far, unless his progress were to be prematurely cut short.

HIM[225] — Oh! You needn't worry, he said: the main thing, the really difficult thing a good father must pay particular attention to, is not so much giving his child vices that will make him rich, or comic quirks that will endear him to the great and powerful — that's what everyone does, even if they haven't got a system like I do, but just teach by example and lecture instead — but showing him where the limits are, the art of avoiding shame, dishonour, and the law; these are dissonances within the social harmony, which you have to learn how to introduce, set up, and pull off. There's nothing so flat as a sequence of perfect chords. What's needed is something sharp, which splits the bundle of rays, and makes them fan out. [226]

ME — I quite agree. Your comparison has taken me away from morals and back to music, which I'd got diverted from in spite of myself; and I am very grateful to you, because, to be perfectly honest, I like you more as a musician than as a moralist.

HIM — And yet I'm well below average at music, whereas at morals, I'm near the top.

ME — I very much doubt that; but even if it were true, I'm a good man, and your principles have nothing in common with mine.

HIM — That's too bad. Oh! If only I had your talents!

ME — Leave my talents out of it, and let's get back to yours.

HIM — If only I knew how to express myself like you! The way I speak makes me sound like a bloody cageful of squawking birds; it's half high society literary, half barrow-boy.

ME — I'm not good at speaking. I only know how to tell the truth, and that doesn't always go down very well, as you know.[227]

HIM — But it's not so I can tell the truth; on the contrary, it's so I can lie better that I'd like to have your talent. If only I knew how to write, how to throw a book together, turn a dedicatory epistle, intoxicate a fool with his own merits, worm my way into the company of women!

ME — All of which, you can do a thousand times better than I can. I am not even worthy of being your pupil.

HIM — So many great qualities gone to waste, and you don't even know what they're worth!

ME — I earn from them what I think their value is.

HIM — If that were true, you wouldn't be wearing that shabby coat, that flimsy waistcoat, those woollen stockings, those clumpy shoes and that antique wig.

ME — Agreed. A man must be really quite inept if he's not rich but will do anything to get rich. But the thing is that there are people like me — bizarre people indeed — who don't regard wealth as the most precious thing in the world.

HIM — Very bizarre. No one is born that way. You have to want to be like that since it's not natural.

ME — In man?

HIM — In man. Everything alive, without exception, seeks to ensure its own well-being at the expense of whatever it is dependent on; and I'm sure that if I let the little savage grow up without me telling him anything, he'd want to be richly dressed, lavishly fed, prized by men, loved by women, and to surround himself with all the pleasures of life.

ME — If the little savage were left to himself, remaining in a state of imbecility, and combining the feeble reasoning abilities of a small infant with the violent passions of a grown man,[228] he'd wring his father's neck and sleep with his mother.[229]

HIM — That just goes to show the necessity of a good education; and who'd argue with that? And what's a good education if it doesn't mean you get to enjoy all sorts of things without getting into danger or difficulty?

ME — I almost entirely agree with you, but let's not get into that.

HIM — Why not?

ME — Because I fear we only appear to agree with each other, and that, were we to get into a discussion of the dangers and difficulties to be avoided, there'd no longer be any agreement between us.

HIM — And what's the problem with that?

ME — Let's drop it, I mean it. I could never make you learn what I know about the subject, but you can easily teach me what I don't know about music, and you do. Dear Rameau, let's talk music; tell me why it is that, given your facility for hearing, remembering, and reproducing the most beautiful passages from the great masters, and given the enthusiasm they inspire in you and which you communicate to others, you've not managed to produce anything of value yourself.

Instead of replying, he began to nod his head, and then, raising his finger to the sky, exclaimed: What star was I born under? What star? Nature smiled when she made Leo,[230] Vinci,[231] Pergolesi, Duni. She had an imposing and a serious air as she was forming dear uncle Rameau, whom we'll have spent ten years calling the 'great Rameau', and soon won't be calling anything at all.[232] When she threw his nephew together, she pulled a face, and then another one, and kept on pulling faces. And as he was saying this, he was pulling all sorts of faces, contemptuous, disdainful, ironic; and he seemed to be squeezing a piece of paste with his fingers, and smiling at the ridiculous shapes he was making. Once he'd finished, he hurled the funny little figure away, and said: That's how she made me and then she cast me down alongside other little figures, some with fat little tummies, short necks, huge eyes bulging out of their heads, looking apoplectic, others with sideways necks; there were dried out ones, with beady eyes and hooked noses; when they saw me they all started killing themselves laughing; and I dug my fists into my sides and split them laughing back, for fools and madmen find each other entertaining; they seek each other out, they are attracted to each other. If, at that moment, the proverb *The foolish man's money is the clever man's inheritance* hadn't already existed, I'd have had to invent it. I felt that nature had put my rightful portion into the purses of the funny little figures, and so I invented thousands of ways to get it back.

ME — I know what those ways are; you've told me about them, and I have been very admiring of them. Yet, with all those talents, why haven't you tried to produce a work of art?

HIM — That reminds me of the kind of thing a man of the world would say to the Abbé Leblanc.[233] The Abbé said: Madame de Pompadour[234] takes me by the hand, leads me as far as the threshold of the Académie française, where she lets my hand go. I fall over and break both my legs... The man of the world replied: Come on now, Abbé, you have to get up and use your head instead... The Abbé retorted: That's what I was trying to do; and guess what I got for it? A bump on the forehead.

After telling this little story, my man started pacing to and fro, looking down, with a pensive and a weary air; he sighed, wept, grieved, raised his hands, and looked up, punched himself in the head so violently that he nearly broke his forehead or his fingers, adding: It seems to me that there must be something in there, but however hard I hit it or shake it, nothing comes out. Then he began shaking his head again, and hitting his forehead even harder, saying: Either there's nobody at home, or they're refusing to answer.

A moment later, he took on an air of pride, lifted his head, placed his right hand over his heart; he strode up and down, saying: I can feel something, yes, I can. He imitated a man getting angry, indignant, being moved, giving orders, imploring; he extemporised speeches that were angry, commiserating, full of hatred or love; he sketched out the characters of the different passions with surprising subtlety and truth. And then he added: That's it, I think. It's coming out now; that's what happens when you find an accoucheur who knows how to get a reaction, to bring on the pains, and get the baby out. When I'm alone, I pick up my pen, I want to write. I bite my nails, I wear my forehead out. Your servant. Good evening. The god has gone out; I had convinced myself that I had some genius; when I get to the end of my line, I read that I'm a fool, a fool, a fool. But how are we supposed to feel, be inspired, think, paint powerful pictures, when we have to frequent the kind of people we are obliged to in order to make a living, when we have to say and listen to the kinds of things we have to, such as this drivel: Today, it was quite charming out on the boulevard. Have you been to see the little marmot? Her acting is quite exquisite. Monsieur So-And-So had the most beautiful dappled grey mount imaginable. Beautiful Madame Whatsherface is beginning to fade; can you get away with wearing your hair like that at forty-five? Little Miss Whatsit is head to toe in diamonds that she got for free. — You mean that she got for a fee? — No, I don't. — Where did you see her? — When I went to see *L'Enfant d'Arlequin perdu et retrouvé* [*Harlequin's Child Lost and Found*].[235] — They did the despair scene as it had never been done before. The Punchinello at the Fair has got lungs on him, but no subtlety, no soul. Madame So-And-So has just given birth to two children at once. One for each father... And you think hearing that, day in day out, is inspiring and leads to great things?

ME — No. It'd be better to shut yourself away in a garret, drink water, eat dry bread, and seek inspiration from within yourself.

HIM — Perhaps, but I'm not brave enough for that; and besides the idea of giving up on happiness when there's no guarantee of success! And what do I do about the name I bear? Rameau! Being called Rameau is quite a burden. Talents aren't like noble titles that can be handed down, and which become more and more illustrious as they go from grandfather to father, from father to son, from son to grandson, without the ancestor impressing any particular merit on his descendant. The old stump ramifies into one great stem of fools; but so what? That's not what talent does. Merely to equal your father's reputation, you need to surpass him in talent. You have to inherit his fibre. I missed out on the fibre, but my wrist is nice and loose; the bow works, and the pot is simmering away. It might not be glory, but it is good stock.

ME — If I were you, I wouldn't take that as read; I'd have a go.

HIM — And you think I haven't been trying? I was barely fifteen when I first said to myself: What's up, Rameau? You're dreaming. What are you dreaming of? Of having done something or doing something to excite universal admiration. Sure, all you have to do is blow and move your fingers. All you need is a duck, and hey presto, golden eggs. When I was a bit older, I was still saying the same thing as I'd said when I was a child. Today, I'm still saying it, and I'm still waiting around the statue of Memnon.[236]

ME — What are talking about with your statue of Memnon?

HIM — It's obvious, I'd have thought. Around the statue of Memnon, there were countless other ones, all equally struck by the sun's rays; but his was the only one that resonated. If it's a poet you're after, there's De Voltaire; and who else? De Voltaire; and in third place? De Voltaire; and in fourth? De Voltaire. If it's a composer, there's Rinaldo di Capua,[237] there's Hasse,
there's Pergolesi, there's Alberti, there's Tartini,[238] there's Locatelli,[239] there's 18
Terradellas, there's my uncle, there's that little Duni who doesn't look like much, but who has feeling, God yes, who understands the voice and is very expressive. The rest of them, surrounding this little group of Memnons, are no better than pairs of ears stuck on the end of a stick. And so we're beggars, poor beggars, so poor that it's a blessing. Oh! Mister Philosopher, poverty is a terrible thing. I can see her now, crouching down with her mouth wide open, trying to catch a few drips of the icy water leaking from the barrel of the Danaides.[240] I don't know whether it sharpens the wits of a philosopher; but it damn well freezes the head of a poet. Not much good singing goes on under that barrel. And if you can get yourself under there, you're one of the lucky ones! I used to be, but I couldn't work out how to hold on to it. I'd made that foolish mistake once already. I went on a journey to Bohemia, Germany, Switzerland, Holland, Flanders; I went to the devil and the back of beyond.

ME — Beneath the leaky barrel?

HIM — Beneath the leaky barrel; it was a wealthy, profligate Jew, who loved music and my follies. I musicked away like an angel; I played the fool; I wanted for nothing. My Jew was a man who knew his law, and who followed it to the letter, that is, he sometimes did with his friends, and he always did with people he didn't know. He got involved in some bad business that I must tell you about, because it'll amuse you. In Utrecht,[241] there lived a charming courtesan. The Jew was tempted by the beautiful Christian; he had his courier deliver her a pretty substantial promissory note. The bizarre creature rejected his offer. He was in despair. The courier said to him: Why are you getting in such a state? You want to sleep with a pretty woman; nothing could be simpler, and you could even sleep with a woman who's prettier than the one you're pursuing. Which is to say, my wife, whom I will surrender to you for the same price. No sooner said than done. The courier keeps the promissory note, and my Jew sleeps with the courier's wife. The deadline for paying the promissory note arrives. The Jew allows it to go by and disputes its validity. Trial. The Jew said: This man will never dare to admit what the payment is for, and I shall not pay it. At the hearing, he summons the courier. — This promissory note, who gave it to you? — You did. — Is it for money you lent me? — No. — Is it for merchandise supplied? — No. — Is it for services rendered? — No. It's not about any of that; I am in possession of it; you signed it; and you will pay it. — I did not sign it. — Are you saying I forged it? — You or someone you represent. — I may be a coward, but you're a crook. Believe me, you don't want to push me too far. I'll tell all. I'll lose my honour, but I'll ruin you... The Jew dismissed the threat, and the courier revealed all at the following session. The judgement went against them both; the Jew was sentenced to pay the promissory note, and the money went to the relief of the poor. So I left him. I came back here. What could I do? For if I didn't want to die of hunger, I'd have to do something. All sorts of schemes came to mind. One day, I decided I was leaving the next day to join a travelling band of musicians just as well or ill-suited to play in theatres or orchestras; the next day, I was considering having one of those paintings done that you attach to a pole and plant by a crossroads, where I would stand shouting at the top of my voice, pointing out the different scenes: This is the town where he was born; here he is saying goodbye to his father, the apothecary; here he is arriving in the capital, looking for where his uncle lives; here he is kneeling before his uncle, who sends him packing; here he is with a Jew, et cetera, et cetera. The day after that, I got up, absolutely determined to join the street singers; it's not the worst thing I could have done; we'd have gone and sung outside dear uncle's windows, and he'd have died of rage. I chose to do something else.

At this point, he stopped, and adopted the poses, one after another, of a man holding a violin and endlessly tuning it, a poor devil worn-out with fatigue, who has no strength left, whose legs are giving way beneath him, on the point of expiring unless he's thrown a piece of bread; he indicated the urgency of his need by pointing at his drooping mouth; then he added: You get my point. They threw me a scrap. There were three or four of us starving wretches, and we fought over it; then try and think great thoughts; see if you can create things of beauty when you're in that state of wretchedness.

ME — It'd be difficult.

HIM — I'd taken one tumble after another, and ended up down here. I'd been like a pig in clover. No longer. So I'll have to go back to sawing at the cat-gut, and pointing at my gaping mouth. Nothing is stable in this world. Today, I'm up on top; tomorrow, the wheel has turned and I'm back down below. We are led by unfortunate circumstances, and very badly they lead us too.

Then, gulping down what was left in the bottle and turning to his neighbour, he said: Monsieur, would you, out of the goodness of your heart, give me a little pinch? What a pretty snuffbox you've got there! You wouldn't be a musician, would you? — No. — Lucky you, as they're poor sods deserving of your pity. Fate decreed that I should be one, myself; whereas somewhere, in Montmartre perhaps, in a windmill,[242] there is a miller or a miller's assistant, who'll never hear anything except the clickety-clack of the ratchet, but who might have come up with the most beautiful tunes. Rameau! Get to the mill, off you go, that's the place for you.

ME — Whatever man applies himself to, is what Nature destined him for.

HIM — She has strange blind spots. The vantage point I see things from is not so lofty that things become indistinguishable, that the man pruning a tree with his shears and the caterpillar nibbling at one of its leaves simply look like two insects going about their business. Perch astride the epicycle of Mercury,[243] and from up there, classify, should you so wish — like Réaumur[244] sorting the class of flies into three kinds of female worker, the snippers, the measurers, the spinners — the species of man into various different kinds of male worker, the carpenters, the joiners, the roofers, dancers, singers — that's your business. I won't get involved. I'm in this world and I'm staying in it. But if it's natural to have an appetite, given that everything brings us back to appetite and to my ever-present sensation,

I consider it out of order not always to have something to eat. What a bloody awful economy! Some men are full to bursting while others are as clamorous as their stomachs, their hunger reviving as often as they do, but without a thing to chew on. The worst of it is how need forces you into certain postures. The man in need doesn't walk like other people; he jumps, he crawls, he contorts himself, he drags himself along; he spends his life in positions that he has had to take up and maintain.

ME — What do you mean by positions?

HIM — Go and ask Noverre.[245] There are even more of them in society than his art could ever imitate.

ME — And now you're up there, *astride the epicycle of Mercury*, to use your expression, or rather Montaigne's, looking down at the human species doing its various mimes and dances.

HIM — No, no, I'm not. I'm too heavy to get up there. I leave others to walk about with their heads in the clouds. I'm very down to earth. I look around, and I take up my positions, or I laugh at the positions I see other people taking up. I am an excellent mime artist, as you can judge for yourself.

Then he began to smile, to act the admiring man, the imploring man, the obliging man; right foot forward, left foot back, back bent, head up, hanging on someone else's look, mouth half-open, arms stretched out towards some object; he awaits an order, he receives it; he darts off; he returns, it has been carried out; he says so. He attends to every detail; he picks things up; he places a cushion or a stool beneath someone's feet; he holds a saucer, he moves a chair closer, he opens a door; he closes a window; he draws curtains; he watches the master and mistress; he stands still, his arms by his sides and his legs parallel; he listens; he tries to read their faces; and he adds: That's my mime, and it's more or less the same as what any flatterer, courtier, valet and beggar does.

The follies of this man, the stories of the Abbé Galiani,[246] and the wild imaginings of Rabelais have at times sent me into deep reverie. These three storehouses supply me with ridiculous masks to put on the faces of the most serious of personages; and so I see a prelate as Pantaloon,[247] a high court judge as a satyr,[248] a cenobite as a piglet, a minister as an ostrich, his private secretary as a goose. In your account, said I to my man, there are a good number of beggars in this world; moreover, I don't know anyone who doesn't do a few steps of your dance.

HIM — You're right. There's only one man in the whole of any kingdom who walks upright, and that's the sovereign. Everyone else just takes up positions.

ME — The sovereign? Surely, there's something more to be said on that score. Don't you think he mightn't sometimes find himself next to a little foot, a little chignon, a little nose that mightn't make him do a few moves in the mime? Anyone who needs someone is indigent and takes up a position. The King takes up a position before his mistress and before God; he dances his steps in the mime. The minister does all the steps of the courtier, flatterer, valet and beggar in front of his King. Crowds of ambitious people dance your positions, in hundreds of different ways, each more base than the next, in front of the minister. The noble-born Abbé in his bands and long robes[249] does his at least once a week, in front of the keeper of the list of benefices. Good God, what you're calling the beggar's mime show is the rhythm the earth moves to. Everyone has a little Hus and a Bertin.

HIM — I find that consoling.

But while I was speaking, he was hilariously doing the positions of the characters as I mentioned them; for instance, for the little Abbé, he held his hat under his arm, and his breviary in his left hand; with his right, he held up the train of his robe; he walked forward, with his head slightly tilted to one shoulder, eyes looking down, in such a perfect imitation of a hypocrite that I thought I was watching the author of the *Réfutations* in front of the Bishop of Orleans.[250] When I mentioned the flatterers and the ambitious people, he lay flat on his stomach on the ground. It was Bouret in the office of the Auditor-General.[251]

ME — That's superbly executed, I tell him. But nonetheless there is one person who is exempt from dancing the mime. And that's the philosopher who has nothing and asks for nothing.

HIM — And where is such an animal to be found? If he has nothing, he'll suffer; if he doesn't ask for anything, he won't get anything, and then he'll always be suffering.

ME — No he won't. Diogenes couldn't have cared less about his needs.

HIM — But you need clothes.

ME — No you don't. He went about naked.

HIM — Sometimes it was cold in Athens.

ME — Not as cold as it is here.

HIM — There were things to eat.

ME — I'm sure there were.

HIM — At whose expense?

ME — Nature's. What does the savage turn to? To the earth, the animals, the fish, the trees, the plants, the roots, the streams.

HIM — Nasty food.

ME — But plentiful.

HIM — A bit basic.

ME — Yet it's the basis for ours.[252]

HIM — But you must agree that the art of our cooks, pastry chefs, meat roasters, caterers, confectioners does something for it. Given the austere diet your Diogenes followed, his organs can't have misbehaved very often.

ME — How wrong you are. What used to be the cynic's habit is now the monk's habit, and it had the same virtues. The Cynics were the Carmelites and the Franciscans of Athens.[253]

HIM — I've got you there. Diogenes must therefore have danced the mime; if he didn't do it in front of Pericles, then he must have done it in front of Laïs or Phryne.[254]

ME — Wrong again. Other people had to pay a lot of money to sleep with the courtesan but she gave herself to him for the sheer pleasure of it.

HIM — But what would happen when the courtesan was busy, and the cynic in a hurry?

ME — He'd go back into his barrel and get by without her.

HIM — And are you suggesting I copy him?

ME — I'm as sure as I can be that it'd be better than crawling or abasing and prostituting yourself.

HIM — But I need a good bed, good food, a warm coat in winter, a light one in summer; rest, money and plenty of other things besides, which I would rather owe to the generosity of others than have to work for.

ME — That's because you're a layabout, a greedy pig, a coward, and a real old scumbag.

HIM — I believe I told you that myself.

ME — Things in life doubtless have their price; but you don't realize how high a price you're paying for them. You are dancing, you have danced, and you will keep on dancing the vile mime.

HIM — That is true. But it didn't cost me much, and it doesn't cost me anything anymore. And that's why it'd be a bad idea for me to adopt a different posture, which in any case I'd find painful, and would be unable to keep up. But I see from what you're saying that my poor little wife was some species of philosopher. She was as brave as a lion. Sometimes we went without bread and didn't have a penny. We'd sold almost all our clothes. I had thrown myself on the end of the bed, and was racking my brains to come up with anyone who might lend me some money that I wouldn't pay back. She, meanwhile, happy as a lark, sat herself down at her harpsichord, and accompanied herself as she sang. She warbled like a nightingale; it's a great shame you never heard her. When I was playing in some concert,[255] I'd bring her along. On the way, I would say to her: Do make sure, Madame, that everyone admires you; show off your talent and your charms. Show us your brio. Give us a crescendo. We arrived; she sang; she showed her brio; she gave us a crescendo.[256] Alas! I lost her, poor little thing. Apart from her talent, what she also had was a mouth so tiny it couldn't even take a little finger; teeth like a string of pearls; eyes, feet, skin, cheeks, tits, legs like a gazelle, thighs and a bottom you'd want to sculpt. Sooner or later, she'd have had a Tax Farmer[257] at the very least. The way she walked! The arse on her! Oh God, her arse!

And now here he is doing his wife's walk. He took little steps; he flung his head back; he played with his fan; he waggled his backside furiously; it was the funniest and most ridiculous caricature of our little coquettes.

Then taking up the thread of his speech, he added:

I took her out in public everywhere, walking in the Tuileries,[258] in the Palais Royal, along the Boulevards. There was no way she was ever going to stay with me. When she crossed the street, in the morning, without her hat on and in the little cropped jacket that stopped short of her arse, you'd have stopped and stared, and you could easily have held her waist in one hand. Those following her, watching her trip along on her little feet, sizing up that large arse with its contours outlined by her flimsy skirts, would speed up; she'd let them get close; then she'd spin round and fix her two big, black, sparkling eyes on them, and bring them up short. The fact was that the head was as good as the tail. But alas! I lost her; and my great expectations all vanished into thin air with her. I'd only taken her for that, I'd confided all my schemes in her; and she had too much foresight not to see that they were bound to succeed, and too much sense not to approve of them.

And now he's weeping and wailing, saying: No, no, I'll never get over her loss. I've since become a man of the cloth.

ME — Out of sorrow?

HIM — If you like. But the truth is, so I could wear my dog bowl on my head...[259] But look how late it is, it's time for me to go to the Opera.

ME — What's on?

HIM — The Dauvergne opera.[260] There are some quite good things in his music; what a pity he didn't come up with them first. Amongst the illustrious dead, there are always some who'll drive the living to despair. What do you expect? *Quisque suos patimur manes.*[261] But it's half-past five, and I can hear the bell ringing for the Abbé de Canaye's[262] vespers, and mine too. Adieu, Mister Philosopher, is it not true that I'm still the same as I was before?

ME — Alas! Yes it is, unfortunately.

HIM — Let's hope I only have that misfortune for another forty years or so. He who laughs last laughs longest.

DIDEROT

LE

NEVEU DE RAMEAU

SATYRE

publiée pour la première fois sur le manuscrit original autographe

Avec une introduction et des notes

PAR

GEORGES MONVAL

Accompagnée d'une Notice sur les premières éditions de l'ouvrage et de la Vie de Jean-François Rameau

PAR

ER. THOINAN

PARIS

LIBRAIRIE PLON

E. PLON, NOURRIT ET Cie, IMPRIMEURS-ÉDITEURS

Rue Garancière, 10

MDCCCXCI

Fig. 2b Georges Monval, *Le Neveu de Rameau, Satyre, publiée pour la première fois sur le manuscrit original* [...] (Paris: Plon, 1891), title page. Image compliments of the Master and Fellows of Trinity College, Cambridge. Public Domain.

Le Neveu de Rameau*

Satire 2de[1]

Vertumnis, quotquot sunt, natus iniquis

Horat., lib. II, Satyr, VII.[2]

Qu'il fasse beau, qu'il fasse laid, c'est mon habitude d'aller sur les cinq heures
du soir me promener au Palais-Royal.[3] C'est moi qu'on voit, toujours seul,
rêvant sur le banc d'Argenson,[4] Je m'entretiens avec moi-même de politique,
d'amour, de goût ou de philosophie. J'abandonne mon esprit à tout son
libertinage. Je le laisse maître de suivre la première idée sage ou folle qui
se présente, comme on voit dans l'allée de Foy, nos jeunes dissolus marcher
sur les pas d'une courtisane à l'air éventé, au visage riant, à l'œil vif, au nez
retroussé, quitter celle-ci pour une autre, les attaquant toutes et ne s'attachant
à aucune. Mes pensées, ce sont mes catins. Si le temps est trop froid, ou trop
pluvieux, je me réfugie au café de la Régence ; là je m'amuse à voir jouer aux
échecs. Paris est l'endroit du monde, et le café de la Régence est l'endroit de
Paris où l'on joue le mieux à ce jeu. C'est chez Rey que font assaut Legal le
profond,[5] Philidor le subtil,[6] le solide Mayot ; qu'on voit les coups les plus 1♪

* The French text utilised is that published by Georges Monval: *Le Neveu de Rameau, Satyre, publiée pour la première fois sur le manuscrit original autographe, avec une introduction, accompagnée d'une notice sur les premières éditions de l'ouvrage et de la vie de Jean-François Rameau par Er[nest] Thoinan* (Paris: Plon, 1891), freely available online at http://gallica.bnf.fr/ark:/12148/bpt6k5699166t. This text has been collated on the editions by Jean Fabre, Droz, 1950, and Henri Coulet, 1989 (in *Œuvres complètes de Diderot*, known as 'DPV', vol. XII), and also on a microfilm of the autograph manuscript, kindly furnished by the Morgan Library and Museum, New York. The spelling has been modernised; for the punctuation, we [MH] avoided the use of inverted commas, which would have obscured the floating movement of the text between direct and indirect speech.

 http://dx.doi.org/10.11647/OBP.0098.02

surprenants et qu'on entend les plus mauvais propos ; car si l'on peut être homme d'esprit et grand joueur d'échecs, comme Legal, on peut être aussi un grand joueur d'échecs et un sot, comme Foubert et Mayot.[7] Un après-dîner, j'étais là, regardant beaucoup, parlant peu, et écoutant le moins que je pouvais, lorsque je fus abordé par un des plus bizarres personnages de ce pays où Dieu n'en a pas laissé manquer. C'est un composé de hauteur et de bassesse, de bon sens et de déraison. Il faut que les notions de l'honnête et du déshonnête soient bien étrangement brouillées dans sa tête, car il montre ce que la nature lui a donné de bonnes qualités sans ostentation, et ce qu'il en a reçu de mauvaises, sans pudeur. Au reste, il est doué d'une organisation forte, d'une chaleur d'imagination singulière, et d'une vigueur de poumons peu commune. Si vous le rencontrez jamais et que son originalité ne vous arrête pas, ou vous mettrez vos doigts dans vos oreilles, ou vous vous enfuirez. Dieux, quels terribles poumons ! Rien ne dissemble plus de lui que lui-même. Quelquefois, il est maigre et hâve comme un malade au dernier degré de la consomption ; on compterait ses dents à travers ses joues ; on dirait qu'il a passé plusieurs jours sans manger, ou qu'il sort de la Trappe. Le mois suivant, il est gras et replet, comme s'il n'avait pas quitté la table d'un financier, ou qu'il eût été renfermé dans un couvent de Bernardins.[8] Aujourd'hui, en linge sale, en culotte déchirée, couvert de lambeaux, presque sans souliers, il va la tête basse, il se dérobe, on serait tenté de l'appeler pour lui donner l'aumône. Demain, poudré, chaussé, frisé, bien vêtu, il marche la tête haute, il se montre, et vous le prendriez au peu près pour un honnête homme. Il vit au jour la journée. Triste ou gai, selon les circonstances. Son premier soin, le matin, quand il est levé, est de savoir où il dînera ; après dîner, il pense où il ira souper. La nuit amène aussi son inquiétude. Ou il regagne, à pied, un petit grenier qu'il habite, à moins que l'hôtesse ennuyée d'attendre son loyer, ne lui en ait redemandé la clef ; ou il se rabat dans une taverne du faubourg où il attend le jour, entre un morceau de pain et un pot de bière. Quand il n'a pas six sols dans sa poche, ce qui lui arrive quelquefois, il a recours soit à un fiacre de ses amis, soit au cocher d'un grand seigneur qui lui donne un lit sur de la paille, à côté de ses chevaux. Le matin, il a encore une partie de son matelas dans ses cheveux. Si la saison est douce, il arpente toute la nuit le Cours ou les Champs-Élysées.[9] Il reparaît avec le jour, à la ville, habillé de la veille pour le lendemain, et du lendemain quelquefois pour le reste de la semaine. Je n'estime pas ces originaux-là. D'autres en font leurs connaissances familières, même leurs amis. Ils m'arrêtent une fois l'an, quand je les rencontre, parce que leur caractère tranche avec celui des autres, et qu'ils rompent cette fastidieuse uniformité que notre éducation, nos conventions de société, nos bienséances d'usage ont introduite. S'il en paraît un dans une compagnie, c'est un grain de levain qui fermente et qui restitue à chacun une portion de son individualité naturelle. Il secoue, il agite, il fait approuver ou blâmer ; il fait sortir la vérité ; il fait connaître les gens de bien ; il démasque les coquins ; c'est alors que l'homme de bon sens écoute, et démêle son monde.

Je connaissais celui-ci de longue main. Il fréquentait dans une maison dont son talent lui avait ouvert la porte. Il y avait une fille unique. Il jurait au père et à la mère qu'il épouserait leur fille. Ceux-ci haussaient les épaules, lui riaient au nez, lui disaient qu'il était fou, et je vis le moment que la chose était faite. Il m'empruntait quelques écus que je lui donnais. Il s'était introduit, je ne sais comment, dans quelques maisons honnêtes, où il avait son couvert, mais à la condition qu'il ne parlerait pas, sans en avoir obtenu la permission. Il se taisait, et mangeait de rage. Il était excellent à voir dans cette contrainte. S'il lui prenait envie de manquer au traité, et qu'il ouvrît la bouche, au premier mot tous les convives s'écriaient : O Rameau ! Alors la fureur étincelait dans ses yeux, et il se remettait à manger avec plus de rage. Vous étiez curieux de savoir le nom de l'homme, et vous le savez. C'est le neveu de ce musicien célèbre[10] qui nous a délivrés du plain-chant de Lulli[11] que nous psalmodions depuis plus de cent ans, qui a tant écrit de visions inintelligibles et de vérités apocalyptiques sur la théorie de la musique, où ni lui ni personne n'entendit jamais rien, et de qui nous avons un certain nombre d'opéras où il y a de l'harmonie, des bouts de chants, des idées décousues, du fracas, des vols, des triomphes, des lances, des gloires,[12] des murmures, des victoires à perte d'haleine, des airs de danse qui dureront éternellement, et qui, après avoir enterré le Florentin, sera enterré par les virtuoses italiens, ce qu'il pressentait et le rendait sombre, triste, hargneux ; car personne n'a autant d'humeur, pas même une jolie femme qui se lève avec un bouton sur le nez, qu'un auteur menacé de survivre à sa réputation, témoins Marivaux[13] et Crébillon le fils.[14]

Il m'aborde. Ah ! ah ! vous voilà, monsieur le philosophe ; et que faites-vous ici parmi ce tas de fainéants ? Est-ce que vous perdez aussi votre temps à pousser le bois ? C'est ainsi qu'on appelle par mépris jouer aux échecs ou aux dames.

MOI — Non, mais quand je n'ai rien de mieux à faire, je m'amuse à regarder un instant ceux qui le poussent bien.

LUI — En ce cas, vous vous amusez rarement ; excepté Legal et Philidor, le reste n'y entend rien.

MOI — Et M. de Bissy donc ?[15]

LUI — Celui-là est en joueur d'échecs ce que Mlle Clairon est en acteur. Ils savent de ces jeux, l'un et l'autre, tout ce qu'on en peut apprendre.[16]

MOI — Vous êtes difficile ; et je vois que vous ne faites grâce qu'aux hommes sublimes.

LUI — Oui, aux échecs, aux dames, en poésie, en éloquence, en musique et autres fadaises comme cela. À quoi bon la médiocrité dans ces genres ?

MOI — À peu de chose, j'en conviens. Mais c'est qu'il faut qu'il y ait un grand nombre d'hommes qui s'y appliquent pour faire sortir l'homme de génie. Il est un dans la multitude. Mais laissons cela. Il y a une éternité que je ne vous ai vu. Je ne pense guère à vous, quand je ne vous vois pas. Mais vous me plaisez toujours à revoir. Qu'avez-vous fait ?

LUI — Ce que vous, moi et tous les autres font : du bien, du mal, et rien. Et puis j'ai eu faim, et j'ai mangé, quand l'occasion s'en est présentée ; après avoir mangé, j'ai eu soif, et j'ai bu quelquefois. Cependant la barbe me venait, et quand elle a été venue, je l'ai fait raser.

MOI — Vous avez mal fait. C'est la seule chose qui vous manque pour être un sage.

LUI — Oui-da. J'ai le front grand et ridé, l'œil ardent, le nez saillant, les joues larges, le sourcil noir et fourni, la bouche bien fendue, la lèvre rebordée et la face carrée. Si ce vaste menton était couvert d'une longue barbe, savez-vous que cela figurerait très bien en bronze ou en marbre ?

MOI — À côté d'un César, d'un Marc Aurèle, d'un Socrate.

LUI — Non. Je serais mieux entre Diogène[17] et Phryné[18] Je suis effronté comme l'un, et je fréquente volontiers chez les autres.

MOI — Vous portez-vous toujours bien ?

LUI — Oui, ordinairement ; mais pas merveilleusement aujourd'hui.

MOI — Comment ? vous voilà avec un ventre de Silène[19] et un visage…

LUI — Un visage qu'on prendrait pour son antagoniste. C'est que l'humeur qui fait sécher mon cher oncle engraisse apparemment son cher neveu.

MOI — À propos de cet oncle, le voyez-vous quelquefois ?

LUI — Oui, passer dans la rue.

MOI — Est-ce qu'il ne vous fait aucun bien ?

LUI — S'il en fait à quelqu'un, c'est sans s'en douter. C'est un philosophe dans son espèce. Il ne pense qu'à lui ; le reste de l'univers lui est comme d'un clou à soufflet. Sa fille et sa femme n'ont qu'à mourir quand elles voudront, pourvu que les cloches de la paroisse qu'on sonnera pour elles continuent de résonner la douzième et la dix-septième,[20] tout sera bien. Cela est heureux pour lui ; et c'est ce que je prise particulièrement dans les gens de génie. Ils ne sont bons qu'à une chose. Passé cela, rien. Ils ne savent ce que c'est d'être citoyens, pères, mères, frères, parents, amis. Entre nous, il faut leur ressembler de tout point, mais ne pas désirer que la graine en soit commune. Il faut des hommes ; mais pour des hommes de génie, point. Non, ma foi, il n'en faut point. Ce sont eux qui changent la face du globe ; et dans les plus petites choses, la sottise est si commune et si puissante qu'on ne la réforme pas sans charivari. Il s'établit partie de ce qu'ils ont imaginé, partie reste comme il était ; de là deux évangiles, un habit d'Arlequin. La sagesse du moine de Rabelais est la vraie sagesse pour son repos et pour celui des autres : faire son devoir tellement quellement, toujours dire du bien de monsieur le prieur, et laisser aller le monde à sa fantaisie. Il va bien, puisque la multitude en est contente. Si je savais l'histoire, je vous montrerais que le mal est toujours venu ici-bas par quelque homme de génie. Mais je ne sais pas l'histoire, parce que je ne sais rien. Le diable m'emporte si j'ai jamais rien appris, et si, pour n'avoir rien appris, je m'en trouve plus mal. J'étais un jour à la table d'un ministre du roi de France qui a de l'esprit comme quatre ;[21] hé bien, il nous démontra clair comme un et un font deux, que rien n'était plus utile aux peuples que le mensonge, rien de plus nuisible que la vérité. Je ne me rappelle pas bien ses preuves, mais il s'ensuivait évidemment que les gens de génie sont détestables, et que si un enfant apportait en naissant, sur son front, la caractéristique de ce dangereux présent de la nature, il faudrait ou l'étouffer, ou le jeter au cagnard.

MOI — Cependant ces personnages-là, si ennemis du génie, prétendent tous en avoir.

LUI — Je crois bien qu'ils le pensent au-dedans d'eux-mêmes, mais je ne crois pas qu'ils osassent l'avouer.

MOI — C'est par modestie. Vous conçûtes donc là une terrible haine contre le génie.

LUI — À n'en jamais revenir.

MOI — Mais j'ai vu un temps que vous vous désespériez de n'être qu'un homme commun. Vous ne serez jamais heureux, si le pour et le contre vous afflige également. Il faudrait prendre son parti, et y demeurer attaché. Tout en convenant avec vous que les hommes de génie sont communément singuliers, ou, comme dit le proverbe, qu'il n'y a point de grands esprits sans un grain de folie, on n'en reviendra pas. On méprisera les siècles qui n'en auront pas produit. Ils feront l'honneur des peuples chez lesquels ils auront existé ; tôt ou tard, on leur élève des statues, et on les regarde comme les bienfaiteurs du genre humain. N'en déplaise au ministre sublime que vous m'avez cité, je crois que si le mensonge peut servir un moment, il est nécessairement nuisible à la longue, et qu'au contraire, la vérité sert nécessairement à la longue, bien qu'il puisse arriver qu'elle nuise dans le moment. D'où je serais tenté de conclure que l'homme de génie qui décrie une erreur générale, ou qui accrédite une grande vérité, est toujours un être digne de notre vénération.[22] Il peut arriver que cet être soit la victime du préjugé et des lois ; mais il y a deux sortes de lois, les unes d'une équité, d'une généralité absolues, d'autres bizarres, qui ne doivent leur sanction qu'à l'aveuglement ou la nécessité des circonstances. Celles-ci ne couvrent le coupable qui les enfreint que d'une ignominie passagère, ignominie que le temps reverse sur les juges et sur les nations, pour y rester à jamais. De Socrate ou du magistrat qui lui fit boire la ciguë, quel est aujourd'hui le déshonoré ?

LUI — Le voilà bien avancé ! en a-t-il été moins condamné ? en a-t-il moins été mis à mort ? en a-t-il moins été un citoyen turbulent ? par le mépris d'une mauvaise loi, en a-t-il moins encouragé les fous, au mépris des bonnes ? en a-t-il moins été un particulier audacieux et bizarre ? Vous n'étiez pas éloigné tout à l'heure d'un aveu peu favorable aux hommes de génie.

MOI — Écoutez-moi, cher homme. Une société ne devrait point avoir de mauvaises lois, et si elle n'en avait que de bonnes, elle ne serait jamais dans le cas de persécuter un homme de génie. Je ne vous ai pas dit que le génie fût indivisiblement attaché à la méchanceté, ni la méchanceté au génie. Un sot sera plus souvent un méchant qu'un homme d'esprit. Quand un homme de génie serait communément d'un commerce dur, difficile, épineux, insupportable, quand même ce serait un méchant, qu'en concluriez-vous ?

LUI — Qu'il est bon à noyer.

MOI — Doucement, cher homme. Ça, dites-moi, je ne prendrai pas votre oncle pour exemple, c'est un homme dur, c'est un brutal ; il est sans humanité, il est avare. Il est mauvais père, mauvais époux, mauvais oncle ; mais il n'est pas assez décidé que ce soit un homme de génie, qu'il ait poussé son art fort loin, et qu'il soit question de ses ouvrages dans dix ans. Mais Racine ? Celui-là certes avait du génie, et ne passait pas pour un trop bon homme. Mais de Voltaire ?[23]

LUI — Ne me pressez pas, car je suis conséquent.

MOI — Lequel des deux préféreriez-vous ? ou qu'il eût été un bon homme, identifié avec son comptoir, comme Briasson,[24] ou avec son aune, comme Barbier,[25] faisant régulièrement tous les ans un enfant légitime à sa femme, bon mari, bon père, bon oncle, bon voisin, honnête commerçant, mais rien de plus ; ou qu'il eût été fourbe, traître, ambitieux, envieux, méchant, mais auteur d'*Andromaque*, de *Britannicus*, d'*Iphigénie*, de *Phèdre*, d'*Athalie* ?

LUI — Pour lui, ma foi, peut-être que de ces deux hommes, il eût mieux valu qu'il eût été le premier.

MOI — Cela est même infiniment plus vrai que vous ne le sentez.

LUI — Oh ! vous voilà, vous autres ! Si nous disons quelque chose de bien, c'est comme des fous ou des inspirés, par hasard. Il n'y a que vous autres qui vous entendiez. Oui, monsieur le philosophe, je m'entends, et je m'entends ainsi que vous vous entendez.

MOI — Voyons ; eh bien ! pourquoi pour lui ?

LUI — C'est que toutes ces belles choses-là qu'il a faites ne lui ont pas rendu vingt mille francs ; et que s'il eût été un bon marchand en soie de la rue Saint-Denis ou Saint-Honoré, un bon épicier en gros, un apothicaire bien achalandé, il eût amassé une fortune immense, et qu'en l'amassant il n'y aurait eu sorte de plaisirs dont il n'eût joui ; qu'il aurait donné de temps en temps la pistole à un pauvre diable de bouffon comme moi qui l'aurait fait rire, qui lui aurait procuré dans l'occasion une jeune fille qui l'aurait désennuyé de l'éternelle cohabitation avec sa femme ; que nous aurions fait d'excellents repas chez lui, joué gros jeu, bu d'excellents vins, d'excellentes liqueurs, d'excellents cafés, fait des parties de campagne ; et vous voyez que je m'entendais. Vous riez. Mais laissez-moi dire. Il eût été mieux pour ses entours.

MOI — Sans contredit ; pourvu qu'il n'eût pas employé d'une façon déshonnête l'opulence qu'il aurait acquise par un commerce légitime ; qu'il eût éloigné de sa maison tous ces joueurs, tous ces parasites, tous ces fades complaisants, tous ces fainéants, tous ces pervers inutiles, et qu'il eût fait assommer à coups de bâton, par ses garçons de boutique, l'homme officieux qui soulage, par la variété, les maris du dégoût d'une cohabitation habituelle avec leurs femmes.

LUI — Assommer, monsieur, assommer ! On n'assomme personne dans une ville bien policée C'est un état honnête. Beaucoup de gens, même titrés, s'en mêlent. Et à quoi diable voulez-vous donc qu'on emploie son argent, si ce n'est à avoir bonne table, bonne compagnie, bons vins, belles femmes, plaisirs de toutes les couleurs, amusements de toutes les espèces ? J'aimerais autant être gueux que de posséder une grande fortune sans aucune de ces jouissances. Mais revenons à Racine. Cet homme n'a été bon que pour des inconnus et que pour le temps où il n'était plus.

MOI — D'accord. Mais pesez le mal et le bien. Dans mille ans d'ici, il fera verser des larmes ; il sera l'admiration des hommes dans toutes les contrées de la terre. Il inspirera l'humanité, la commisération, la tendresse ; on demandera qui il était, de quel pays, et on l'enviera à la France. Il a fait souffrir quelques êtres qui ne sont plus, auxquels nous ne prenons presque aucun intérêt ; nous n'avons rien à redouter ni de ses vices, ni de ses défauts. Il eût été mieux sans doute qu'il eût reçu de la nature les vertus d'un homme de bien, avec les talents d'un grand homme. C'est un arbre qui a fait sécher quelques arbres plantés dans son voisinage, qui a étouffé les plantes qui croissaient à ses pieds ; mais il a porté sa cime jusque dans la nue ; ses branches se sont étendues au loin ; il a prêté son ombre à ceux qui venaient, qui viennent et qui viendront se reposer autour de son tronc majestueux ; il a produit des fruits d'un goût exquis et qui se renouvellent sans cesse.[26] Il serait à souhaiter que de Voltaire eût encore la douceur de Duclos,[27] l'ingénuité de l'abbé Trublet,[28] la droiture de l'abbé d'Olivet ;[29] mais puisque cela ne se peut, regardons la chose du côté vraiment intéressant ; oublions pour un moment le point que nous occupons dans l'espace et dans la durée, et étendons notre vue sur les siècles à venir, les régions les plus éloignées et les peuples à naître. Songeons au bien de notre espèce. Si nous ne sommes pas assez généreux, pardonnons au moins à la nature d'avoir été plus sage que nous. Si vous jetez de l'eau froide sur la tête de Greuze,[30] vous éteindrez peut-être son talent avec sa vanité. Si vous rendez de Voltaire moins sensible à la critique, il ne saura plus descendre dans l'âme de Mérope.[31] Il ne vous touchera plus.

LUI — Mais si la nature était aussi puissante que sage, pourquoi ne les a-t-elle pas faits aussi bons qu'elle les a faits grands ?

MOI — Mais ne voyez-vous pas qu'avec un pareil raisonnement vous renversez l'ordre général, et que si tout ici-bas était excellent, il n'y aurait rien d'excellent ?[32]

LUI — Vous avez raison. Le point important est que vous et moi nous soyons, et que nous soyons vous et moi. Que tout aille d'ailleurs comme il pourra. Le meilleur ordre des choses, à mon avis, est celui où j'en devais être, et foin du plus parfait des mondes, si je n'en suis pas. J'aime mieux être, et même être impertinent raisonneur, que de n'être pas.

MOI — Il n'y a personne qui ne pense comme vous, et qui ne fasse le procès à l'ordre qui est, sans s'apercevoir qu'il renonce à sa propre existence.

LUI — Il est vrai.

MOI — Acceptons donc les choses comme elles sont. Voyons ce qu'elles nous coûtent et ce qu'elles nous rendent, et laissons là le tout que nous ne connaissons pas assez pour le louer ou le blâmer, et qui n'est peut-être ni bien ni mal, s'il est nécessaire, comme beaucoup d'honnêtes gens l'imaginent.[33]

LUI — Je n'entends pas grand-chose à tout ce que vous me débitez là. C'est apparemment de la philosophie ; je vous préviens que je ne m'en mêle pas.

Tout ce que je sais, c'est que je voudrais bien être un autre, au hasard d'être un homme de génie, un grand home. Oui, il faut que j'en convienne, il y a là quelque chose qui me le dit. Je n'en ai jamais entendu louer un seul que son éloge ne m'ait fait secrètement enrager. Je suis envieux. Lorsque j'apprends de leur vie privée quelque trait qui les dégrade, je l'écoute avec plaisir. Cela nous rapproche. J'en supporte plus aisément ma médiocrité. Je me dis : Certes, tu n'aurais jamais fait *Mahomet*, mais ni l'éloge du Maupeou.[34] J'ai donc été, je suis donc fâché d'être médiocre. Oui, oui, je suis médiocre et fâché. Je n'ai jamais entendu jouer l'ouverture des *Indes galantes*,[35] jamais entendu chanter *Profonds abîmes du Ténare*,[36] *Nuit, éternelle nuit*, sans me dire avec douleur : 'Voilà ce que tu ne feras jamais'. J'étais donc jaloux de mon oncle ; et s'il y avait eu, à sa mort, quelques belles pièces de clavecin dans son portefeuille, je n'aurais pas balancé à rester moi et à être lui.

MOI — S'il n'y a que cela qui vous chagrine, cela n'en vaut pas trop la peine.

LUI — Ce n'est rien, ce sont des moments qui passent.

(Puis il se remettait à chanter l'ouverture des *Indes* galantes et l'air *Profonds abîmes*, et il ajoutait :)

LUI — Le quelque chose qui est là et qui me parle, me dit : Rameau, tu voudrais bien avoir fait ces deux morceaux-là ; si tu avais fait ces deux morceaux-là, tu en ferais bien deux autres ; et quand tu en aurais fait un certain nombre, on te jouerait, on te chanterait partout ; quand tu marcherais, tu aurais la tête droite, la conscience te rendrait témoignage à toi-même de ton propre mérite, les autres te désigneraient du doigt. On dirait : C'est lui qui a fait les jolies gavottes ; et il chantait les gavottes, puis, avec l'air d'un homme touché, qui nage dans la joie et qui en a les yeux humides, il ajoutait en se frottant les mains : Tu aurais une bonne maison, et il en mesurait l'étendue avec ses bras, un bon lit, et il s'y étendait nonchalamment, de bons vins, qu'il goûtait en faisant claquer sa langue contre son palais, un bon équipage, et il levait le pied pour y monter, de jolies femmes, à qui il prenait déjà la gorge et qu'il regardait voluptueusement ; cent faquins me viendraient encenser tous les jours ; et il croyait les voir autour de lui ; il voyait Palissot,[37] Poinsinet,[38] les Fréron père et fils,[39] La Porte ;[40] il les entendait, il se rengorgeait, les approuvait, leur souriait, les dédaignait, les méprisait, les chassait, les rappelait ; puis il continuait : Et c'est ainsi que l'on te dirait le matin que tu es un grand homme ; tu lirais dans l'histoire des *Trois Siècles*[41] que tu es un grand homme ; tu serais convaincu le soir que tu es un grand homme ; et le grand homme, Rameau le neveu, s'endormirait au doux murmure de l'éloge qui retentirait dans son oreille ; même en dormant, il aurait l'air satisfait : sa poitrine se dilaterait, s'élèverait, s'abaisserait avec aisance, il ronflerait comme un grand homme ; et en parlant ainsi, il se laissait aller mollement sur une banquette ; il fermait les yeux, et il imitait le sommeil heureux qu'il imaginait. Après avoir goûté quelques instants la douceur de ce repos, il se réveillait, étendait ses bras, bâillait, se frottait les yeux, et cherchait encore autour de lui ses adulateurs insipides.

MOI — Vous croyez donc que l'homme heureux a son sommeil ?

LUI — Si je le crois ! Moi, pauvre hère, lorsque le soir j'ai regagné mon grenier et que je me suis fourré dans mon grabat, je suis ratatiné sous ma couverture, j'ai la poitrine étroite et la respiration gênée ; c'est une espèce de plainte faible qu'on entend à peine, au lieu qu'un financier fait retentir son appartement et étonne toute sa rue. Mais ce qui m'afflige aujourd'hui, ce n'est pas de ronfler et de dormir mesquinement, comme un misérable.

MOI — Cela est pourtant triste.

LUI — Ce qui m'est arrivé l'est bien davantage.

MOI — Qu'est-ce donc ?

LUI — Vous avez toujours pris quelque intérêt à moi, parce que je suis un bon diable, que vous méprisez dans le fond, mais qui vous amuse.

MOI — C'est la vérité.

LUI — Et je vais vous le dire.

Avant que de commencer, il pousse un profond soupir et porte ses deux mains à son front. Ensuite, il reprend un air tranquille et me dit :

Vous savez que je suis un ignorant, un sot, un fou, un impertinent, un paresseux, ce que nos Bourguignons[42] appellent un fieffé truand, un escroc, un gourmand...

MOI — Quel panégyrique !

LUI — Il est vrai de tout point. Il n'y en a pas un mot à rabattre. Point de contestation là-dessus, s'il vous plaît. Personne ne me connaît mieux que moi, et je ne dis pas tout.

MOI — Je ne veux point vous fâcher, et je conviendrai de tout.

LUI — Hé bien, je vivais avec des gens qui m'avaient pris en gré, précisément parce que j'étais doué, à un rare degré, de toutes ces qualités.

MOI — Cela est singulier. Jusqu'à présent, j'avais cru ou qu'on se les cachait à soi-même ou qu'on se les pardonnait, et qu'on les méprisait dans les autres.

LUI — Se les cacher, est-ce qu'on le peut ? Soyez sûr que, quand Palissot est seul et qu'il revient sur lui-même, il se dit bien d'autres choses. Soyez sûr qu'en tête-à-tête avec son collègue, ils s'avouent franchement qu'ils ne sont que deux insignes maroufles. Les mépriser dans les autres ! mes gens étaient plus équitables, et leur caractère me réussissait merveilleusement auprès d'eux. J'étais comme un coq en pâte. On me fêtait. On ne me perdait pas un moment sans me regretter. J'étais leur petit Rameau, leur joli Rameau, leur Rameau le fou, l'impertinent, l'ignorant, le paresseux, le gourmand, le bouffon, la grosse bête. Il n'y avait pas une de ces épithètes familières qui ne me valût un sourire, une caresse, un petit coup sur l'épaule, un soufflet, un coup de pied, à table un bon morceau qu'on me jetait sur mon assiette, hors de table, une liberté que je prenais sans conséquence, car moi, je suis sans conséquence. On fait de moi, avec moi, devant moi tout ce qu'on veut, sans que je m'en formalise ; et les petits présents qui me pleuvaient ? Le grand chien que je suis, j'ai tout perdu ! J'ai tout perdu pour avoir eu le sens commun une fois, une seule fois en ma vie. Ah ! si cela m'arrive jamais !

MOI — De quoi s'agissait-il donc ?

LUI — C'est une sottise incomparable, incompréhensible, irrémissible.

MOI — Quelle sottise encore ?

LUI — Rameau, Rameau, vous avait-on pris pour cela ? La sottise d'avoir eu un peu de goût, un peu d'esprit, un peu de raison. Rameau, mon ami, cela vous apprendra à rester ce que Dieu vous fit et ce que vos protecteurs vous voulaient. Aussi l'on vous a pris par les épaules, on vous a conduit à la porte, on vous a dit : Faquin, tirez, ne reparaissez plus ; cela veut avoir du sens, de la raison, je crois ! Tirez ! Nous avons de ces qualités-là, de reste. Vous vous en êtes allé en vous mordant les doigts ; c'est votre langue maudite qu'il fallait mordre auparavant. Pour ne vous en être pas avisé, vous voilà sur le pavé, sans le sol, et ne sachant où donner de la tête. Vous étiez nourri à bouche que veux-tu, et vous retournerez au regrat; bien logé, et vous serez trop heureux si l'on vous rend votre grenier ; bien couché, et la paille vous attend entre le cocher de monsieur de Soubise[43] et l'ami Robbé.[44] Au lieu d'un sommeil doux et tranquille comme vous l'aviez, vous entendrez d'une oreille le hennissement et le piétinement des chevaux, de l'autre le bruit mille fois plus insupportable des vers secs, durs et barbares. Malheureux, mal avisé, possédé d'un million de diables !

MOI — Mais n'y aurait-il pas moyen de se rapatrier ? La faute que vous avez commise est-elle si impardonnable ? À votre place, j'irais retrouver mes gens. Vous leur êtes plus nécessaire que vous ne croyez.

LUI — Ho ! je suis sûr qu'à présent qu'ils ne m'ont pas pour les faire rire, ils s'ennuient comme des chiens.

MOI — J'irais donc les retrouver. Je ne leur laisserais pas le temps de se passer de moi, de se tourner vers quelque amusement honnête ; car qui sait ce qui peut arriver ?

LUI — Ce n'est pas là ce que je crains ; cela n'arrivera pas.

MOI — Quelque sublime que vous soyez, un autre peut vous remplacer.

LUI — Difficilement.

MOI — D'accord. Cependant j'irais avec ce visage défait, ces yeux égarés, ce col débraillé, ces cheveux ébouriffés, dans l'état vraiment tragique où vous voilà. Je me jetterais aux pieds de la divinité.[45] Je me collerais la face contre terre, et sans me relever, je lui dirais d'une voix basse et sanglotante : Pardon, madame ! pardon ! je suis un indigne, un infâme. Ce fut un malheureux instant ; car vous savez que je ne suis pas sujet à avoir du sens commun, et je vous promets de n'en avoir de ma vie.

Ce qu'il y a de plaisant, c'est que, tandis que je lui tenais ce discours, il en exécutait la pantomime. Il s'était prosterné ; il avait collé son visage contre terre, il paraissait tenir entre ses deux mains le bout d'une pantoufle, il pleurait, il sanglotait, il disait : Oui, ma petite reine, oui, je le promets, je n'en aurai de ma vie, de ma vie. Puis se relevant brusquement, il ajouta d'un ton sérieux et réfléchi :

LUI — Oui, vous avez raison. Je crois que c'est le mieux. Elle est bonne. M. Viellard[46] dit qu'elle est si bonne ! Moi je sais un peu qu'elle l'est. Mais cependant aller s'humilier devant une guenon ! Crier miséricorde aux pieds d'une misérable petite histrionne que les sifflets du parterre ne cessent de
2♪ poursuivre ! Moi Rameau, fils de M. Rameau, apothicaire de Dijon, qui est
un homme de bien et qui n'a jamais fléchi le genou devant qui que ce soit !
3♪ Moi, Rameau, le neveu de celui qu'on appelle le grand Rameau,[47] qu'on voit
4♪ se promener droit et les bras en l'air au Palais-Royal, depuis que monsieur
Carmontelle l'a dessiné courbé et les mains sous les basques de son habit ![48]
Moi qui ai composé des pièces de clavecin que personne ne joue, mais qui seront peut-être les seules qui passeront à la postérité qui les jouera ; moi ! moi enfin ! j'irais !... Tenez, monsieur, cela ne se peut. Et mettant sa main droite sur sa poitrine, il ajoutait : Je me sens là quelque chose qui s'élève et qui me dit : Rameau, tu n'en feras rien. Il faut qu'il y ait une certaine dignité attachée à la nature de l'homme, que rien ne peut étouffer. Cela se réveille à propos de bottes, oui, à propos de bottes, car il y a d'autres jours où il ne m'en coûterait rien pour être vil tant qu'on voudrait ; ces jours-là, pour un liard, je baiserais le cul à la petite Hus.[45]

MOI — Hé ! mais, l'ami, elle est blanche, jolie, jeune, douce, potelée ; et c'est un acte d'humilité auquel un plus délicat que vous pourrait quelquefois s'abaisser.

LUI — Entendons-nous ; c'est qu'il y a baiser le cul au simple, et baiser le cul au figuré. Demandez au gros Bergier qui baise le cul de Mme de La Marck[49] au simple et au figuré ; et ma foi, le simple et le figuré me déplairaient également là.

MOI — Si l'expédient que je vous suggère ne vous convient pas, ayez donc le courage d'être gueux.

LUI — Il est dur d'être gueux, tandis qu'il y a tant de sots opulents aux dépens desquels on peut vivre. Et puis le mépris de soi ; il est insupportable.

MOI — Est-ce que vous connaissez ce sentiment-là ?

LUI — Si je le connais ! Combien de fois je me suis dit : Comment, Rameau, il y a dix mille bonnes tables à Paris, à quinze ou vingt couverts chacune, et de ces couverts-là il n'y en a pas un pour toi ! Il y a des bourses pleines d'or qui se versent de droite et de gauche, et il n'en tombe pas une pièce sur toi ! Mille petits beaux esprits sans talent, sans mérite ; mille petites créatures sans charmes ; mille plats intrigants sont bien vêtus, et tu irais tout nu ? Et tu serais imbécile à ce point ? Est-ce que tu ne saurais pas flatter comme un autre ? Est-ce que tu ne saurais pas mentir, jurer, parjurer, promettre, tenir ou manquer comme un autre ? Est-ce que tu ne saurais pas te mettre à quatre pattes comme un autre ? Est-ce que tu ne saurais pas favoriser l'intrigue de madame et porter le billet doux de monsieur comme un autre ? Est-ce que tu ne saurais pas encourager ce jeune homme à parler à mademoiselle et persuader à mademoiselle de l'écouter, comme un autre ? Est-ce que tu ne saurais pas faire entendre à la fille d'un de nos bourgeois qu'elle est mal mise, que de belles boucles d'oreilles, un peu de rouge, des dentelles, une robe à la polonaise,[50] lui siéraient à ravir ? Que ces petits pieds-là ne sont pas faits pour marcher dans la rue ? Qu'il y a un beau monsieur, jeune et riche, qui a un habit galonné d'or, un superbe équipage, six grands laquais, qui l'a vue en passant, qui la trouve charmante, et qui depuis ce jour-là en a perdu le boire et le manger ; qu'il n'en dort plus, et qu'il en mourra ? Mais mon papa ? — Bon, bon, votre papa ! il s'en fâchera d'abord un peu. — Et maman qui me recommande tant d'être honnête fille ? qui me dit qu'il n'y a rien dans ce monde que l'honneur ? — Vieux propos qui ne signifient rien. — Et mon confesseur ? — Vous ne le verrez plus ; ou si vous persistez dans la fantaisie d'aller lui faire l'histoire de vos amusements, il vous en coûtera quelques livres de sucre et de café. — C'est un homme sévère qui m'a déjà refusé l'absolution pour la chanson, *Viens dans ma cellule*.[51] — C'est que vous n'aviez rien à lui donner… Mais quand vous lui apparaîtrez en dentelles… — J'aurai donc des dentelles ? — Sans doute et de toutes les sortes… en belles boucles de diamants… — J'aurai donc de belles boucles de diamants ? — Oui. — Comme celles de cette marquise qui vient quelquefois prendre des gants dans notre boutique ? — Précisément ; dans un bel équipage avec des chevaux gris pommelés, deux grands laquais, un petit nègre, et le coureur en avant ; du rouge, des mouches, la queue portée. — Au bal ? — Au bal… à l'Opéra, à la Comédie…[52] Déjà le cœur lui tressaillit de joie. Tu joues avec un papier entre tes doigts. Qu'est cela ? — Ce n'est rien. — Il me semble que si. — C'est un billet. — Et pour qui ? — Pour vous, si vous étiez un peu curieuse. — Curieuse ? Je le suis beaucoup. Voyons. Elle lit. Une entrevue, cela ne se peut. — En allant à la messe. — Maman m'accompagne toujours ; mais s'il venait ici un peu matin ; je me lève la première et je suis au comptoir avant qu'on soit levé. Il vient, il plaît ; un beau jour à la brune, la petite disparaît, et l'on me compte mes deux mille écus... Et quoi ! tu possèdes ce talent-là et tu manques de pain ? N'as-tu pas de honte, malheureux ? Je me rappelais un tas de coquins qui ne m'allaient pas à la cheville et qui regorgeaient de richesses. J'étais en surtout de baracan, et ils étaient couverts de velours ; ils s'appuyaient sur la canne à pomme d'or et en bec de corbin, et ils avaient l'aristote ou le platon au doigt. Qu'étaient-ce pourtant ? la plupart de misérables croquenotes ; aujourd'hui, ce sont des espèces de seigneurs. Alors je me sentais du courage, l'âme élevée, l'esprit subtil, et capable de tout. Mais ces heureuses dispositions apparemment ne duraient pas ; car, jusqu'à présent, je n'ai pu faire un certain chemin. Quoi qu'il en soit, voilà le texte de mes fréquents soliloques que vous pouvez paraphraser à votre fantaisie, pourvu que vous en concluiez que je connais le mépris de soi-même, ou ce tourment de la conscience qui naît de l'inutilité des dons que le ciel nous a départis ; c'est le plus cruel de tous. Il vaudrait presque autant que l'homme ne fût pas né.

Je l'écoutais, et à mesure qu'il faisait la scène du proxénète et de la jeune fille qu'il séduisait, l'âme agitée de deux mouvements opposés, je ne savais si je m'abandonnerais à l'envie de rire. ou au transport de l'indignation. Je souffrais. Vingt fois un éclat de rire empêcha ma colère d'éclater ; vingt fois la colère qui s'élevait au fond de mon cœur se termina par un éclat de rire. J'étais confondu de tant de sagacité et de tant de bassesse, d'idées si justes et alternativement si fausses, d'une perversité si générale de sentiments, d'une turpitude si complète, et d'une franchise si peu commune. Il s'aperçut du conflit qui se passait en moi : Qu'avez-vous ? me dit-il.

MOI — Rien.

LUI — Vous me paraissez troublé.

MOI — Je le suis aussi.

LUI — Mais enfin que me conseillez-vous ?

MOI — De changer de propos. Ah malheureux ! dans quel état d'abjection vous êtes né ou tombé.

LUI — J'en conviens. Mais cependant que mon état ne vous touche pas trop. Mon projet, en m'ouvrant à vous, n'était point de vous affliger. Je me suis fait chez ces gens quelque épargne. Songez que je n'avais besoin de rien, mais de rien absolument, et que l'on m'accordait tant pour mes menus plaisirs.

Alors il recommença à se frapper le front avec un de ses poings, à se mordre la lèvre, et rouler au plafond ses yeux égarés, ajoutant : Mais c'est une affaire faite. J'ai mis quelque chose de côté. Le temps s'est écoulé, et c'est toujours autant d'amassé.

MOI — Vous voulez dire de perdu ?

LUI — Non, non, d'amassé. On s'enrichit à chaque instant. Un jour de moins à vivre ou un écu de plus, c'est tout un. Le point important est d'aller aisément, librement, agréablement, copieusement tous les soirs à la garde-robe. *O stercus pretiosum* ![53] Voilà le grand résultat de la vie dans tous les états. Au dernier moment, tous sont également riches, et Samuel Bernard[54] qui, à force de vols, de pillages, de banqueroutes, laisse vingt-sept millions en or, et Rameau qui ne laissera rien, Rameau à qui la charité fournira la serpillière dont on l'enveloppera. Le mort n'entend pas sonner les cloches. C'est en vain que cent prêtres s'égosillent pour lui, qu'il est précédé et suivi d'une longue file de torches ardentes, son âme ne marche pas à côté du maître des cérémonies. Pourrir sous du marbre, pourrir sous de la terre, c'est toujours pourrir. Avoir autour de son cercueil les Enfants rouges et les Enfants bleus,[55] ou n'avoir personne, qu'est-ce que cela fait ? Et puis vous voyez bien ce poignet, il était raide comme un diable. Ces dix doigts, c'étaient autant de bâtons fichés dans un métacarpe de bois, et ces tendons, c'étaient de vieilles cordes à boyau plus sèches, plus roides, plus inflexibles que celles qui ont servi à la roue d'un tourneur. Mais je vous les ai tant tourmentées, tant brisées, tant rompues. Tu ne veux pas aller ; et moi, mordieu, je dis que tu iras ; et cela sera.

Et tout en disant cela, de la main droite, il s'était saisi les doigts et le poignet de la main gauche et il les renversait en dessus, en dessous ; l'extrémité des doigts touchait au bras ; les jointures en craquaient ; je craignais que les os n'en demeurassent disloqués.

MOI — Prenez garde, lui dis-je, vous allez vous estropier.

LUI — Ne craignez rien, ils y sont faits ; depuis dix ans je leur en ai bien donné d'une autre façon. Malgré qu'ils en eussent, il a bien fallu que les bougres s'y accoutumassent et qu'ils apprissent à se placer sur les touches et à voltiger sur les cordes. Aussi à présent cela va. Oui, cela va.

En même temps il se met dans l'attitude d'un joueur de violon ; il fredonne
5♪ de la voix un allegro de Locatelli ;[56] son bras droit imite le mouvement de l'archet, sa main gauche et ses doigts semblent se promener sur la longueur du manche ; s'il fait un ton faux, il s'arrête, il remonte ou baisse la corde ; il la pince de l'ongle pour s'assurer qu'elle est juste ; il reprend le morceau où il l'a laissé ; il bat la mesure du pied, il se démène de la tête, des pieds, des mains, des bras, du corps. Comme vous avez vu quelquefois, au Concert spirituel,[57] Ferrari ou Chiabran, ou quelque autre virtuose, dans les mêmes convulsions, m'offrant l'image du même supplice et me causant à peu près la même peine ; car n'est-ce pas une chose pénible à voir que le tourment dans celui qui s'occupe à me peindre le plaisir ? Tirez entre cet homme et moi un rideau qui me le cache, s'il faut qu'il me montre un patient appliqué à la question. Au milieu de ses agitations et de ses cris, s'il se présentait une tenue, un de ces endroits harmonieux où l'archet se meut lentement sur plusieurs cordes à la fois, son visage prenait l'air de l'extase, sa voix s'adoucissait, il s'écoutait avec ravissement. Il est sûr que les accords résonnaient dans ses oreilles et dans les miennes. Puis remettant son instrument sous son bras gauche de la même main dont il le tenait, et laissant tomber sa main droite avec son archet : Hé bien, me disait-il, qu'en pensez-vous ?

MOI — À merveilles.

LUI — Cela va, ce me semble, cela résonne à peu près comme les autres.

Et aussitôt il s'accroupit comme un musicien qui se met au clavecin. Je vous demande grâce pour vous et pour moi, lui dis-je.

LUI — Non, non ; puisque je vous tiens, vous m'entendrez. Je ne veux point d'un suffrage qu'on m'accorde sans savoir pourquoi. Vous me louerez d'un ton plus assuré, et cela me vaudra quelque écolier.

MOI — Je suis si peu répandu, et vous allez vous fatiguer en pure perte.

LUI — Je ne me fatigue jamais.

Comme je vis que je voudrais inutilement avoir pitié de mon homme, car la sonate sur le violon l'avait mis tout en eau, je pris le parti de le laisser faire. Le voilà donc assis au clavecin, les jambes fléchies, la tête élevée vers le plafond où l'on eût dit qu'il voyait une partition notée, chantant, préludant, exécutant une pièce d'Alberti[58] ou de Galuppi,[59] je ne sais lequel des deux. 6
Sa voix allait comme le vent et ses doigts voltigeaient sur les touches, tantôt laissant le dessus pour prendre la basse ; tantôt quittant la partie d'accompagnement pour revenir au dessus. Les passions se succédaient sur son visage ; on y distinguait la tendresse, la colère, le plaisir, la douleur ; on sentait les piano, les forte, et je suis sûr qu'un plus habile que moi aurait reconnu le morceau au mouvement, au caractère, à ses mines et à quelques traits de chant qui lui échappaient par intervalle. Mais, ce qu'il y avait de bizarre, c'est que de temps en temps il tâtonnait, se reprenait comme s'il eût manqué, et se dépitait de n'avoir plus la pièce dans les doigts.

Enfin, vous voyez, dit-il en se redressant, et en essuyant les gouttes de sueur qui descendaient le long de ses joues, que nous savons aussi placer un triton, une quinte superflue, et que l'enchaînement des dominantes nous est familier. Ces passages enharmoniques, dont le cher oncle a fait tant de train, ce n'est pas la mer à boire, nous nous en tirons.[60]

MOI — Vous vous êtes donné bien de la peine pour me montrer que vous étiez fort habile ; j'étais homme à vous croire sur votre parole.

LUI — Fort habile ? ho ! non ; pour mon métier, je le sais à peu près, et c'est plus qu'il ne faut. Car dans ce pays-ci, est-ce qu'on est obligé de savoir ce qu'on montre ?

MOI — Pas plus que de savoir ce qu'on apprend.

LUI — Cela est juste, morbleu ! et très juste ! Là, monsieur le philosophe, la main sur la conscience, parlez net. Il y eut un temps où vous n'étiez pas cossu comme aujourd'hui.[61]

MOI — Je ne le suis pas encore trop.

LUI — Mais vous n'iriez plus au Luxembourg,[62] en été, vous vous en souvenez...

MOI — Laissons cela, oui, je m'en souviens.

LUI — En redingote de peluche grise…

MOI — Oui, oui.

LUI — Éreintée par un des côtés ; avec la manchette déchirée et les bas de laine noirs et recousus par-derrière avec du fil blanc.

MOI — Et oui, oui, tout comme il vous plaira.

LUI — Que faisiez-vous alors dans l'allée des Soupirs ?

MOI — Une assez triste figure.

LUI — Au sortir de là, vous trottiez sur le pavé.

MOI — D'accord.

LUI — Vous donniez des leçons de mathématiques.

MOI — Sans en savoir un mot : n'est-ce pas là que vous en vouliez venir ?

LUI — Justement.

MOI — J'apprenais en montrant aux autres, et j'ai fait quelques bons écoliers.

LUI — Cela se peut ; mais il n'en est pas de la musique comme de l'algèbre ou de la géométrie. Aujourd'hui que vous êtes un gros monsieur…

MOI — Pas si gros.

LUI — Que vous avez du foin dans vos bottes…

MOI — Très peu.

LUI — Vous donnez des maîtres à votre fille.

MOI — Pas encore. C'est sa mère qui se mêle de son éducation ; car il faut avoir la paix chez soi.

LUI — La paix chez soi ? Morbleu ! on ne l'a que quand on est le serviteur ou le maître, et c'est le maître qu'il faut être. J'ai eu une femme. Dieu veuille avoir son âme ; mais quand il lui arrivait quelquefois de se rebéquer, je m'élevais sur mes ergots, je déployais mon tonnerre, je disais comme Dieu : Que la lumière se fasse ; et la lumière était faite. Aussi en quatre années de temps nous n'avons pas eu dix fois un mot, l'un plus haut que l'autre. Quel âge a votre enfant ?

MOI — Cela ne fait rien à l'affaire.

LUI — Quel âge a votre enfant ?

MOI — Et que diable ! laissons là mon enfant et son âge et revenons aux maîtres qu'elle aura.

LUI — Pardieu ! je ne sache rien de si têtu qu'un philosophe. En vous suppliant très humblement, ne pourrait-on savoir de monseigneur le philosophe quel âge à peu près peut avoir mademoiselle sa fille ?

MOI — Supposez-lui huit ans.[63]

LUI — Huit ans ! Il y a quatre ans que cela devrait avoir les doigts sur les touches.

MOI — Mais peut-être ne me souciais-je pas trop de faire entrer dans le plan de son éducation une étude qui occupe si longtemps et qui sert si peu.

LUI — Et que lui apprendrez-vous donc, s'il vous plaît ?

MOI — À raisonner juste, si je puis ; chose si peu commune parmi les hommes, et plus rare encore parmi les femmes.

LUI — Et laissez-la déraisonner tant qu'elle voudra, pourvu qu'elle soit jolie, amusante et coquette.

MOI — Puisque la nature a été assez ingrate envers elle pour lui donner une organisation délicate avec une âme sensible, et l'exposer aux mêmes peines de la vie que si elle avait une organisation forte et un cœur de bronze, je lui apprendrai, si je puis, à les supporter avec courage.

LUI — Et laissez-la pleurer, souffrir, minauder, avoir des nerfs agacés comme les autres, pourvu qu'elle soit jolie, amusante et coquette. Quoi ! point de danse ?[64]

MOI — Pas plus qu'il n'en faut pour faire une révérence, avoir un maintien décent, se bien présenter et savoir marcher.

LUI — Point de chant ?

MOI — Pas plus qu'il n'en faut pour bien prononcer.

LUI — Point de musique ?

MOI — S'il y avait un bon maître d'harmonie, je la lui confierais volontiers, deux heures par jour, pendant un ou deux ans, pas davantage.

LUI — Et à la place des choses essentielles que vous supprimez ?

MOI — Je mets de la grammaire, de la fable, de l'histoire, de la géographie, un peu de dessin et beaucoup de morale.

LUI — Combien il me serait facile de vous prouver l'inutilité de toutes ces connaissances là dans un monde tel que le nôtre ; que dis-je l'inutilité, peut-être le danger. Mais je m'en tiendrai pour ce moment à une question : ne lui faudra-t-il pas un ou deux maîtres ?

MOI — Sans doute.

LUI — Ah ! nous y revoilà. Et ces maîtres, vous espérez qu'ils sauront la grammaire, la fable, l'histoire, la géographie, la morale, dont ils lui donneront des leçons ? Chansons, mon cher maître, chansons ; s'ils possédaient ces choses assez pour les montrer, ils ne les montreraient pas.

MOI — Et pourquoi ?

LUI — C'est qu'ils auraient passé leur vie à les étudier. Il faut être profond dans l'art ou dans la science pour en bien posséder les éléments. Les ouvrages classiques ne peuvent être bien faits que par ceux qui ont blanchi sous le harnais. C'est le milieu et la fin qui éclairassent les ténèbres du commencement. Demandez à votre ami, M. d'Alembert,[65] le coryphée de la science mathématique, s'il serait trop bon pour en faire des éléments. Ce n'est qu'après trente à quarante ans d'exercice que mon oncle a entrevu les premières lueurs de la théorie musicale.

MOI — Ô fou, archifou ! m'écriai-je, comment se fait-il que dans ta mauvaise tête il se trouve des idées si justes pêle-mêle avec tant d'extravagances ?

LUI — Qui diable sait cela ? C'est le hasard qui vous les jette, et elles demeurent. Tant y a que quand on ne sait pas tout, on ne sait rien de bien. On ignore où une chose va, d'où une autre vient, où celle-ci ou celle-là veulent être placées ; laquelle doit passer la première, ou sera mieux la seconde. Montre-t-on bien sans la méthode ? Et la méthode, d'où naît-elle ? Tenez, mon philosophe, j'ai dans la tête que la physique sera toujours une pauvre science, une goutte d'eau prise avec la pointe d'une aiguille dans le vaste océan, un grain détaché de la chaîne des Alpes. Et les raisons des phénomènes ? En vérité, il vaudrait autant ignorer que de savoir si peu et si mal ; et c'était précisément où j'en étais, lorsque je me fis maître d'accompagnement et de composition. À quoi rêvez-vous ?

MOI — Je rêve que tout ce que vous venez de dire est plus spécieux que solide. Mais laissons cela. Vous avez montré, dites-vous, l'accompagnement et la composition ?

LUI — Oui.

MOI — Et vous n'en saviez rien du tout ?

LUI — Non, ma foi ; et c'est pour cela qu'il y en avait de pires que moi : ceux qui croyaient savoir quelque chose. Au moins je ne gâtais ni le jugement ni les mains des enfants. En passant de moi à un bon maître, comme ils n'avaient rien appris, du moins ils n'avaient rien à désapprendre, et c'était toujours autant d'argent et de temps épargnés.

MOI — Comment faisiez-vous ?

LUI — Comme ils font tous. J'arrivais, je me jetais dans une chaise : Que le temps est mauvais ! que le pavé est fatigant ! Je bavardais quelques nouvelles : Mlle Lemierre[66] devait faire un rôle de vestale dans l'opéra nouveau ; mais elle est grosse pour la seconde fois ; on ne sait qui la doublera. Mlle Arnould[67] vient de quitter son petit comte ; on dit qu'elle est en négociation avec Bertin.[45] Le petit comte a pourtant trouvé la porcelaine de M. de Montamy.[68] Il y avait, au dernier Concert des amateurs, une

Italienne qui a chanté comme un ange. C'est un rare corps que ce Préville, il faut le voir dans *Le Mercure galant* ;[69] l'endroit de l'énigme est impayable. Cette pauvre Dumesnil[70] ne sait plus ni ce qu'elle dit ni ce qu'elle fait. Allons, mademoiselle, prenez votre livre. Tandis que mademoiselle, qui ne se presse pas, cherche son livre qu'elle a égaré, qu'on appelle une femme de chambre, qu'on gronde, je continue : La Clairon est vraiment incompréhensible. On parle d'un mariage fort saugrenu : c'est celui de Mlle... comment l'appelez-vous ? une petite créature qu'il entretenait, à qui il a fait deux ou trois enfants, qui avait été entretenue par tant d'autres. — Allons, Rameau, cela ne se peut ; vous radotez. — Je ne radote point. On dit même que la chose est faite. Le bruit court que de Voltaire est mort ; tant mieux. — Et pourquoi tant mieux ? — C'est qu'il va nous donner quelque bonne folie. C'est son usage que de mourir une quinzaine auparavant. Que vous dirai-je encore ? Je disais quelques polissonneries que je rapportais des maisons où j'avais été, car nous sommes tous grands colporteurs. Je faisais le fou. On m'écoutait. On riait. On s'écriait : Il est toujours charmant. Cependant le livre de mademoiselle s'était enfin retrouvé sous un fauteuil où il avait été traîné, mâchonné, déchiré par un jeune doguin, ou par un petit chat. Elle se mettait à son clavecin. D'abord elle y faisait du bruit toute seule. Ensuite je m'approchais, après avoir fait à la mère un signe d'approbation. La mère : Cela ne va pas mal ; on n'aurait qu'à vouloir, mais on ne veut pas. On aime mieux perdre son temps à jaser, à chiffonner, à courir, à je ne sais quoi. Vous n'êtes pas sitôt parti, que le livre est fermé pour ne le rouvrir qu'à votre retour. Aussi vous ne la grondez jamais... Cependant, comme il fallait faire quelque chose, je lui prenais les mains que je lui plaçais autrement. Je me dépitais, je criais : Sol, sol, sol ; mademoiselle, c'est un sol. — La mère : Mademoiselle, est-ce que vous n'avez point d'oreilles ? Moi qui ne suis pas au clavecin, et qui ne vois pas sur votre livre, je sens qu'il faut un sol. Vous donnez une peine infinie à monsieur. Je ne conçois pas sa patience. Vous ne retenez rien de ce qu'il vous dit. Vous n'avancez point... Alors je rabattais un peu les coups, et hochant de la tête, je disais : Pardonnez-moi, madame, pardonnez-moi. Cela pourrait aller mieux si mademoiselle voulait, si elle étudiait un peu ; mais cela ne va pas mal. — La mère : À votre place, je la tiendrais un an sur la même pièce. — Ho ! pour cela, elle n'en sortira pas qu'elle ne soit au-dessus de toutes les difficultés ; et cela ne sera pas si long que madame le croit. — La mère : Monsieur Rameau, vous la flattez. Vous êtes trop bon. Voilà de sa leçon la seule chose qu'elle retiendra et qu'elle saura bien me répéter dans l'occasion. L'heure se passait. Mon écolière me présentait le petit cachet avec la grâce du bras et la révérence qu'elle avait apprise du maître à danser. Je le mettais dans ma poche, pendant que la mère disait : Fort bien, mademoiselle. Si Javillier[71] était là, il vous applaudirait. Je bavardais encore un moment par bienséance ; je disparaissais ensuite, et voilà ce qu'on appelait alors une leçon d'accompagnement.

MOI — Et aujourd'hui c'est donc autre chose ?

LUI — Vertudieu ! je le crois. J'arrive. Je suis grave. Je me hâte d'ôter mon manchon. J'ouvre le clavecin. J'essaye les touches. Je suis toujours pressé : si l'on me fait attendre un moment, je crie comme si l'on me volait un écu. Dans une heure d'ici il faut que je sois là ; dans deux heures chez Mme la duchesse une telle. Je suis attendu à dîner chez une belle marquise ; et au sortir de là, c'est un concert chez M. le baron de Bacq,[72] rue Neuve-des-Petits-Champs.

MOI — Et cependant vous n'êtes attendu nulle part ?

LUI — Il est vrai.

MOI — Et pourquoi employer toutes ces petites viles ruses-là ?

LUI — Viles ! et pourquoi, s'il vous plaît ? Elles sont d'usage dans mon état ; je ne m'avilis point en faisant comme tout le monde. Ce n'est pas moi qui les ai inventées, et je serais bizarre et maladroit de ne pas m'y conformer. Vraiment, je sais bien que si vous allez appliquer à cela certains principes généraux de je ne sais quelle morale qu'ils ont tous à la bouche, et qu'aucun d'eux ne pratique, il se trouvera que ce qui est blanc sera noir et que ce qui est noir sera blanc. Mais, monsieur le philosophe, il y a une conscience générale, comme il y a une grammaire générale, et puis des exceptions dans chaque langue, que vous appelez, je crois, vous autres savants, des… aidez-moi donc, des…

MOI — Idiotismes.[73]

LUI — Tout juste. Eh bien, chaque état a ses exceptions à la conscience générale, auxquelles je donnerais volontiers le nom d'idiotismes de métier.

MOI — J'entends. Fontenelle[74] parle bien, écrit bien, quoique son style fourmille d'idiotismes français.

LUI — Et le souverain, le ministre, le financier, le magistrat, le militaire, l'homme de lettres, l'avocat, le procureur, le commerçant, le banquier, l'artisan, le maître à chanter, le maître à danser, sont de fort honnêtes gens, quoique leur conduite s'écarte en plusieurs points de la conscience générale, et soit remplie d'idiotismes moraux. Plus l'institution des choses est ancienne, plus il y a d'idiotismes ; plus les temps sont malheureux, plus les idiotismes se multiplient. Tant vaut l'homme, tant vaut le métier ; et réciproquement, à la fin, tant vaut le métier, tant vaut l'homme. On fait donc valoir le métier tant qu'on peut.

MOI — Ce que je conçois clairement à tout cet entortillage, c'est qu'il y a peu de métiers honnêtement exercés, ou peu d'honnêtes gens dans leurs métiers.

LUI — Bon ! il n'y en a point ; mais en revanche il y a peu de fripons hors de leur boutique ; et tout irait assez bien, sans un certain nombre de gens qu'on appelle assidus, exacts, remplissant rigoureusement leurs devoirs, stricts, ou, ce qui revient au même, toujours dans leurs boutiques, et faisant leur métier depuis le matin jusqu'au soir, et ne faisant que cela. Aussi sont-ils les seuls qui deviennent opulents et qui soient estimés.

MOI — À force d'idiotismes.

LUI — C'est cela ; je vois que vous m'avez compris. Or donc un idiotisme de presque tous les états, car il y en a de communs à tous les pays, à tous les temps, comme il y a des sottises communes, un idiotisme commun est de se procurer le plus de pratiques que l'on peut ; une sottise commune est de croire que le plus habile est celui qui en a le plus. Voilà deux exceptions à la conscience générale auxquelles il faut se plier. C'est une espèce de crédit. Ce n'est rien en soi ; mais cela vaut par l'opinion. On a dit que *bonne renommée valait mieux que ceinture dorée*. Cependant qui a bonne renommée n'a pas ceinture dorée, et je vois qu'aujourd'hui qui a ceinture dorée ne manque guère de renommée. Il faut, autant qu'il est possible, avoir le renom et la ceinture. Et c'est mon objet, lorsque je me fais valoir par ce que vous qualifiez d'adresses viles, d'indignes petites ruses. Je donne ma leçon, et je la donne bien : voilà la règle générale. Je fais croire que j'en ai plus à donner que la journée n'a d'heures, voilà l'idiotisme.

MOI — Et la leçon, vous la donnez bien ?

LUI — Oui, pas mal, passablement. La basse fondamentale du cher oncle a bien simplifié tout cela. Autrefois je volais l'argent de mon écolier ; oui, je le volais, cela est sûr. Aujourd'hui je le gagne, du moins comme les autres.

MOI — Et le voliez-vous sans remords ?

LUI — Ho, sans remords ! On dit que *si un voleur vole l'autre, le diable s'en rit*. Les parents regorgeaient d'une fortune acquise Dieu sait comment ; c'étaient des gens de cour, des financiers, de gros commerçants, des banquiers, des gens d'affaires. Je les aidais à restituer, moi et une foule d'autres qu'ils employaient comme moi. Dans la nature, toutes les espèces se dévorent ; toutes les conditions se dévorent dans la société. Nous faisons justice les uns des autres sans que la loi s'en mêle. La Deschamps autrefois, aujourd'hui la Guimard[75] venge le prince du financier, et c'est la marchande de mode, le bijoutier, le tapissier, la lingère, l'escroc, la femme de chambre, le cuisinier, le bourrelier qui vengent le financier de la Deschamps[76]. Au milieu de tout cela, il n'y a que l'imbécile ou l'oisif qui soit lésé sans avoir vexé personne, et c'est fort bien fait. D'où vous voyez que ces exceptions à la conscience générale, ou ces idiotismes moraux dont on fait tant de bruit sous la dénomination de *tours du bâton*, ne sont rien, et qu'à tout, il n'y a que le coup d'œil qu'il faut avoir juste.

MOI — J'admire le vôtre.

LUI — Et puis la misère. La voix de la conscience et de l'honneur est bien faible, lorsque les boyaux crient. Suffit que si je deviens jamais riche, il faudra bien que je restitue, et que je suis bien résolu à restituer de toutes les manières possibles, par la table, par le jeu, par le vin, par les femmes.

MOI — Mais j'ai peur que vous ne deveniez jamais riche.

LUI — Moi, j'en ai le soupçon.

MOI — Mais s'il en arrivait autrement, que feriez-vous ?

LUI — Je ferais comme tous les gueux revêtus ; je serais le plus insolent maroufle qu'on eût encore vu. C'est alors que je me rappellerais tout ce qu'ils m'ont fait souffrir, et je leur rendrais bien les avanies qu'ils m'ont faites. J'aime à commander, et je commanderai. J'aime qu'on me loue, et l'on me louera. J'aurai à mes gages toute la troupe villemorienne,[77] et je leur dirai, comme on me l'a dit : Allons, faquins, qu'on m'amuse, et l'on m'amusera ; Qu'on me déchire les honnêtes gens, et on les déchirera, si l'on en trouve encore ; et puis nous aurons des filles, nous nous tutoierons quand nous serons ivres ; nous nous enivrerons, nous ferons des contes, nous aurons toutes sortes de travers et de vices. Cela sera délicieux. Nous prouverons que de Voltaire est sans génie : que Buffon,[78] toujours guindé sur des échasses, n'est qu'un déclamateur ampoulé ; que Montesquieu[79] n'est qu'un bel esprit ; nous reléguerons d'Alembert dans ses mathématiques,[80] nous en donnerons sur dos et ventre à tous ces petits Catons comme vous, qui nous méprisent par envie, dont la modestie est le manteau de l'orgueil, et dont la sobriété est la loi du besoin. Et de la musique ? C'est alors que nous en ferons.

MOI — Au digne emploi que vous feriez de la richesse, je vois combien c'est grand dommage que vous soyez gueux. Vous vivriez là d'une manière bien honorable pour l'espèce humaine, bien utile à vos concitoyens, bien glorieuse pour vous.

LUI — Mais je crois que vous vous moquez de moi. Monsieur le philosophe, vous ne savez pas à qui vous vous jouez ; vous ne vous doutez pas que dans ce moment je représente la partie la plus importante de la ville et de la cour. Nos opulents dans tous les états ou se sont dit à eux-mêmes ou ne se sont pas dit les mêmes choses que je vous ai confiées ; mais le fait est que la vie que je mènerais à leur place est exactement la leur. Voilà où vous en êtes, vous autres. Vous croyez que le même bonheur est fait pour tous. Quelle étrange vision ! Le vôtre suppose un certain tour d'esprit romanesque que nous n'avons pas, une âme singulière, un goût particulier. Vous décorez cette bizarrerie du nom de vertu, vous l'appelez philosophie. Mais la vertu, la philosophie sont-elles faites pour tout le monde ? En a qui peut, en conserve qui peut. Imaginez l'univers sage et philosophe ; convenez qu'il serait diablement triste. Tenez, vive la philosophie, vive la sagesse de Salomon : boire de bon vin, se gorger de mets délicats, se rouler sur de jolies femmes, se reposer dans des lits bien mollets. Excepté cela, le reste n'est que vanité.

MOI — Quoi ! défendre sa patrie ?

LUI — Vanité ![81] Il n'y a plus de patrie : je ne vois d'un pôle à l'autre que des tyrans et des esclaves.

MOI — Servir ses amis ?

LUI — Vanité ! Est-ce qu'on a des amis ? Quand on en aurait, faudrait-il en faire des ingrats ? Regardez-y bien, et vous verrez que c'est presque toujours là ce qu'on recueille des services rendus. La reconnaissance est un fardeau, et tout fardeau est fait pour être secoué.

MOI — Avoir un état dans la société et en remplir les devoirs ?

LUI — Vanité ! Qu'importe qu'on ait un état ou non, pourvu qu'on soit riche, puisqu'on ne prend un état que pour le devenir. Remplir ses devoirs, à quoi cela mène-t-il ? à la jalousie, au trouble, à la persécution. Est-ce ainsi qu'on s'avance ? Faire sa cour, morbleu ! faire sa cour, voir les grands, étudier leurs goûts, se prêter à leurs fantaisies, servir leurs vices, approuver leurs injustices : voilà le secret.

MOI — Veiller à l'éducation de ses enfants ?

LUI — Vanité ! C'est l'affaire d'un précepteur.

MOI — Mais si ce précepteur, pénétré de vos principes, néglige ses devoirs, qui est-ce qui en sera châtié ?

LUI — Ma foi, ce ne sera pas moi, mais peut-être un jour le mari de ma fille ou la femme de mon fils.

MOI — Mais si l'un et l'autre se précipitent dans la débauche et les vices ?

LUI — Cela est de leur état.

MOI — S'ils se déshonorent ?

LUI — Quoi qu'on fasse, on ne peut se déshonorer quand on est riche.

MOI — S'ils se ruinent ?

LUI — Tant pis pour eux.

MOI — Je vois que si vous vous dispensez de veiller à la conduite de votre femme, de vos enfants, de vos domestiques, vous pourriez aisément négliger vos affaires.

LUI — Pardonnez-moi ; il est quelquefois difficile de trouver de l'argent, et il est prudent de s'y prendre de loin.

MOI — Vous donnerez peu de soin à votre femme ?

LUI — Aucun, s'il vous plaît. Le meilleur procédé, je crois, qu'on puisse avoir avec sa chère moitié, c'est de faire ce qui lui convient. À votre avis, la société ne serait-elle pas fort amusante, si chacun y était à sa chose ?

MOI — Pourquoi pas ? la soirée n'est jamais plus belle pour moi que quand je suis content de ma matinée.

LUI — Et pour moi aussi.

MOI — Ce qui rend les gens du monde si délicats sur leurs amusements, c'est leur profonde oisiveté.

LUI — Ne croyez pas cela ; ils s'agitent beaucoup.

MOI — Comme ils ne se lassent jamais, ils ne se délassent jamais.

LUI — Ne croyez pas cela ; ils sont sans cesse excédés.

MOI — Le plaisir est toujours une affaire pour eux, et jamais un besoin.

LUI — Tant mieux ; le besoin est toujours une peine.

MOI — Ils usent tout. Leur âme s'hébète. L'ennui s'en empare. Celui qui leur ôterait la vie au milieu de leur abondance accablante, les servirait. C'est qu'ils ne connaissent du bonheur que la partie qui s'émousse le plus vite. Je ne méprise pas les plaisirs des sens. J'ai un palais aussi, et il est flatté d'un mets délicat ou d'un vin délicieux. J'ai un cœur et des yeux, et j'aime à voir une jolie femme, j'aime à sentir sous ma main la fermeté et la rondeur de sa gorge, à presser ses lèvres des miennes, à puiser la volupté dans ses regards, et à en expirer entre ses bras. Quelquefois, avec mes amis, une partie de débauche, même un peu tumultueuse, ne me déplaît pas. Mais, je ne vous le dissimulerai pas, il m'est infiniment plus doux encore d'avoir secouru le malheureux, d'avoir terminé une affaire épineuse, donné un conseil salutaire, fait une lecture agréable, une promenade avec un homme ou une femme chère à mon cœur, passé quelques heures instructives avec mes enfants, écrit une bonne page, rempli les devoirs de mon état, dit à celle que j'aime quelques choses tendres et douces qui amènent ses bras autour de mon cou. Je connais telle action que je voudrais avoir faite pour tout ce que je possède. C'est un sublime ouvrage que *Mahomet* ;[82] j'aimerais mieux avoir réhabilité la mémoire des Calas.[83] Un homme de ma connaissance s'était réfugié à Carthagène.[84] C'était un cadet de famille, dans un pays où la coutume transfère tout le bien aux aînés. Là il apprend que son aîné, enfant gâté, après avoir dépouillé son père et sa mère, trop faciles, de tout ce qu'ils possédaient, les avait expulsés de leur château, et que les bons vieillards languissaient indigents, dans une petite ville de la province. Que fait alors ce cadet qui, traité durement par ses parents, était allé tenter la fortune au loin ? Il leur envoie des secours ; il se hâte d'arranger ses affaires. Il revient opulent. Il ramène son père et sa mère dans leur domicile. Il marie ses sœurs. Ah ! mon cher Rameau, cet homme regardait cet intervalle comme le plus heureux de sa vie. C'est les larmes aux yeux qu'il m'en parlait ; et moi, je sens, en vous faisant ce récit, mon cœur se troubler de joie, et le plaisir me couper la parole.

LUI — Vous êtes des êtres bien singuliers !

MOI — Vous êtes des êtres bien à plaindre, si vous n'imaginez pas qu'on s'est élevé au-dessus du sort, et qu'il est impossible d'être malheureux à l'abri de deux belles actions telles que celle-ci.

LUI — Voilà une espèce de félicité avec laquelle j'aurai de la peine à me familiariser, car on la rencontre rarement. Mais, à votre compte, il faudrait donc être d'honnêtes gens ?

MOI — Pour être heureux ? assurément.

LUI — Cependant je vois une infinité d'honnêtes gens qui ne sont pas heureux, et une infinité de gens qui sont heureux sans être honnêtes.

MOI — Il vous semble.

LUI — Et n'est-ce pas pour avoir eu du sens commun et de la franchise un moment, que je ne sais où aller souper ce soir ?

MOI — Hé non ! c'est pour n'en avoir pas toujours eu ; c'est pour n'avoir pas senti de bonne heure qu'il fallait d'abord se faire une ressource indépendante de la servitude.

LUI — Indépendante ou non, celle que je me suis faite est au moins la plus aisée.

MOI — Et la moins sûre et la moins honnête.

LUI — Mais la plus conforme à mon caractère de fainéant, de sot, de vaurien.

MOI — D'accord.

LUI — Et que puisque je puis faire mon bonheur par des vices qui me sont naturels, que j'ai acquis sans travail, que je conserve sans effort, qui cadrent avec les mœurs de ma nation, qui sont du goût de ceux qui me protègent, et plus analogues à leurs petits besoins particuliers que des vertus qui les gêneraient en les accusant depuis le matin jusqu'au soir, il serait bien singulier que j'allasse me tourmenter comme une âme damnée, pour me bistourner et me faire autre que je ne suis, pour me donner un caractère étranger au mien, des qualités très estimables, j'y consens, pour ne pas disputer, mais qui me coûteraient beaucoup à acquérir, à pratiquer, ne me mèneraient à rien, peut-être à pis que rien, par la satire continuelle des riches auprès desquels les gueux comme moi ont à chercher leur vie. On loue la vertu, mais on la hait, mais on la fuit, mais elle gèle de froid, et dans ce monde, il faut avoir les pieds chauds. Et puis cela me donnerait de l'humeur, infailliblement ; car pourquoi voyons-nous si fréquemment les dévots si durs, si fâcheux, si insociables ? C'est qu'ils se sont imposé une tâche qui ne leur est pas naturelle. Ils souffrent, et quand on souffre, on fait souffrir les autres. Ce n'est pas là mon compte, ni celui de mes protecteurs ; il faut que je sois gai, souple, plaisant, bouffon, drôle. La vertu se fait respecter, et le respect est incommode. La vertu se fait admirer, et l'admiration n'est pas amusante. J'ai affaire à des gens qui s'ennuient, et il faut que je les fasse rire. Or c'est le ridicule et la folie qui font rire, il faut donc que je sois ridicule et fou ; et quand la nature ne m'aurait pas fait tel, le plus court serait de le paraître. Heureusement je n'ai pas besoin d'être hypocrite ; il y en a déjà tant de toutes les couleurs, sans compter ceux qui le sont avec eux-mêmes. Ce chevalier de La Morlière,[85] qui retape son chapeau sur son oreille, qui porte la tête au vent, qui vous regarde le passant par-dessus l'épaule, qui fait battre une longue épée sur sa cuisse, qui a l'insulte toute prête pour celui qui n'en porte point, et qui semble adresser un défi à tout venant, que fait-il ? tout ce qu'il peut pour se persuader qu'il est homme de cœur, mais il est lâche. Offrez-lui une croquignole sur le bout du nez, et il la recevra en douceur. Voulez-vous lui faire baisser le ton ? élevez-le. Montrez-lui votre canne ou appliquez votre pied entre ses fesses, tout étonné de se trouver un lâche, il vous demandera qui est-ce qui vous l'a appris, d'où vous le savez. Lui-même l'ignorait le moment précédent ; une longue et habituelle singerie de bravoure lui en avait imposé. Il avait tant fait les mines qu'il se croyait la chose. Et cette femme qui se mortifie, qui visite les prisons, qui assiste à toutes les assemblées de charité, qui marche les yeux baissés, qui n'oserait regarder un homme en face, sans cesse en garde contre la séduction de ses sens ; tout cela empêche-t-il que son cœur ne brûle, que des soupirs ne lui échappent, que son tempérament ne s'allume, que les désirs ne l'obsèdent, et que son imagination ne lui retrace, la nuit et le jour, les scènes du *Portier des Chartreux*,[86] les *Postures*[87] de l'Arétin ? Alors que devient-elle ? qu'en pense sa femme de chambre lorsqu'elle se lève en chemise et qu'elle vole au secours de sa maîtresse qui se meurt ? Justine, allez vous recoucher, ce n'est pas vous que votre maîtresse appelle dans son délire. Et l'ami Rameau, s'il se mettait un jour à marquer du mépris pour la fortune, les femmes, la bonne chère, l'oisiveté, à catoniser,[88] que serait-il ? un hypocrite. Il faut que Rameau soit ce qu'il est : un brigand heureux avec des brigands opulents, et non un fanfaron de vertu ou même un homme vertueux, rongeant sa croûte de pain, seul, ou à côté des gueux. Et pour le trancher net, je ne m'accommode point de votre félicité, ni du bonheur de quelques visionnaires comme vous.

MOI — Je vois, mon cher, que vous ignorez ce que c'est, et que vous n'êtes pas même fait pour l'apprendre.

LUI — Tant mieux, mordieu ! tant mieux. Cela me ferait crever de faim, d'ennui, et de remords peut-être.

MOI — D'après cela, le seul conseil que j'aie à vous donner, c'est de rentrer bien vite dans la maison d'où vous vous êtes imprudemment fait chasser.

LUI — Et de faire ce que vous ne désapprouvez pas au simple, et ce qui me répugne un peu au figuré ?

MOI — C'est mon avis.

LUI — Indépendamment de cette métaphore qui me déplaît dans ce moment, et qui ne me déplaira pas dans un autre.

MOI — Quelle singularité !

LUI — Il n'y a rien de singulier à cela. Je veux bien être abject, mais je veux que ce soit sans contrainte.[89] Je veux bien descendre de ma dignité… Vous riez ?

MOI — Oui, votre dignité me fait rire.

LUI — Chacun a la sienne ; je veux bien oublier la mienne, mais à ma discrétion et non à l'ordre d'autrui. Faut-il qu'on puisse me dire : Rampe, et que je sois obligé de ramper ? C'est l'allure du ver, c'est mon allure ; nous la suivons l'un et l'autre quand on nous laisse aller, mais nous nous redressons quand on nous marche sur la queue. On m'a marché sur la queue, et je me redresserai. Et puis vous n'avez pas d'idée de la pétaudière dont il s'agit. Imaginez un mélancolique et maussade personnage, dévoré de vapeurs, enveloppé dans deux ou trois tours de robe de chambre, qui se déplaît à lui-même, à qui tout déplaît, qu'on fait à peine sourire en se disloquant le corps et l'esprit en cent manières diverses, qui considère froidement les grimaces plaisantes de mon visage et celles de mon jugement qui sont plus plaisantes encore ; car, entre nous, ce père Noël,[90] ce vilain bénédictin, si renommé pour les grimaces, malgré ses succès à la Cour, n'est, sans me vanter ni lui non plus, à comparaison de moi qu'un polichinelle de bois. J'ai beau me tourmenter pour atteindre au sublime des Petites-Maisons, rien n'y fait. Rira-t-il ? ne rira-t-il pas ? voilà ce que je suis forcé de me dire au milieu de mes contorsions, et vous pouvez juger combien cette incertitude nuit au talent. Mon hypocondre, la tête renfoncée dans un bonnet de nuit qui lui couvre les yeux, a l'air d'une pagode[91] immobile à laquelle on aurait attaché un fil au menton, d'où il descendrait jusque sous son fauteuil. On attend que le fil se tire, et il ne se tire point, ou s'il arrive que la mâchoire s'entrouvre, c'est pour articuler un mot désolant, un mot qui vous apprend que vous n'avez point été aperçu, et que toutes vos singeries sont perdues ; ce mot est la réponse à une question que vous lui aurez faite il y a quatre jours ; ce mot dit, le ressort mastoïde se détend, et la mâchoire se referme.

Puis il se mit à contrefaire son homme ; il s'était placé dans une chaise, la tête fixe, le chapeau jusque sur ses paupières, les yeux à demi clos, les bras pendants, remuant sa mâchoire comme un automate, et disant : Oui, vous avez raison, Mademoiselle, il faut mettre de la finesse là. C'est que cela décide, que cela décide toujours et sans appel, le soir, le matin, à la toilette, à dîner, au café, au jeu, au théâtre, à souper, au lit, et, Dieu me le pardonne, je crois entre les bras de sa maîtresse. Je ne suis pas à portée d'entendre ces dernières décisions-ci, mais je suis diablement las des autres. Triste, obscur, et tranché, comme le destin, tel est notre patron.

Vis-à-vis, c'est une bégueule qui joue l'importance, à qui l'on se résoudrait à dire qu'elle est jolie, parce qu'elle l'est encore, quoiqu'elle ait sur le visage quelques gales par-ci par-là, et qu'elle coure après le volume de Mme Bouvillon.[92] J'aime les chairs quand elles sont belles ; mais aussi trop est trop, et le mouvement est si essentiel à la matière ![93] *Item*, elle est plus méchante, plus fière et plus bête qu'une oie. *Item*, elle veut avoir de l'esprit. *Item*, il faut lui persuader qu'on lui en croit comme à personne. *Item*, cela ne sait rien, et cela décide aussi. *Item*, il faut applaudir à ces décisions des pieds et des mains, sauter d'aise, se transir d'admiration : Que cela est beau, délicat, bien dit, finement vu, singulièrement senti ! où les femmes prennent-elles cela ? Sans étude, par la seule force de l'instinct, par la seule lumière naturelle : cela tient du prodige. Et puis qu'on vienne nous dire que l'expérience, l'étude, la réflexion, l'éducation y font quelque chose, et autres pareilles sottises, et pleurer de joie. Dix fois dans la journée se courber, un genou fléchi en devant, l'autre jambe tirée en arrière. Les bras étendus vers la déesse, chercher son désir dans ses yeux, rester suspendu à sa lèvre, attendre son ordre et partir comme un éclair. Qui est-ce qui peut s'assujettir à un rôle pareil, si ce n'est le misérable qui trouve là, deux ou trois fois la semaine, de quoi calmer la tribulation de ses intestins ? Que penser des autres, tels que le Palissot, le Fréron, les Poinsinet, le Baculard[94] qui ont quelque chose, et dont les bassesses ne peuvent s'excuser par le borborygme d'un estomac qui souffre ?

MOI — Je ne vous aurais jamais cru si difficile.

LUI — Je ne le suis pas. Au commencement je voyais faire les autres, et je faisais comme eux, même un peu mieux, parce que je suis plus franchement impudent, meilleur comédien, plus affamé, fourni de meilleurs poumons. Je descends apparemment en droite ligne du fameux Stentor.[95]

Et pour me donner une juste idée de la force de ce viscère, il se mit à tousser d'une violence à ébranler les vitres du café, et à suspendre l'attention des joueurs d'échecs.

MOI — Mais à quoi bon ce talent ?

LUI — Vous ne le devinez pas ?

MOI — Non, je suis un peu borné.

LUI — Supposez la dispute engagée et la victoire incertaine : je me lève, et déployant mon tonnerre, je dis : Cela est comme mademoiselle l'assure. C'est là ce qui s'appelle juger. Je le donne en cent à tous nos beaux esprits. L'expression est de génie. Mais il ne faut pas toujours approuver de la même manière. On serait monotone. On aurait l'air faux. On deviendrait insipide. On ne se sauve de là que par du jugement, de la fécondité ; il faut savoir préparer et placer ces tons majeurs et péremptoires, saisir l'occasion et le moment ;[96] lors, par exemple, qu'il y a partage entre les sentiments, que la dispute s'est élevée à son dernier degré de violence, qu'on ne s'entend plus, que tous parlent à la fois, il faut être placé à l'écart, dans l'angle de l'appartement le plus éloigné du champ de bataille, avoir préparé son explosion par un long silence, et tomber subitement, comme une comminge au milieu des contendants. Personne n'a eu cet art comme moi. Mais où je suis surprenant, c'est dans l'opposé ; j'ai des petits tons que j'accompagne d'un sourire, une variété infinie de mines approbatives ; là, le nez, la bouche, le front, les yeux entrent en jeu ; j'ai une souplesse de reins, une manière de contourner l'épine du dos, de hausser ou de baisser les épaules, d'étendre les doigts, d'incliner la tête, de fermer les yeux et d'être stupéfait comme si j'avais entendu descendre du ciel une voix angélique et divine. C'est là ce qui flatte. Je ne sais si vous saisissez bien toute l'énergie de cette dernière attitude-là. Je ne l'ai point inventée, mais personne ne m'a surpassé dans l'exécution. Voyez, voyez.

MOI — Il est vrai que cela est unique.

LUI — Croyez-vous qu'il y ait cervelle de femme un peu vaine qui tienne à cela ?

MOI — Non. Il faut convenir que vous avez porté le talent de faire des fous et de s'avilir aussi loin qu'il est possible.

LUI — Ils auront beau faire, tous tant qu'ils sont, ils n'en viendront jamais là. Le meilleur d'entre eux, Palissot, par exemple, ne sera jamais qu'un bon écolier. Mais si ce rôle amuse d'abord, et si l'on goûte quelque plaisir à se moquer en dedans de la bêtise de ceux qu'on enivre, à la longue cela ne pique plus ; et puis, après un certain nombre de découvertes, on est forcé de se répéter. L'esprit et l'art ont leurs limites. Il n'y a que Dieu ou quelques génies rares pour qui la carrière s'étend à mesure qu'ils y avancent. Bouret[97] en est un peut-être : il y a de celui-ci des traits qui m'en donnent à moi, oui, à moi-même, la plus sublime idée. Le petit chien, le Livre de la Félicité, les flambeaux sur la route de Versailles sont de ces choses qui me confondent et m'humilient ; ce serait capable de dégoûter du métier.

MOI — Que voulez-vous dire avec votre petit chien ?

LUI — D'où venez-vous donc ? Quoi ! sérieusement, vous ignorez comment cet homme rare s'y prit pour détacher de lui et attacher au garde des Sceaux[98] un petit chien qui plaisait à celui-ci ?

MOI — Je l'ignore, je le confesse.

LUI — Tant mieux. C'est une des plus belles choses qu'on ait imaginées ; toute l'Europe en a été émerveillée, et il n'y a pas un courtisan dont elle n'ait excité l'envie. Vous qui ne manquez pas de sagacité, voyons comment vous vous y seriez pris à sa place. Songez que Bouret était aimé de son chien ; songez que le vêtement bizarre du ministre effrayait le petit animal ; songez qu'il n'avait que huit jours pour vaincre les difficultés. Il faut connaître toutes les conditions du problème pour bien sentir le mérite de la solution. Hé bien !

MOI — Eh bien ! il faut que je vous avoue que, dans ce genre, les choses les plus faciles m'embarrasseraient.

LUI — Écoutez, me dit-il en me frappant un petit coup sur l'épaule, car il est familier, écoutez et admirez. Il se fait faire un masque qui ressemble au garde des Sceaux ; il emprunte d'un valet de chambre la volumineuse simarre.[99] Il se couvre le visage du masque. Il endosse la simarre. Il appelle son chien, il le caresse. Il lui donne la gimblette.[100] Puis tout à coup changeant de décoration, ce n'est plus le garde des Sceaux ; c'est Bouret qui appelle son chien et qui le fouette. En moins de deux ou trois jours de cet exercice continué du matin au soir, le chien sait fuir Bouret le fermier général et courir à Bouret le garde des Sceaux. Mais je suis trop bon, vous êtes un profane qui ne méritez pas d'être instruit de miracles qui s'opèrent à côté de vous.

MOI — Malgré cela, je vous prie, le livre, les flambeaux ?

LUI — Non, non. Adressez-vous aux pavés qui vous diront ces choses-là, et profitez de la circonstance qui nous a rapprochés, pour apprendre des choses que personne ne sait que moi.

MOI — Vous avez raison.

LUI — Emprunter la robe et la perruque, j'avais oublié la perruque, du garde des Sceaux ! Se faire un masque qui lui ressemble ! Le masque surtout me tourne la tête. Aussi cet homme jouit-il de la plus haute considération ; aussi possède-t-il des millions. Il y a des croix de Saint-Louis[101] qui n'ont pas de pain ; aussi pourquoi courir après la croix, au hasard de se faire échiner, et ne pas se tourner vers un état sans péril qui ne manque jamais sa récompense ? Voilà ce qui s'appelle aller au grand. Ces modèles-là sont décourageants. On a pitié de soi, et l'on s'ennuie. Le masque ! le masque ! Je donnerais un de mes doigts pour avoir trouvé le masque.

MOI — Mais avec cet enthousiasme pour les belles choses et cette fertilité de génie que vous possédez, est-ce que vous n'avez rien inventé ?

LUI — Pardonnez-moi ; par exemple, l'attitude admirative du dos dont je vous ai parlé ; je la regarde comme mienne, quoiqu'elle puisse peut-être m'être contestée par des envieux. Je crois bien qu'on l'a employée auparavant ; mais qui est-ce qui a senti combien elle était commode pour rire en dessous de l'impertinent qu'on admirait ? J'ai plus de cent façons d'entamer la séduction d'une jeune fille, à côté de sa mère, sans que celle-ci s'en aperçoive, et même de la rendre complice. À peine entrais-je dans la carrière, que je dédaignai toutes les manières vulgaires de glisser un billet doux. J'ai dix moyens de me le faire arracher, et parmi ces moyens j'ose me flatter qu'il y en a de nouveaux. Je possède surtout le talent d'encourager un jeune homme timide ; j'en ai fait réussir qui n'avaient ni esprit ni figure. Si cela était écrit, je crois qu'on m'accorderait quelque génie.

MOI — Vous ferait un honneur singulier.

LUI — Je n'en doute pas.

MOI — À votre place, je jetterais ces choses-là sur le papier. Ce serait dommage qu'elles se perdissent.

LUI — Il est vrai ; mais vous ne soupçonnez pas combien je fais peu de cas de la méthode et des préceptes. Celui qui a besoin d'un protocole n'ira jamais loin. Les génies lisent peu, pratiquent beaucoup, et se font d'eux-mêmes. Voyez César, Turenne,[102] Vauban,[103] la marquise de Tencin, son frère le cardinal, et le secrétaire de celui-ci, l'abbé Trublet.[104] Et Bouret ? Qui est-ce qui a donné des leçons à Bouret ? Personne. C'est la nature qui forme ces hommes rares-là. Croyez-vous que l'histoire du chien et du masque soit écrite quelque part ?

MOI — Mais à vos heures perdues, lorsque l'angoisse de votre estomac vide ou la fatigue de votre estomac surchargé éloigne le sommeil…

LUI — J'y penserai. Il vaut mieux écrire de grandes choses que d'en exécuter de petites. Alors l'âme s'élève, l'imagination s'échauffe, s'enflamme et s'étend, au lieu qu'elle se rétrécit à s'étonner, auprès de la petite Hus, des applaudissements que ce sot public s'obstine à prodiguer à cette minaudière de Dangeville[105] qui joue si platement, qui marche presque courbée en deux sur la scène, qui a l'affectation de regarder sans cesse dans les yeux de celui à qui elle parle et de jouer en dessous, et qui prend elle-même ses grimaces pour de la finesse, son petit trotter pour de la grâce ; à cette emphatique Clairon qui est plus maigre, plus apprêtée, plus étudiée, plus empesée qu'on ne saurait dire. Cet imbécile parterre les claque à tout rompre,[106] et ne s'aperçoit pas que nous sommes un peloton d'agréments ; il est vrai que le peloton grossit un peu, mais qu'importe ? que nous avons la plus belle peau, les plus beaux yeux, le plus joli bec, peu d'entrailles à la vérité, une démarche qui n'est pas légère, mais qui n'est pas non plus aussi gauche qu'on le dit. Pour le sentiment, en revanche, il n'y en a aucune à qui nous ne damions le pion.

MOI — Comment dites-vous tout cela ? Est-ce ironie ou vérité ?

LUI — Le mal est que ce diable de sentiment est tout en dedans, et qu'il n'en transpire pas une lueur au-dehors. Mais moi qui vous parle, je sais, et je sais bien qu'elle en a. Si ce n'est pas cela précisément, c'est quelque chose comme cela. Il faut voir, quand l'humeur nous prend, comme nous traitons les valets, comme les femmes de chambre sont souffletées, comme nous menons à grands coups de pied les Parties casuelles, pour peu qu'elles s'écartent du respect qui nous est dû. C'est un petit diable, vous dis-je, tout plein de sentiment et de dignité… Oh çà, vous ne savez où vous en êtes, n'est-ce pas ?

MOI — J'avoue que je ne saurais démêler si c'est de bonne foi ou méchamment que vous parlez. Je suis un bon homme ; ayez la bonté d'en user avec moi plus rondement, et de laisser là votre art.

LUI — Cela, c'est ce que nous débitons à la petite Hus, de la Dangeville et de la Clairon, mêlé par-ci par-là de quelques mots qui vous donnassent l'éveil. Je consens que vous me preniez pour un vaurien, mais non pour un sot, et il n'y aurait qu'un sot ou un homme perdu d'amour qui pût dire sérieusement tant d'impertinences.

MOI — Mais comment se résout-on à les dire ?

LUI — Cela ne se fait pas tout d'un coup ; mais petit à petit on y vient. *Ingenii largitor venter.*[107]

MOI — Il faut être pressé d'une cruelle faim.

LUI — Cela se peut. Cependant, quelque fortes qu'elles vous paraissent, croyez que ceux à qui elles s'adressent sont plutôt accoutumés à les entendre que nous à les hasarder.

MOI — Est-ce qu'il y a là quelqu'un qui ait le courage d'être de votre avis ?

LUI — Qu'appelez-vous quelqu'un ? C'est le sentiment et le langage de toute la société.

MOI — Ceux d'entre vous qui ne sont pas de grands vauriens, doivent être de grands sots.

LUI — Des sots, là ? je vous jure qu'il n'y en a qu'un, c'est celui qui nous fête pour lui en imposer.

MOI — Mais comment s'en laisse-t-on si grossièrement imposer ? Car enfin la supériorité des talents de la Dangeville et de la Clairon est décidée.

LUI — On avale à pleine gorgée le mensonge qui nous flatte, et l'on boit goutte à goutte une vérité qui nous est amère. Et puis nous avons l'air si pénétré, si vrai !

MOI — Il faut cependant que vous ayez péché une fois contre les principes de l'art, et qu'il vous soit échappé par mégarde quelques-unes de ces vérités amères qui blessent ; car en dépit du rôle misérable, abject, vil, abominable que vous faites, je crois qu'au fond vous avez l'âme délicate.

LUI — Moi, point du tout. Que le diable m'emporte si je sais au fond ce que je suis. En général, j'ai l'esprit rond comme une boule, et le caractère franc comme l'osier ; jamais faux, pour peu que j'aie intérêt d'être vrai, jamais vrai pour peu que j'aie intérêt d'être faux. Je dis les choses comme elles me viennent ; sensées, tant mieux ; impertinentes, on n'y prend pas garde. J'use en plein de mon franc parler. Je n'ai pensé de ma vie, ni avant que de dire, ni en disant, ni après avoir dit. Aussi je n'offense personne.

MOI — Cela vous est pourtant arrivé avec les honnêtes gens chez qui vous viviez, et qui avaient pour vous tant de bontés.

LUI — Que voulez-vous ? C'est un malheur, un mauvais moment, comme il y en a dans la vie. Point de félicité continue ; j'étais trop bien, cela ne pouvait durer. Nous avons, comme vous savez, la compagnie la plus nombreuse et la mieux choisie. C'est une école d'humanité, le renouvellement de l'antique hospitalité. Tous les poètes qui tombent, nous les ramassons. Nous eûmes Palissot après sa *Zara*,[108] Bret après *Le Faux Généreux*,[109] tous les musiciens décriés, tous les auteurs qu'on ne lit point, toutes les actrices sifflées, tous les acteurs hués, un tas de pauvres honteux, plats parasites à la tête desquels j'ai l'honneur d'être, brave chef d'une troupe timide. C'est moi qui les exhorte à manger la première fois qu'ils viennent ; c'est moi qui demande à boire pour eux. Ils tiennent si peu de place ! Quelques jeunes gens déguenillés qui ne savent où donner de la tête, mais qui ont de la figure ; d'autres scélérats qui cajolent le patron et qui l'endorment, afin de glaner après lui sur la patronne. Nous paraissons gais ; mais au fond nous avons tous de l'humeur et grand appétit. Des loups ne sont pas plus affamés ; des tigres ne sont pas plus cruels. Nous dévorons comme des loups, lorsque la terre a été longtemps couverte de neige ; nous déchirons comme des tigres tout ce qui réussit. Quelquefois les cohues Bertin, Monsauge et Villemorien[110] se réunissent, c'est alors qu'il se fait un beau bruit dans la ménagerie. Jamais on ne vit ensemble tant de bêtes tristes, acariâtres, malfaisantes et courroucées. On n'entend que les noms de Buffon, de Duclos, de Montesquieu, de Rousseau,[111] de Voltaire, de d'Alembert, de Diderot, et Dieu sait de quelles épithètes ils sont accompagnés. Nul n'aura de l'esprit s'il n'est aussi sot que nous.[112] C'est là que le plan de la comédie des *Philosophes*[113] a été conçu ; la scène du colporteur, c'est moi qui l'ai fournie, d'après *La Théologie en quenouille*.[114] Vous n'êtes pas épargné là plus qu'un autre.

MOI — Tant mieux ! Peut-être me fait-on plus d'honneur que je n'en mérite. Je serais humilié si ceux qui disent du mal de tant d'habiles et honnêtes gens s'avisaient de dire du bien de moi.

LUI — Nous sommes beaucoup, et il faut que chacun paye son écot. Après le sacrifice des grands animaux nous immolons les autres.

MOI — Insulter la science et la vertu pour vivre, voilà du pain bien cher.

LUI — Je vous l'ai déjà dit, nous sommes sans conséquence. Nous injurions tout le monde et nous n'affligeons personne. Nous avons quelquefois le pesant abbé d'Olivet, le gros abbé Leblanc,[115] l'hypocrite Batteux.[116] Le gros abbé n'est méchant qu'avant dîner. Son café pris, il se jette dans un fauteuil, les pieds appuyés contre la tablette de la cheminée, et s'endort comme un vieux perroquet sur son bâton. Si le vacarme devient violent, il bâille, il étend ses bras, il frotte ses yeux, et dit : Hé bien ! qu'est-ce, qu'est-ce ? — Il s'agit de savoir si Piron[117] a plus d'esprit que de Voltaire. — Entendons-nous. C'est de l'esprit que vous dites ? Il ne s'agit pas de goût ; car du goût, votre Piron ne s'en doute pas. — Ne s'en doute pas ? — Non. Et puis, nous voilà embarqués dans une dissertation sur le goût. Alors le patron fait signe de la main qu'on l'écoute, car c'est surtout de goût qu'il se pique. Le goût, dit-il… le goût est une chose… Ma foi, je ne sais quelle chose il disait que c'était ; ni lui non plus.

Nous avons quelquefois l'ami Robbé. Il nous régale de ses contes cyniques, des miracles des convulsionnaires[118] dont il a été le témoin oculaire, et de quelques chants de son poème sur un sujet qu'il connaît à fond. Je hais ses vers, mais j'aime à l'entendre réciter : il a l'air d'un énergumène. Tous s'écrient autour de lui : Voilà ce qu'on appelle un poète ! Entre nous, cette poésie-là n'est qu'un charivari de toutes sortes de bruits confus, le ramage barbare des habitants de la tour de Babel.

Il nous vient aussi un certain niais qui a l'air plat et bête, mais qui a de l'esprit comme un démon et qui est plus malin qu'un vieux singe.[119] C'est une de ces figures qui appellent la plaisanterie, et les nasardes, et que Dieu fit pour la correction des gens qui jugent à la mine, et à qui leur miroir aurait dû apprendre qu'il est aussi aisé d'être un homme d'esprit et d'avoir l'air d'un sot, que de cacher un sot sous une physionomie spirituelle. C'est une lâcheté bien commune que celle d'immoler un bon homme à l'amusement des autres. On ne manque jamais de s'adresser à celui-ci. C'est un piège que nous tendons aux nouveaux venus, et je n'en ai presque pas vu un seul qui n'y donnât.

J'étais quelquefois surpris de la justesse des observations de ce fou sur les hommes et sur les caractères, et je le lui témoignai.

C'est, me répondit-il, qu'on tire parti de la mauvaise compagnie comme du libertinage. On est dédommagé de la perte de son innocence par celle de ses préjugés. Dans la société des méchants, où le vice se montre à masque levé, on apprend à les connaître. Et puis j'ai un peu lu.

MOI — Qu'avez-vous lu ?

LUI — J'ai lu et je lis et relis sans cesse Théophraste, La Bruyère et Molière.

MOI — Ce sont d'excellents livres.

LUI — Ils sont bien meilleurs qu'on ne pense ; mais qui est-ce qui sait les lire ?

MOI — Tout le monde, selon la mesure de son esprit.

LUI — Presque personne. Pourriez-vous me dire ce qu'on y cherche ?

MOI — L'amusement et l'instruction.

LUI — Mais quelle instruction ? Car c'est là le point.

MOI — La connaissance de ses devoirs, l'amour de la vertu, la haine du vice.

LUI — Moi j'y recueille tout ce qu'il faut faire et tout ce qu'il ne faut pas dire. Ainsi quand je lis *L'Avare*, je me dis : Sois avare si tu veux, mais garde-toi de parler comme l'avare. Quand je lis *Le Tartuffe*, je me dis : Sois hypocrite si tu veux, mais ne parle pas comme l'hypocrite. Garde des vices qui te sont utiles ; mais n'en aie ni le ton, ni les apparences qui te rendraient ridicule. Pour se garantir de ce ton, de ces apparences, il faut les connaître ; or, ces auteurs en on fait des peintures excellentes. Je suis moi et je reste ce que je suis, mais j'agis et je parle comme il convient. Je ne suis pas de ces gens qui méprisent les moralistes ; il y a beaucoup à profiter, surtout en ceux qui ont mis la morale en action. Le vice ne blesse les hommes que par intervalle ; les caractères apparents du vice les blessent du matin au soir. Peut-être vaudrait-il mieux être un insolent que d'en avoir la physionomie ; l'insolent de caractère n'insulte que de temps en temps, l'insolent de physionomie insulte toujours. Au reste, n'allez pas imaginer que je sois le seul lecteur de mon espèce. Je n'ai d'autre mérite ici que d'avoir fait, par système, par justesse d'esprit, par une vue raisonnable et vraie, ce que la plupart des autres font par instinct. De là vient que leurs lectures ne les rendent pas meilleurs que moi, mais qu'ils restent ridicules en dépit d'eux ; au lieu que je ne le suis que quand je veux, et que je les laisse alors loin derrière moi : car le même art qui m'apprend à me sauver du ridicule en certaines occasions, m'apprend aussi dans d'autres à l'attraper supérieurement. Je me rappelle alors tout ce que les autres ont dit, tout ce que j'ai lu, et j'y ajoute tout ce qui sort de mon fonds qui est en ce genre d'une fécondité surprenante.

MOI — Vous avez bien fait de me révéler ces mystères ; sans quoi, je vous aurais cru en contradiction.

LUI — Je n'y suis point, car pour une fois où il faut éviter le ridicule, heureusement il y en a cent où il faut s'en donner. Il n'y a point de meilleur rôle auprès des grands que celui de fou. Longtemps il y a eu le fou du roi en titre, en aucun il n'y a eu en titre le sage du roi. Moi, je suis le fou de Bertin et de beaucoup d'autres, le vôtre peut-être dans ce moment, ou peut-être vous le mien : celui qui serait sage n'aurait point de fou ; celui donc qui a un fou n'est pas sage ; s'il n'est pas sage il est fou ; et peut-être, fût-il le roi, le fou de son fou. Au reste, souvenez-vous que dans un sujet aussi variable que les mœurs, il n'y a d'absolument, d'essentiellement, de généralement vrai ou faux, sinon qu'il faut être ce que l'intérêt veut qu'on soit, bon ou mauvais, sage ou fou, décent ou ridicule, honnête ou vicieux. Si par hasard la vertu avait conduit à la fortune, ou j'aurais été vertueux, ou j'aurais simulé la vertu comme un autre. On m'a voulu ridicule, et je me le suis fait ; pour vicieux, nature seule en avait fait les frais. Quand je dis vicieux, c'est pour parler votre langue, car si nous venions à nous expliquer, il pourrait arriver que vous appelassiez vice ce que j'appelle vertu, et vertu ce que j'appelle vice.

Nous avons aussi les auteurs de l'Opéra-Comique, leurs acteurs et leurs actrices, et plus souvent leurs entrepreneurs Corbi, Moette[120]... tous gens de ressource et d'un mérite supérieur.

Et j'oubliais les grands critiques de la littérature, *L'Avant-Coureur,*[121] *Les Petites Affiches,*[122] *L'Année littéraire,*[123] *L'Observateur littéraire,*[124] *Le Censeur hebdomadaire,*[125] toute la clique des feuillistes.

MOI — *L'Année littéraire ! L'Observateur littéraire* ! Cela ne se peut ; ils se détestent.

LUI — Il est vrai ; mais tous les gueux se réconcilient à la gamelle. Ce maudit *Observateur littéraire*, que le diable l'eût emporté lui et ses feuilles ! C'est ce chien de petit prêtre,[126] avare, puant et usurier, qui est la cause de mon désastre. Il parut sur notre horizon hier pour la première fois ; il arriva à l'heure qui nous chasse tous de nos repaires, l'heure du dîner. Quand il fait mauvais temps, heureux celui d'entre nous qui a la pièce de vingt-quatre sols dans sa poche. Tel s'est moqué de son confrère qui était arrivé le matin crotté jusqu'à l'échine et mouillé jusqu'aux os, qui, le soir, rentre chez lui dans le même état. Il y en eut un, je ne sais plus lequel, qui eut, il y a quelques mois, un démêlé violent avec le Savoyard qui s'est établi à notre porte. Ils étaient en compte courant ; le créancier voulait que son débiteur se liquidât, et celui-ci n'était pas en fonds. On sert,[127] on fait les honneurs de la table à l'abbé, on le place au haut bout. J'entre, je l'aperçois. Comment, l'abbé, lui dis-je, vous présidez ? voilà qui est fort bien pour aujourd'hui ; mais demain vous descendrez, s'il vous plaît, d'une assiette, après-demain, d'une autre assiette, et ainsi, d'assiette en assiette, soit à droite, soit à gauche, jusqu'à ce que de la place que j'ai occupée une fois avant vous, Fréron une fois après moi, Dorat[128] une fois après Fréron, Palissot une fois après Dorat, vous deveniez stationnaire à côté de moi, pauvre plat bougre comme vous qui *siedo sempre come un maestoso cazzo fra duoi coglioni.*[129] L'abbé, qui est bon diable, et qui prend tout bien, se mit à rire. Mademoiselle, pénétrée de la vérité de mon observation et de la justesse de ma comparaison, se mit à rire ; tous ceux qui siégeaient à droite et à gauche de l'abbé et qu'il avait reculés d'un cran, se mirent à rire ; tout le monde rit, excepté monsieur qui se fâche, et me tient des propos qui n'auraient rien signifié, si nous avions été seuls : Rameau, vous êtes un impertinent. — Je le sais bien, et c'est à cette condition que vous m'avez reçu. — Un faquin. — Comme un autre. — Un gueux. — Est-ce que je serais ici sans cela ? — Je vous ferai chasser. — Après dîner je m'en irai de moi-même. — Je vous le conseille. On dîna ; je n'en perdis pas un coup de dent. Après avoir bien mangé, bu largement, car, après tout, il n'en aurait été ni plus ni moins, messer Gaster[130] est un personnage contre lequel je n'ai jamais boudé, je pris mon parti, et je me disposais à m'en aller. J'avais engagé ma parole en présence de tant de monde, qu'il fallait bien la tenir. Je fus un temps considérable à rôder dans l'appartement, cherchant ma canne et mon chapeau où ils n'étaient pas, et comptant toujours que le patron se répandrait dans un nouveau torrent d'injures, que quelqu'un s'interposerait, et que nous finirions par nous raccommoder à force de nous fâcher. Je tournais, je tournais ; car moi je n'avais rien sur le cœur ; mais le patron, lui, plus sombre et plus noir que l'Apollon d'Homère lorsqu'il décoche ses traits sur l'armée des Grecs,[131] son bonnet une fois plus renfoncé que de coutume, se promenait en long et en large, le poing sous le menton.[132] Mademoiselle s'approche de moi : Mais, mademoiselle, qu'est-ce qu'il y a donc d'extraordinaire ? Ai-je été différent aujourd'hui de moi-même ? — Je veux qu'il sorte. — Je sortirai, je ne lui ai pas manqué. — Pardonnez-moi ; on invite monsieur l'abbé, et… — C'est lui qui s'est manqué à lui-même en invitant l'abbé, en me recevant, et avec moi tant d'autres bélîtres tels que moi. — Allons, mon petit Rameau, il faut demander pardon à monsieur l'abbé. — Je n'ai que faire de son pardon. — Allons, allons, tout cela s'apaisera... On me prend par la main, on m'entraîne vers le fauteuil de l'abbé ; j'étends les bras, je contemple l'abbé avec une espèce d'admiration, car qui est-ce qui a jamais demandé pardon à l'abbé ? L'abbé, lui dis-je, l'abbé, tout ceci est bien ridicule, n'est-il pas vrai ? Et puis je me mets à rire, et l'abbé aussi. Me voilà donc excusé de ce côté-là ; mais il fallait aborder l'autre, et ce que j'avais à lui dire était une autre paire de manches. Je ne sais plus trop comment je tournai mon excuse... Monsieur, voilà ce fou. — Il y a trop longtemps qu'il me fait souffrir ; je n'en veux plus entendre parler. — Il est fâché. — Oui, je suis très fâché. — Cela ne lui arrivera plus. — Qu'au premier faquin. Je ne sais s'il était dans un de ces jours d'humeur où mademoiselle craint d'en approcher et n'ose le toucher qu'avec ses mitaines de velours, ou s'il entendit mal ce que je disais, ou si je dis mal : ce fut pis qu'auparavant. Que diable ! est-ce qu'il ne me connaît pas ? est-ce qu'il ne sait pas que je suis comme les enfants, et qu'il y a des circonstances où je laisse tout aller sous moi ? Et puis je crois, Dieu me pardonne, que je n'aurais pas un moment de relâche. On userait un pantin d'acier à tirer la ficelle du matin au soir et du soir au matin. Il faut que je les désennuie ; c'est la condition ; mais il faut que je m'amuse quelquefois. Au milieu de cet imbroglio, il me passa par la tête une pensée funeste, une pensée qui me donna de la morgue, une pensée qui m'inspira de la fierté et de l'insolence : c'est qu'on ne pouvait se passer de moi, que j'étais un homme essentiel.

MOI — Oui, je crois que vous leur êtes très utile, mais qu'ils vous le sont encore davantage. Vous ne retrouverez pas, quand vous voudrez, une aussi bonne maison ; mais eux, pour un fou qui leur manque, ils en retrouveront cent.

LUI — Cent fous comme moi ! Monsieur le philosophe, ils ne sont pas si communs. Oui, des plats fous. On est plus difficile en sottise qu'en talent ou en vertu. Je suis rare dans mon espèce, oui, très rare. À présent qu'ils ne m'ont plus, que font-ils ? Ils s'ennuient comme des chiens. Je suis un sac inépuisable d'impertinences. J'avais à chaque instant une boutade qui les faisait rire aux larmes, j'étais pour eux les Petites-Maisons tout entières.

MOI — Aussi vous aviez la table, le lit, l'habit, veste et culotte, les souliers et la pistole par mois.

LUI — Voilà le beau côté, voilà le bénéfice ; mais les charges, vous n'en dites mot. D'abord, s'il était bruit d'une pièce nouvelle, quelque temps qu'il fît, il fallait fureter dans tous les greniers de Paris, jusqu'à ce que j'en eusse trouvé l'auteur ; que je me procurasse la lecture de l'ouvrage, et que j'insinuasse adroitement qu'il y avait un rôle qui serait supérieurement rendu par quelqu'un de ma connaissance... Et par qui, s'il vous plaît ? — Par qui ? belle question ! Ce sont les grâces, la gentillesse, la finesse. — Vous voulez dire Mlle Dangeville ? Par hasard la connaîtriez-vous ? — Oui, un peu ; mais ce n'est pas elle. — Et qui donc ? Je nommais tout bas. — Elle ! — Oui, elle, répétais-je, un peu honteux, car j'ai quelquefois de la pudeur, et à ce nom répété il fallait voir comme la physionomie du poète s'allongeait, et d'autres fois comme on m'éclatait au nez. Cependant, bon gré mal gré qu'il en eût, il fallait que j'amenasse mon homme à dîner ; et lui qui craignait de s'engager, rechignait, remerciait. Il fallait voir comme j'étais traité quand je ne réussissais pas dans ma négociation : j'étais un butor, un sot, un balourd, je n'étais bon à rien ; je ne valais pas le verre d'eau qu'on me donnait à boire. C'était bien pis lorsqu'on jouait, et qu'il fallait aller intrépidement au milieu des huées d'un public qui juge bien, quoi qu'on en dise, faire entendre mes claquements de mains isolés, attacher les regards sur moi, quelquefois dérober les sifflets à l'actrice, et ouïr chuchoter à côté de soi : C'est un des valets déguisés de celui qui couche. Ce maraud-là se taira-t-il ?... On ignore ce qui peut déterminer à cela ; on croit que c'est ineptie, tandis que c'est un motif qui excuse tout.

MOI — Jusqu'à l'infraction des lois civiles.

LUI — À la fin cependant j'étais connu, et l'on disait : Oh ! c'est Rameau. Ma ressource était de jeter quelques mots ironiques qui sauvassent du ridicule mon applaudissement solitaire, qu'on interprétait à contresens. Convenez qu'il faut un puissant intérêt pour braver ainsi le public assemblé, et que chacune de ces corvées valait mieux qu'un petit écu.

MOI — Que ne vous faisiez-vous prêter main-forte ?

LUI — Cela m'arrivait aussi, et je glanais un peu là-dessus. Avant que de se rendre au lieu du supplice, il fallait se charger la mémoire des endroits brillants où il importait de donner le ton. S'il m'arrivait de les oublier et de me méprendre, j'en avais le tremblement à mon retour ; c'était un vacarme dont vous n'avez pas d'idée. Et puis à la maison une meute de chiens à soigner ; il est vrai que je m'étais sottement imposé cette tâche ; des chats dont j'avais la surintendance : j'étais trop heureux si *Micou* me favorisait d'un coup de griffe qui déchirât ma manchette ou ma main. *Criquette* est sujette à la colique ; c'est moi qui lui frotte le ventre. Autrefois, mademoiselle avait des vapeurs ; ce sont aujourd'hui des nerfs. Je ne parle point d'autres indispositions légères dont on ne se gêne pas devant moi. Pour ceci, passe ; je n'ai jamais prétendu contraindre. J'ai lu je ne sais où, qu'un prince surnommé le Grand, restait quelquefois appuyé sur le dossier de la chaise percée de sa maîtresse. On en use à son aise avec ses familiers, et j'en étais ces jours-là plus que personne. Je suis l'apôtre de la familiarité et de l'aisance. Je les prêchais là d'exemple, sans qu'on s'en formalisât ; il n'y avait qu'à me laisser aller. Je vous ai ébauché le patron. Mademoiselle commence à devenir pesante, il faut entendre les bons contes qu'ils en font.

MOI — Vous n'êtes pas de ces gens-là ?

LUI — Pourquoi non ?

MOI — C'est qu'il est au moins indécent de donner des ridicules à ses bienfaiteurs.

LUI — Mais n'est-ce pas pis encore de s'autoriser de ses bienfaits pour avilir son protégé ?

MOI — Mais si le protégé n'était pas vil par lui-même, rien ne donnerait au protecteur cette autorité.

LUI — Mais si les personnages n'étaient pas ridicules par eux-mêmes, on n'en ferait pas de bons contes. Et puis est-ce ma faute s'ils s'encanaillent ? Est-ce ma faute, lorsqu'ils se sont encanaillés, si on les trahit, si on les bafoue ? Quand on se résout à vivre avec des gens comme nous et qu'on a le sens commun, il y a je ne sais combien de noirceurs auxquelles il faut s'attendre. Quand on nous prend, ne nous connaît-on pas pour ce que nous sommes, pour des âmes intéressées, viles et perfides ? Si l'on nous connaît, tout est bien. Il y a un pacte tacite[133] qu'on nous fera du bien, et que tôt ou tard nous rendrons le mal pour le bien qu'on nous aura fait. Ce pacte ne subsiste-t-il pas entre l'homme et son singe ou son perroquet ? Brun[134] jette les hauts cris que Palissot, son convive et son ami, ait fait des couplets contre lui. Palissot a dû faire les couplets, et c'est Brun qui a tort. Poinsinet jette les hauts cris que Palissot ait mis sur son compte les couplets qu'il avait faits contre Brun. Palissot a dû mettre sur le compte de Poinsinet les couplets qu'il avait faits contre Brun, et c'est Poinsinet qui a tort. Le petit abbé Rey[135] jette les hauts cris de ce que son ami Palissot lui a soufflé sa maîtresse auprès de laquelle il l'avait introduit. C'est qu'il ne fallait point introduire un Palissot chez sa maîtresse, ou se résoudre à la perdre ; Palissot a fait son devoir, et c'est l'abbé Rey qui a tort. Le libraire David[136] jette les hauts cris de ce que son associé Palissot a couché ou voulu coucher avec sa femme ; la femme du libraire David jette les hauts cris de ce que Palissot a laissé croire à qui l'a voulu qu'il avait couché avec elle ; que Palissot ait couché ou non avec la femme du libraire, ce qui est difficile à décider, car la femme a dû nier ce qui était, et Palissot a pu laisser croire ce qui n'était pas. Quoi qu'il en soit, Palissot a fait son rôle et c'est David et sa femme qui ont tort. Qu'Helvétius jette les hauts cris que Palissot le traduise sur la scène comme un malhonnête homme, lui à qui il doit encore l'argent qu'il lui prêta pour se faire traiter de la mauvaise santé, se nourrir et se vêtir.[137] A-t-il dû se promettre un autre procédé de la part d'un homme souillé de toutes sortes d'infamies, qui par passe-temps fait abjurer la religion à son ami qui s'empare du bien de ses associés,[138] qui n'a ni foi, ni loi, ni sentiment, qui court à la fortune *per fas et nefas* ; qui compte ses jours par ses scélératesses ; et qui s'est traduit lui-même sur la scène comme un des plus dangereux coquins,[139] impudence dont je ne crois pas qu'il y ait eu dans le passé un premier exemple, ni qu'il y en ait un second dans l'avenir. Non. Ce n'est donc pas Palissot, mais c'est Helvétius qui a tort. Si l'on mène un jeune provincial à la ménagerie de Versailles, et qu'il s'avise par sottise, de passer la main à travers les barreaux de la loge du tigre ou de la panthère ; si le jeune homme laisse son bras dans la gueule de l'animal féroce ; qui est-ce qui a tort ? Tout cela est écrit dans le pacte tacite. Tant pis pour celui qui l'ignore ou l'oublie. Combien je justifierais par ce pacte universel et sacré, de gens qu'on accuse de méchanceté ; tandis que c'est soi qu'on devrait accuser de sottise ! Oui, grosse comtesse,[140] c'est vous qui avez tort, lorsque vous rassemblez autour de vous ce qu'on appelle parmi les gens de votre sorte des espèces,[141] et que ces espèces vous font des vilenies, vous en font faire, et vous exposent au ressentiment des honnêtes gens. Les honnêtes gens font ce qu'ils doivent ; les espèces aussi ; et c'est vous qui avez tort de les accueillir. Si Bertinhus[142] vivait doucement, paisiblement avec sa maîtresse ; si par l'honnêteté de leurs caractères, ils s'étaient fait des connaissances honnêtes ; s'ils avaient appelé autour d'eux des hommes à talents, des gens connus dans la société par leur vertu ; s'ils avaient réservé pour une petite compagnie éclairée et choisie les heures de distraction qu'ils auraient dérobées à la douceur d'être ensemble, de s'aimer, de se le dire dans le silence de la retraite ; croyez-vous qu'on en eût fait ni bons ni mauvais contes. Que leur est-il donc arrivé ? ce qu'ils méritaient. Ils ont été punis de leur imprudence v ; et c'est nous que la Providence avait destinés de toute éternité à faire justice des Bertins du jour,[143] et ce sont nos pareils d'entre nos neveux qu'elle a destinés à faire justice des Monsauge et des Bertin à venir. Mais tandis que nous exécutons ses justes décrets sur la sottise, vous qui nous peignez tels que nous sommes, vous exécutez ses justes décrets sur nous. Que penseriez-vous de nous, si nous prétendions, avec des mœurs honteuses, jouir de la considération publique ? Que nous sommes des insensés. Et ceux qui s'attendent à des procédés honnêtes de la part de gens nés vicieux, de caractères vils et bas, sont-ils sages ? Tout a son vrai loyer dans ce monde. Il y a deux procureurs généraux, l'un à votre porte, qui châtie les délits contre la société ; la nature est l'autre. Celle-ci connaît de tous les vices qui échappent aux lois. Vous vous livrez à la débauche des femmes, vous serez hydropique. Vous êtes crapuleux ; vous serez poumonique. Vous ouvrez votre porte à des marauds et vous vivez avec eux ; vous serez trahis, persiflés, méprisés. Le plus court est de se résigner à l'équité de ces jugements ; et de se dire à soi-même, c'est bien fait, de secouer ses oreilles et de s'amender, ou de rester ce qu'on est, mais aux conditions susdites.

MOI — Vous avez raison.

LUI — Au demeurant, de ces mauvais contes, moi, je n'en invente aucun ; je m'en tiens au rôle de colporteur. Ils disent qu'il y a quelques jours, sur les cinq heures du matin, on entendit un vacarme enragé ; toutes les sonnettes étaient en branle ; c'étaient les cris interrompus et sourds d'un homme qui étouffe : À moi, moi, je suffoque, je meurs. Ces cris partaient de l'appartement du patron. On arrive, on le secourt. Notre grosse créature dont la tête était égarée, qui n'y était plus, qui ne voyait plus, comme il arrive dans ce moment, continuait de presser son mouvement, s'élevait sur ses deux mains, et du plus haut qu'elle pouvait, laissait retomber sur les parties casuelles un poids de deux à trois cents livres, animé de toute la vitesse que donne la fureur du plaisir. On eut beaucoup de peine à le dégager de là. Que diable de fantaisie à un petit marteau de se placer sous une lourde enclume ?

MOI — Vous êtes un polisson. Parlons d'autre chose. Depuis que nous causons, j'ai une question sur la lèvre.

LUI — Pourquoi l'avoir arrêtée là si longtemps ?

MOI — C'est que j'ai craint qu'elle ne fût indiscrète.

LUI — Après ce que je viens de vous révéler, j'ignore quel secret je puis avoir pour vous.

MOI — Vous ne doutez pas du jugement que je porte de votre caractère ?

LUI — Nullement. Je suis à vos yeux un être très abject, très méprisable et je le suis aussi quelquefois aux miens ; mais rarement. Je me félicite plus souvent de mes vices que je ne m'en blâme. Vous êtes plus constant dans votre mépris.

MOI — Il est vrai ; mais pourquoi me montrer toute votre turpitude ?

LUI — D'abord, c'est que vous en connaissiez une bonne partie, et que je voyais plus à gagner qu'à perdre à vous avouer le reste.

MOI — Comment cela, s'il vous plaît ?

LUI — S'il importe d'être sublime en quelque genre, c'est surtout en mal.[144] On crache sur un petit filou, mais on ne peut refuser une sorte de considération à un grand criminel : son courage vous étonne, son atrocité vous fait frémir. On prise en tout l'unité de caractère.

MOI — Mais cette estimable unité de caractère, vous ne l'avez pas encore. Je vous trouve de temps en temps vacillant dans vos principes. Il est incertain si vous tenez votre méchanceté de la nature ou de l'étude, et si l'étude vous a porté aussi loin qu'il est possible.

LUI — J'en conviens ; mais j'y ai fait de mon mieux. N'ai-je pas eu la modestie de reconnaître des êtres plus parfaits que moi ? Ne vous ai-je pas parlé de Bouret avec l'admiration la plus profonde ? Bouret est le premier homme du monde dans mon esprit.

MOI — Mais immédiatement après Bouret, c'est vous ?

LUI — Non.

MOI — C'est donc Palissot ?

LUI — C'est Palissot, mais ce n'est pas Palissot seul.

MOI — Et qui peut être digne de partager le second rang avec lui ?

LUI — Le renégat d'Avignon.[145]

MOI — Je n'ai jamais entendu parler de ce renégat d'Avignon, mais ce doit être un homme bien étonnant.

LUI — Aussi l'est-il.

MOI — L'histoire des grands personnages m'a toujours intéressé.

LUI — Je le crois bien. Celui-ci vivait chez un bon et honnête de ces descendants d'Abraham, promis au père des croyants en nombre égal à celui des étoiles.

MOI — Chez un juif ?

LUI — Chez un juif. Il en avait surpris d'abord la commisération, ensuite la bienveillance, enfin la confiance la plus entière ; car voilà comme il en arrive toujours : nous comptons tellement sur nos bienfaits, qu'il est rare que nous cachions notre secret à celui que nous avons comblé de nos bontés. Le moyen qu'il n'y ait pas des ingrats, quand nous exposons l'homme à la tentation de l'être impunément ? C'est une réflexion juste que notre juif ne fit pas. Il confia donc au renégat qu'il ne pouvait en conscience manger du cochon. Vous allez voir tout le parti qu'un esprit fécond sut tirer de cet aveu. Quelques mois se passèrent pendant lesquels notre renégat redoubla d'attachement. Quand il crut son juif bien touché, bien captivé, bien convaincu par ses soins qu'il n'avait pas un meilleur ami dans toutes les tribus d'Israël... Admirez la circonspection de cet homme. Il ne se hâte pas. Il laisse mûrir la poire avant que de secouer la branche. Trop d'ardeur pouvait faire échouer son projet. C'est qu'ordinairement la grandeur de caractère résulte de la balance naturelle de plusieurs qualités opposées.[146]

MOI — Et laissez là vos réflexions, et continuez votre histoire.

LUI — Cela ne se peut. Il y a des jours où il faut que je réfléchisse. C'est une maladie qu'il faut abandonner à son cours. Où en étais-je ?

MOI — À l'intimité bien établie entre le juif et le renégat.

LUI — Alors la poire était mûre... Mais vous ne m'écoutez pas, à quoi rêvez-vous ?

MOI — Je rêve à l'inégalité de votre ton tantôt haut, tantôt bas.

LUI — Est-ce que le ton de l'homme vicieux peut être un ? Il arrive un soir chez son bon ami, l'air effaré, la voix entrecoupée, le visage pâle comme la mort, tremblant de tous ses membres. — Qu'avez-vous ? — Nous sommes perdus. — Perdus, et comment ? — Perdus, vous dis-je ; perdus sans ressource. — Expliquez-vous. — Un moment, que je me remette de mon effroi. — Allons, remettez-vous, lui dit le juif, au lieu de lui dire : Tu es un fieffé fripon, je ne sais ce que tu as à m'apprendre, mais tu es un fieffé fripon ; tu joues la terreur.

MOI — Et pourquoi devait-il lui parler ainsi ?

LUI — C'est qu'il était faux et qu'il avait passé la mesure.[147] Cela est clair pour moi, et ne m'interrompez pas davantage. — Nous sommes perdus, perdus, sans ressource ! Est-ce que vous ne sentez pas l'affectation de ces perdus répétés ? Un traître nous a déférés à la sainte Inquisition, vous comme juif, moi comme renégat, comme un infâme renégat. Voyez comme le traître ne rougit pas de se servir des expressions les plus odieuses. Il faut plus de courage qu'on ne pense pour s'appeler de son nom. Vous ne savez pas ce qu'il en coûte pour en venir là.

MOI — Non, certes. Mais cet infâme renégat ?...

LUI — Est faux, mais c'est une fausseté bien adroite. Le juif s'effraye, il s'arrache la barbe, il se roule à terre, il voit les sbires à sa porte, il se voit affublé du san-bénito,[148] il voit son autodafé[149] préparé. — Mon ami, mon tendre ami, mon unique ami, quel parti prendre ? — Quel parti ? De se montrer, d'affecter la plus grande sécurité, de se conduire comme à l'ordinaire. La procédure de ce tribunal est secrète, mais lente. Il faut user de ses délais pour tout vendre. J'irai louer ou je ferai louer un bâtiment par un tiers ; oui, par un tiers, ce sera le mieux. Nous y déposerons votre fortune ; car c'est à votre fortune principalement qu'ils en veulent ; et nous irons, vous et moi, chercher sous un autre ciel la liberté de servir notre Dieu et de suivre en sûreté la loi d'Abraham et de notre conscience. Le point important dans la circonstance périlleuse où nous nous trouvons est de ne point faire d'imprudence. — Fait et dit. Le bâtiment est loué et pourvu de vivres et de matelots. La fortune du juif est à bord. Demain à la pointe du jour, ils mettent à la voile. Ils peuvent souper gaiement et dormir en sûreté. Demain ils échappent à leurs persécuteurs. Pendant la nuit, le renégat se lève, dépouille le juif de son portefeuille, de sa bourse et de ses bijoux, se rend à bord, et le voilà parti. Et vous croyez que c'est là tout ? Bon ! vous n'y êtes pas. Lorsqu'on me raconta cette histoire, moi, je devinai ce que je vous ai tu, pour essayer votre sagacité. Vous avez bien fait d'être un honnête homme ; vous n'auriez été qu'un friponneau. Jusqu'ici le renégat n'est que cela. C'est un coquin méprisable à qui personne ne voudrait ressembler.

Le sublime de sa méchanceté, c'est d'avoir été lui-même le délateur de son bon ami l'Israélite, dont la sainte Inquisition s'empara à son réveil, et dont, quelques jours après, on fit un beau feu de joie. Et ce fut ainsi que le renégat devint tranquille possesseur de la fortune de ce descendant maudit de ceux qui ont crucifié Notre Seigneur.

MOI — Je ne sais lequel des deux me fait le plus d'horreur, ou de la scélératesse de votre renégat, ou du ton dont vous en parlez.

LUI — Et voilà ce que je vous disais : l'atrocité de l'action vous porte au-delà du mépris, et c'est la raison de ma sincérité. J'ai voulu que vous connussiez jusqu'où j'excellais dans mon art, vous arracher l'aveu que j'étais au moins original dans mon avilissement, me placer dans votre tête sur la ligne des grands vauriens et m'écrier ensuite : *Vivat Mascarillus, fourbum imperator !* Allons, gai, monsieur le philosophe, chorus : *Vivat Mascarillus, fourbum imperator.*

Et là-dessus, il se mit à faire un chant en fugue, tout à fait singulier. Tantôt la mélodie était grave et pleine de majesté, tantôt légère et folâtre ; dans un instant, il imitait la basse, dans un autre, une des parties du dessus ; il m'indiquait, de son bras et de son col allongés, les endroits des tenues, et s'exécutait, se composait à lui-même un chant de triomphe où l'on voyait qu'il s'entendait mieux en bonne musique qu'en bonnes mœurs.[150]

Je ne savais, moi, si je devais rester ou fuir, rire ou m'indigner. Je restai, dans le dessein de tourner la conversation sur quelque sujet qui chassât de mon âme l'horreur dont elle était remplie. Je commençais à supporter avec peine la présence d'un homme qui discutait une action horrible, un exécrable forfait, comme un connaisseur en peinture ou en poésie examine les beautés d'un ouvrage de goût, ou comme un moraliste ou un historien relève et fait éclater les circonstances d'une action héroïque. Je devins sombre, malgré moi. Il s'en aperçut et me dit :

LUI — Qu'avez-vous ? Est-ce que vous vous trouvez mal ?

MOI — Un peu ; mais cela passera.

LUI — Vous avez l'air soucieux d'un homme tracassé de quelque idée fâcheuse.

MOI — C'est cela.

Après un moment de silence de sa part et de la mienne, pendant lequel il se promenait en sifflant et en chantant, pour le ramener à son talent, je lui dis : Que faites-vous à présent ?

LUI — Rien.

MOI — Cela est très fatigant.

LUI — J'étais déjà suffisamment bête. J'ai été entendre cette musique de Duni[151] et de nos autres jeunes faiseurs, qui m'a achevé.

MOI — Vous approuvez donc ce genre ?

LUI — Sans doute.

MOI — Et vous trouvez de la beauté dans ces nouveaux chants ?[152]

LUI — Si j'y en trouve ! Pardieu, je vous en réponds. Comme cela est déclamé ! Quelle vérité ! Quelle expression !

MOI — Tout art d'imitation a son modèle dans la nature. Quel est le modèle du musicien quand il fait un chant ?

LUI — Pourquoi ne pas prendre la chose de plus haut ? Qu'est-ce qu'un chant ?

MOI — Je vous avouerai que cette question est au-dessus de mes forces. Voilà comme nous sommes tous. Nous n'avons dans la mémoire que des mots que nous croyons entendre, par l'usage fréquent et l'application même juste que nous en faisons ; dans l'esprit, que des notions vagues.[153] Quand je prononce le mot chant, je n'ai pas des notions plus nettes que vous et la plupart de vos semblables quand ils disent réputation, blâme, honneur, vice, vertu, pudeur, décence, honte, ridicule.

LUI — Le chant est une imitation, par les sons, d'une échelle inventée par l'art ou inspirée par la nature, comme il vous plaira, ou par la voix ou par l'instrument, des bruits physiques ou des accents de la passion ; et vous voyez qu'en changeant là-dedans les choses à changer, la définition conviendrait exactement à la peinture, à l'éloquence, à la sculpture et à la poésie.[154] Maintenant, pour en venir à votre question, quel est le modèle du musicien ou du chant ? C'est la déclamation, si le modèle est vivant et pensant ; c'est le bruit, si le modèle est inanimé. Il faut considérer la déclamation comme une ligne, et le chant comme une autre ligne, qui serpenterait[155] sur la première. Plus cette déclamation, type du chant, sera forte et vraie, plus le chant qui s'y conforme la coupera en un plus grand nombre de points ; plus le chant sera vrai ; et plus il sera beau. Et c'est ce qu'ont très bien senti nos jeunes musiciens. Quand on entend : *Je suis un pauvre diable*, on croit reconnaître la plainte d'un avare ; s'il ne chantait pas, c'est sur les mêmes tons qu'il parlerait à la terre, quand il lui confie son or et qu'il lui dit : Ô *terre, reçois mon trésor*.[156] Et cette petite fille qui sent palpiter son cœur, qui rougit, qui se trouble et qui supplie monseigneur de la laisser partir, s'exprimerait-elle autrement ? Il y a dans ces ouvrages toutes sortes de caractères, une variété infinie de déclamation. Cela est sublime ; c'est moi qui vous le dis. Allez, allez entendre le morceau où le jeune homme qui se sent mourir s'écrie : *Mon cœur s'en va* ![157] Écoutez le chant ; écoutez la symphonie, et vous me direz après quelle différence il y a entre les vraies voies d'un moribond et le tour de ce chant.[158] Vous verrez si la ligne de la mélodie ne coïncide pas tout entière avec la ligne de la déclamation. Je ne vous parle pas de la mesure, qui est encore une des conditions du chant ; je m'en tiens à l'expression, et il n'y a rien de plus évident que le passage suivant que j'ai lu quelque part :[159] *Musices seminarium accentus*, l'accent est la pépinière de la mélodie. Jugez de là de quelle difficulté et de quelle importance il est de savoir bien faire le récitatif. Il n'y a point de bel air dont on ne puisse faire un beau récitatif, et point de beau récitatif dont un habile homme ne puisse tirer un bel air.[160] Je ne voudrais pas assurer que celui qui récite bien chantera bien ; mais je serais surpris que celui qui chante bien, ne sût pas bien réciter. Et croyez tout ce que je vous dis là ; car c'est le vrai.

MOI — Je ne demanderais pas mieux que de vous en croire, si je n'étais arrêté par un petit inconvénient.

LUI — Et cet inconvénient ?

MOI — C'est que si cette musique est sublime, il faut que celle du divin Lulli,[161] de Campra,[162] de Destouches,[163] de Mouret, et même, soit dit entre nous, celle du cher oncle, soit un peu plate.

lui, s'approchant de mon oreille, me répondit : — Je ne voudrais pas être
entendu, car il y a ici beaucoup de gens qui me connaissent ; c'est qu'elle
l'est aussi. Ce n'est pas que je me soucie du cher oncle, puisque cher il y a.
C'est une pierre. Il me verrait tirer la langue d'un pied qu'il ne me donnerait
pas un verre d'eau ; mais il a beau faire, à l'octave, à la septième : Hon, hon ;
hin, hin ; tu, tu, tu, turelututu,[164] avec un charivari de diable ; ceux qui
commencent à s'y connaître et qui ne prennent plus du tintamarre pour de
la musique, ne s'accommoderont jamais de cela. On devait défendre par une
ordonnance de police à quelque personne, de quelque qualité ou condition
7 qu'elle fût, de faire chanter le *Stabat* du Pergolèse.[165] Ce *Stabat*, il fallait le
faire brûler par la main du bourreau. Ma foi, ces maudits bouffons avec
leur *Servante maîtresse*,[166] leur *Tracollo*, [167] nous en ont donné rudement dans
le cul. Autrefois, un *Tancrède*,[168] un *Issé*,[169] une *Europe galante*,[170] *Les Indes*,[171] et
Castor,[172] *Les Talents lyriques*,[173] allaient à quatre, cinq, six mois. On ne voyait
point la fin des représentations d'une *Armide*.[174] À présent tout cela vous
8 tombe les uns sur les autres, comme des capucins de cartes. Aussi Rebel et
Francœur[175] jettent-ils feu et flamme. Ils disent que tout est perdu, qu'ils
9 sont ruinés, et que si l'on tolère plus longtemps cette canaille chantante de
la foire, la musique nationale est au diable, et que l'Académie royale du cul-de-sac n'a qu'à fermer boutique. Il y a bien quelque chose de vrai là-dedans.
Les vieilles perruques qui viennent là depuis trente à quarante ans, tous les vendredis, au lieu de s'amuser comme ils ont fait par le passé, s'ennuient et bâillent sans trop savoir pourquoi.[176] Ils se le demandent et ne sauraient se répondre. Que ne s'adressent-ils à moi ? La prédiction de Duni s'accomplira, et du train que cela prend, je veux mourir si dans quatre à cinq ans à dater du *Peintre amoureux de son modèle*,[177] il y a un chat à fesser dans le célèbre impasse.[178] Les bonnes gens, ils ont renoncé à leurs symphonies pour jouer des symphonies italiennes. Ils ont cru qu'ils feraient leurs oreilles à celles-ci, sans conséquence pour leur musique vocale,[179] comme si la symphonie n'était pas au chant, à un peu de libertinage près inspiré par l'étendue de l'instrument et la mobilité des doigts, ce que le chant est à la déclamation réelle.[180] Comme si le violon n'était pas le singe du chanteur, qui deviendra un jour, lorsque le difficile prendra la place du beau, le singe du violon.[181] Le premier qui joua Locatelli fut l'apôtre de la nouvelle musique. À d'autres, à d'autres. On nous accoutumera à l'imitation des accents de la passion ou des phénomènes de la nature, par le chant et la voix, par l'instrument, car voilà toute l'étendue de l'objet de la musique, et nous conserverons notre goût pour les vols, les lances, les gloires, les triomphes, les victoires ?[182] *Va-t'en voir s'ils viennent, Jean*.[183] Ils ont imaginé qu'ils pleureraient ou riraient à des scènes de tragédie ou de comédie musiquées ; qu'on porterait

à leurs oreilles les accents de la fureur, de la haine, de la jalousie, les vraies plaintes de l'amour, les ironies, les plaisanteries du théâtre italien ou  français, et qu'ils resteraient admirateurs de *Ragonde*[184] et de *Platée*.[185] Je t'en réponds : tarare, ponpon ; qu'ils éprouveraient sans cesse avec quelle facilité,  quelle flexibilité, quelle mollesse, l'harmonie, la prosodie, les ellipses, les inversions de la langue italienne se prêtaient à l'art, au mouvement, à l'expression, aux tours du chant et à la valeur mesurée des sons, et qu'ils continueraient d'ignorer combien la leur est roide, sourde, lourde, pesante, pédantesque et monotone.[186] Eh ! oui, oui. Ils se sont persuadé qu'après avoir mêlé leurs larmes aux pleurs d'une mère qui se désole sur la mort de son fils, après avoir frémi de l'ordre d'un tyran qui ordonne un meurtre, ils ne s'ennuieraient pas de leur féerie, de leur insipide mythologie, de leurs petits madrigaux doucereux[187] qui ne marquent pas moins le mauvais goût du poète, que la misère de l'art qui s'en accommode. Les bonnes gens ! cela n'est pas et ne peut être. Le vrai, le bon, le beau ont leurs droits.[188] On les conteste, mais on finit par admirer. Ce qui n'est pas marqué à ce coin, on l'admire un temps ; mais on finit par bâiller. Bâillez donc, messieurs, bâillez à votre aise. Ne vous gênez pas. L'empire de la nature et de ma trinité, contre laquelle les portes de l'enfer ne prévaudront jamais : le vrai, qui est le père et qui engendre le bon qui est le fils, d'où procède le beau qui est le Saint-Esprit, s'établit tout doucement. Le dieu étranger se place humblement sur l'autel à côté de l'idole du pays ; peu à peu, il s'y affermit ; un beau jour il pousse du coude son camarade, et patatras, voilà l'idole en bas.[189] C'est comme cela qu'on dit que les jésuites ont planté le christianisme à la Chine et aux Indes. Et ces jansénistes ont beau dire, cette méthode politique qui marche à son but sans bruit, sans effusion de sang, sans martyr, sans un toupet de cheveux arraché, me semble la meilleure.[190]

MOI — Il y a de la raison, à peu près, dans tout ce que vous venez de dire.

LUI — De la raison ! Tant mieux. Je veux que le diable m'emporte, si j'y tâche. Cela va comme je te pousse. Je suis comme les musiciens de l'Impasse, quand mon oncle parut. Si j'adresse à la bonne heure, c'est qu'un garçon charbonnier parlera toujours mieux de son métier que toute une académie, et que tous les Duhamel[191] du monde.

Et puis le voilà qui se met à se promener, en murmurant dans son gosier quelques-uns des airs de *L'Ile des fous*,[192] du *Peintre amoureux de son modèle*,[193] du *Maréchal-ferrant*, de *La Plaideuse*,[194] et de temps en temps il s'écriait, en levant les mains et les yeux au ciel : Si cela est beau, mordieu !

si cela est beau ! Comment peut-on porter à sa tête une paire d'oreilles et faire une pareille question ? Il commençait à entrer en passion et à chanter tout bas. Il élevait le ton à mesure qu'il se passionnait davantage ; vinrent ensuite les gestes, les grimaces du visage et les contorsions du corps ; et je dis : Bon, voilà la tête qui se perd, et quelque scène nouvelle qui se prépare ; en effet, il part d'un éclat de voix : *Je suis un pauvre misérable*[195]... *Monseigneur, monseigneur, laissez-moi partir... O terre, reçois mon or, conserve bien mon trésor... Mon âme, mon âme, ma vie ! Ô terre !... Le voilà le petit ami, le voilà le petit ami ! Aspettare e non venire... A Zerbina penserete... Sempre in contrasti con te si sta*[196].... Il entassait et brouillait ensemble trente airs italiens, français, tragiques, comiques, de toutes sortes de caractères ;[197] tantôt avec une voix de basse-taille, il descendait jusqu'aux enfers ; tantôt s'égosillant et contrefaisant le fausset, il déchirait le haut des airs, imitant de la démarche, du maintien, du geste, les différents personnages chantants ; successivement furieux, radouci, impérieux, ricaneur. Ici c'est une jeune fille qui pleure, et il en rend toute la minauderie ; là, il est prêtre, il est roi, il est tyran, il menace, il commande, il s'emporte ; il est esclave, il obéit. Il s'apaise, il se désole, il se plaint, il rit ; jamais hors de ton, de mesure, du sens des paroles et du caractère de l'air. Tous les pousse-bois avaient quitté leurs échiquiers et s'étaient rassemblés autour de lui. Les fenêtres du café étaient occupées en dehors par les passants qui s'étaient arrêtés au bruit. On faisait des éclats de rire à entrouvrir le plafond. Lui n'apercevait rien ; il continuait, saisi d'une aliénation d'esprit, d'un enthousiasme si voisin de la folie qu'il est incertain qu'il en revienne, s'il ne faudra pas le jeter dans un fiacre et le mener droit aux Petites-Maisons,[198] en chantant un lambeau des *Lamentations* de Jomelli.[199] Il répétait avec une précision, une vérité et une chaleur incroyables les plus beaux endroits de chaque morceau ; ce beau récitatif obligé[200] où le prophète peint la désolation de Jérusalem, il l'arrosa d'un torrent de larmes qui en arrachèrent de tous les yeux. Tout y était, et la délicatesse du chant, et la force de l'expression, et la douleur. Il insistait sur les endroits où le musicien s'était particulièrement montré comme un grand maître ; s'il quittait la partie du chant, c'était pour prendre celle des instruments qu'il laissait subitement pour revenir à la voix, entrelaçant l'une à l'autre de manière à conserver les liaisons et l'unité du tout ; s'emparant de nos âmes, et les tenant suspendues dans la situation la plus singulière que j'aie jamais éprouvée... Admirais-je ? Oui, j'admirais ! Étais-je touché de pitié ? J'étais touché de pitié ; mais une teinte de ridicule était fondue dans ces sentiments, et les dénaturait.[201]

Mais vous vous seriez échappé en éclats de rire à la manière dont il contrefaisait les différents instruments. Avec des joues renflées et bouffies, et un son rauque et sombre, il rendait les cors et les bassons ; il prenait un son éclatant et nasillard pour les hautbois ; précipitant sa voix avec une rapidité incroyable pour les instruments à cordes dont il cherchait les sons les plus approchés ; il sifflait les petites flûtes, il recoulait les traversières ; criant, chantant, se démenant comme un forcené, faisant lui seul les danseurs, les danseuses, les chanteurs, les chanteuses, tout un orchestre, tout un théâtre lyrique, et se divisant en vingt rôles divers ; courant, s'arrêtant avec l'air d'un énergumène, étincelant des yeux, écumant de la bouche. Il faisait une chaleur à périr, et la sueur qui suivait les plis de son front et la longueur de ses joues, se mêlait à la poudre de ses cheveux, ruisselait et sillonnait le haut de son habit. Que ne lui vis-je pas faire ? Il pleurait, il riait, il soupirait ; il regardait, ou attendri, ou tranquille, ou furieux ; c'était une femme qui se pâme de douleur ; c'était un malheureux livré à tout son désespoir ; un temple qui s'élève ; des oiseaux qui se taisent au soleil couchant ; des eaux ou qui murmurent dans un lieu solitaire et frais, ou qui descendent en torrent du haut des montagnes ; un orage, une tempête, la plainte de ceux qui vont périr, mêlée au sifflement des vents, au fracas du tonnerre ; c'était la nuit avec ses ténèbres, c'était l'ombre et le silence, car le silence même se peint par des sons.[202] Sa tète était tout à fait perdue. Épuisé de fatigue, tel qu'un homme qui sort d'un profond sommeil ou d'une longue distraction, il resta immobile, stupide, étonné. Il tournait ses regards autour de lui, comme un homme égaré, qui cherche à reconnaître le lieu où il se trouve. Il attendait le retour de ses forces et de ses esprits ; il essuyait machinalement son visage. Semblable à celui qui verrait à son réveil, son lit environné d'un grand nombre de personnes ; dans un entier oubli ou dans une profonde ignorance de ce qu'il a fait, il s'écria dans le premier moment : Hé bien, messieurs, qu'est-ce qu'il y a ? D'où viennent vos ris et votre surprise ? Qu'est-ce qu'il y a ? Ensuite il ajouta : Voilà ce qu'on doit appeler de la musique et un musicien ! Cependant, messieurs, il ne faut pas mépriser certains morceaux de Lulli. Qu'on fasse mieux la scène *Ah ! j'attendrai*[203] sans changer les paroles, j'en défie. Il ne faut pas mépriser quelques endroits de Campra, les airs de violon de mon oncle, ses gavottes, ses entrées de soldats, de prêtres, de sacrificateurs... *Pâles flambeaux, nuit plus affreuse que les ténèbres*[204]... *Dieu du Tartare, Dieu de l'oubli*[205]... Là, il enflait sa voix ; il soutenait ses sons ; les voisins se mettaient aux fenêtres ; nous mettions nos doigts dans nos oreilles. Il ajoutait : C'est ici qu'il faut des poumons, un

grand organe, un volume d'air. Mais avant peu, serviteur à l'Assomption ;
le carême et les Rois sont passés.[206] Ils ne savent pas encore ce qu'il faut
13 mettre en musique, ni par conséquent ce qui convient au musicien. La
poésie lyrique est encore à naître. Mais ils y viendront à force d'entendre le
14 Pergolèse, le Saxon,[207] Terradoglias,[208] Traetta,[209] et les autres ;[210] à force de
15 lire le Métastase,[211] il faudra bien qu'ils y viennent.

MOI — Quoi donc ! est-ce que Quinault, La Motte, Fontenelle[212] n'y ont rien entendu ?

LUI — Non pour le nouveau style.[213] Il n'y a pas six vers de suite dans tous leurs charmants poèmes qu'on puisse musiquer. Ce sont des sentences ingénieuses, des madrigaux légers, tendres et délicats ; mais pour savoir combien cela est vide de ressource pour notre art, le plus violent de tous, sans en excepter celui de Démosthène, faites-vous réciter ces morceaux, combien ils vous paraîtront froids, languissants, monotones. C'est qu'il n'y a rien là qui puisse servir de modèle au chant. J'aimerais autant avoir à musiquer les *Maximes de La Rochefoucauld* ou les *Pensées de Pascal*.[214] C'est au cri animal de la passion à dicter la ligne qui nous convient. Il faut que ces expressions soient pressées les unes sur les autres ; il faut que la phrase soit courte ; que le sens en soit coupé, suspendu ; que le musicien puisse disposer du tout et de chacune de ses parties ; en omettre un mot ou le répéter ; y en ajouter un qui lui manque ; la tourner et retourner comme un polype, sans la détruire ; ce qui rend la poésie lyrique française beaucoup plus difficile que dans les langues à inversions, qui présentent d'elles-mêmes tous ces avantages… *Barbare, cruel, plonge ton poignard dans mon sein. Me voilà prête à recevoir le coup fatal. Frappe. Ose… Ah ! je languis, je meurs… Un feu secret s'allume dans mes sens… Cruel amour, que veux-tu de moi ?… Laisse-moi la douce paix dont j'ai joui… Rends-moi la raison…*[215] Il faut que les passions soient fortes ; la tendresse du musicien et du poète lyrique doit être extrême. L'air est presque toujours la péroraison de la scène. Il nous faut des exclamations, des interjections, des suspensions, des interruptions, des affirmations, des négations ; nous appelons, nous invoquons, nous crions, nous gémissons, nous pleurons, nous rions franchement. Point d'esprit, point d'épigrammes, point de ces jolies pensées. Cela est trop loin de la simple nature. Or n'allez pas croire que le jeu des acteurs de théâtre et leur déclamation puissent nous servir de modèles. Fi donc ! il nous le faut plus énergique, moins maniéré, plus vrai. Les discours simples, les voix communes de la passion nous sont d'autant plus nécessaires que la langue sera plus monotone, aura moins d'accent. Le cri animal ou de l'homme passionné leur en donne.

Tandis qu'il me parlait ainsi, la foule qui nous environnait, ou n'entendant rien, ou prenant peu d'intérêt à ce qu'il disait, parce qu'en général l'enfant comme l'homme, et l'homme comme l'enfant, aime mieux s'amuser que s'instruire, s'était retirée ; chacun était à son jeu ; et nous étions restés seuls dans notre coin. Assis sur une banquette, la tête appuyée contre le mur, les bras pendants, les yeux à demi fermés, il me dit : Je ne sais ce que j'ai ; quand je suis venu ici, j'étais frais et dispos, et me voilà roué, brisé, comme si j'avais fait dix lieues. Cela m'a pris subitement.

MOI — Voulez-vous vous rafraîchir ?

LUI — Volontiers. Je me sens enroué. Les forces me manquent ; et je souffre un peu de la poitrine. Cela m'arrive presque tous les jours comme cela, sans que je sache pourquoi.

MOI — Que voulez-vous ?

LUI — Ce qui vous plaira ; je ne suis pas difficile ; l'indigence m'a appris à m'accommoder de tout.

On nous sert de la bière, de la limonade. Il en remplit un grand verre qu'il vide deux ou trois fois de suite. Puis comme un homme ranimé, il tousse fortement, il se démène, il reprend : Mais à votre avis, seigneur philosophe, n'est-ce pas une bizarrerie bien étrange qu'un étranger, un italien, un Duni, vienne nous apprendre à donner de l'accent à notre musique,[216] à assujettir notre chant à tous les mouvements, à toutes les mesures, à tous les intervalles, à toutes les déclamations, sans blesser la prosodie ? Ce n'était pourtant pas la mer à boire. Quiconque avait écouté un gueux lui demander l'aumône dans la rue, un homme dans le transport de la colère, une femme jalouse et furieuse, un amant désespéré, un flatteur, oui, un flatteur radoucissant son ton, traînant ses syllabes d'une voix mielleuse, en un mot une passion, n'importe laquelle, pourvu que, par son énergie, elle méritât de servir de modèle au musicien, aurait dû s'apercevoir de deux choses : l'une que les syllabes, longues ou brèves, n'ont aucune durée fixe, pas même de rapport déterminé entre leurs durées ; que la passion dispose de la prosodie presque comme il lui plaît ; qu'elle exécute les plus grands intervalles, et que celui qui s'écrie dans le fort de sa douleur : Ah ! malheureux que je suis ! monte la syllabe d'exclamation au ton le plus élevé et le plus aigu, et descend les autres aux tons les plus graves et les plus bas, faisant l'octave ou même un plus grand intervalle, et donnant à chaque son la quantité qui convient au tour de la mélodie, sans que l'oreille soit offensée, sans que ni la syllabe longue ni la syllabe brève aient conservé la longueur ou la brièveté du discours tranquille. Quel chemin nous avons fait depuis le temps où nous citions la parenthèse d'*Armide* : *Le vainqueur de Renaud, Si quelqu'un le peut être* ;[217] l'*Obéissons sans balancer,*[218] des *Indes galantes,* comme des prodiges de déclamation musicale ! À présent ces prodiges-là me font hausser les épaules de pitié. Du train dont l'art s'avance, je ne sais où il aboutira. En attendant, buvons un coup.

Il en boit deux, trois, sans savoir ce qu'il faisait. Il allait se noyer, comme il s'était épuisé, sans s'en apercevoir, si je n'avais déplacé la bouteille qu'il cherchait de distraction. Alors je lui dis :

MOI — Comment se fait-il qu'avec un tact aussi fin, une si grande sensibilité pour les beautés de l'art musical, vous soyez aussi aveugle sur les belles choses en morale, aussi insensible aux charmes de la vertu ?

LUI — C'est apparemment qu'il y a pour les unes un sens que je n'ai pas, une fibre qui ne m'a point été donnée, une fibre lâche qu'on a beau pincer et qui ne vibre pas ; ou peut-être c'est que j'ai toujours vécu avec de bons musiciens et de méchantes gens ; d'où il est arrivé que mon oreille est devenue très fine, et que mon cœur est devenu sourd.[219] Et puis c'est qu'il y avait quelque chose de race. Le sang de mon père et le sang de mon oncle est le même sang. Mon sang est le même que celui de mon père. La molécule paternelle était dure et obtuse, et cette maudite molécule première s'est assimilé tout le reste.

MOI — Aimez-vous votre enfant ?

LUI — Si je l'aime, le petit sauvage ! j'en suis fou.

MOI — Est-ce que vous ne vous occuperez pas sérieusement d'arrêter en lui l'effet de la maudite molécule paternelle ?

LUI — J'y travaillerais, je crois, bien inutilement. S'il est destiné à devenir un homme de bien, je n'y nuirai pas. Mais si la molécule voulait qu'il fût un vaurien comme son père, les peines que j'aurais prises pour en faire un homme honnête lui seraient très nuisibles : l'éducation croisant sans cesse la pente de la molécule, il serait tiré comme par deux forces contraires, et marcherait tout de guingois dans le chemin de la vie, comme j'en vois une infinité, également gauches dans le bien et dans le mal ; c'est ce que nous appelons des espèces, de toutes les épithètes la plus redoutable, parce qu'elle marque la médiocrité, et le dernier degré du mépris. Un grand vaurien est un grand vaurien, mais n'est point une espèce.[220] Avant que la molécule paternelle n'eût repris le dessus et ne l'eût amené à la parfaite abjection où j'en suis, il lui faudrait un temps infini ; il perdrait ses plus belles années. Je n'y fais rien à présent, je le laisse venir. Je l'examine. Il est déjà gourmand, patelin, filou, paresseux, menteur. Je crains bien qu'il ne chasse de race.

MOI — Et vous en ferez un musicien, afin qu'il ne manque rien à la ressemblance ?

LUI — Un musicien ! un musicien ! quelquefois je le regarde en grinçant les dents, et je dis : Si tu devais jamais savoir une note, je crois que je te tordrais le col.

MOI — Et pourquoi cela, s'il vous plaît ?

LUI — Cela ne mène à rien.

MOI — Cela mène à tout.

LUI — Oui, quand on excelle ; mais qui est-ce qui peut se promettre de son enfant qu'il excellera ? Il y a dix mille à parier contre un qu'il ne serait qu'un misérable racleur de cordes comme moi. Savez-vous qu'il serait peut-être plus aisé de trouver un enfant propre à gouverner un royaume, à faire un grand roi, qu'un grand violon !

MOI — Il me semble que les talents agréables, même médiocres, chez un peuple sans mœurs, perdu de débauche et de luxe, avancent rapidement un homme dans le chemin de la fortune. Moi qui vous parle, j'ai entendu la conversation qui suit, entre une espèce de protecteur et une espèce de protégé.[221] Celui-ci avait été adressé au premier comme à un homme obligeant qui pourrait le servir : — Monsieur, que savez-vous ? — Je sais passablement les mathématiques. — Eh bien, montrez les mathématiques ;

après vous être crotté dix à douze ans sur le pavé de Paris, vous aurez droit à quatre cents livres de rente. — J'ai étudié les lois et je suis versé dans le droit. — Si Puffendorf et Grotius[222] revenaient au monde, ils mourraient de faim contre une borne. — Je sais très bien l'histoire et la géographie. — S'il y avait des parents qui eussent à cœur la bonne éducation de leurs enfants, votre fortune serait faite ; mais il n'y en a point. — Je suis assez bon musicien. — Et que ne disiez-vous cela d'abord ? Et pour vous faire voir le parti qu'on peut tirer de ce dernier talent, j'ai une fille. Venez tous les jours depuis sept heures et demie du soir jusqu'à neuf, vous lui donnerez leçon, et je vous donnerai vingt-cinq louis par an. Vous déjeunerez, dînerez, goûterez, souperez avec nous. Le reste de votre journée vous appartiendra ; vous en disposerez à votre profit.

LUI — Et cet homme, qu'est-il devenu ?

MOI — S'il eût été sage, il eût fait fortune, la seule chose qu'il paraît que vous ayez en vue.

LUI — Sans doute. De l'or, de l'or. L'or est tout ; et le reste, sans or, n'est rien. Aussi, au lieu de lui farcir la tête de belles maximes, qu'il faudrait qu'il oubliât sous peine de n'être qu'un gueux, lorsque je possède un louis, ce qui ne m'arrive pas souvent, je me plante devant lui. Je tire le louis de ma poche. Je le lui montre avec admiration. J'élève les yeux au ciel. Je baise le louis devant lui. Et pour lui faire entendre mieux encore l'importance de la pièce sacrée, je lui bégaye de la voix, je lui désigne du doigt tout ce qu'on en peut acquérir, un beau fourreau, un beau toquet, un bon biscuit. Ensuite je mets le louis dans ma poche, je me promène avec fierté ; je relève la basque de ma veste ; je frappe de la main sur mon gousset ; et c'est ainsi que je lui fais concevoir que c'est du louis qui est là, que naît l'assurance qu'il me voit.

MOI — On ne peut rien de mieux. Mais s'il arrivait que profondément pénétré de la valeur du louis, un jour…

LUI — Je vous entends. Il faut fermer les yeux là-dessus. Il n'y a point de principe de morale qui n'ait son inconvénient. Au pis aller, c'est un mauvais quart d'heure et tout est fini.[223]

MOI — Même d'après des vues si courageuses et si sages, je persiste à croire qu'il serait bon d'en faire un musicien. Je ne connais pas de moyen d'approcher plus rapidement des grands, de servir leurs vices et de mettre à profit les siens.

LUI — Il est vrai ; mais j'ai des projets d'un succès plus prompt et plus sûr. Ah ! si c'était aussi bien une fille ! Mais comme on ne fait pas ce qu'on veut, il faut prendre ce qui vient, en tirer le meilleur parti, et pour cela ne pas donner bêtement, comme la plupart des pères qui ne feraient rien de pis quand ils auraient médité le malheur de leurs enfants, l'éducation de Lacédémone à un enfant destiné à vivre à Paris.[224] Si elle est mauvaise, c'est la faute des mœurs de ma nation, et non la mienne. En répondra qui pourra. Je veux que mon fils soit heureux ; ou, ce qui revient au même, honoré, riche et puissant. Je connais un peu les voies les plus faciles d'arriver à ce but, et je les lui enseignerai de bonne heure. Si vous me blâmez, vous autres sages, la multitude et le succès m'absoudront. Il aura de l'or ; c'est moi qui vous le dis. S'il en a beaucoup, rien ne lui manquera, pas même votre estime et votre respect.

MOI — Vous pourriez vous tromper.

LUI — Ou il s'en passera, comme bien d'autres.

Il y avait dans tout cela beaucoup de ces choses qu'on pense, d'après lesquelles on se conduit ; mais qu'on ne dit pas. Voilà, en vérité, la différence la plus marquée entre mon homme et la plupart de nos entours. Il avouait les vices qu'il avait, que les autres ont ; mais il n'était pas hypocrite. Il n'était ni plus ni moins abominable qu'eux, il était seulement plus franc, et plus conséquent ; et quelquefois profond dans sa dépravation. Je tremblais de ce que son enfant deviendrait sous un pareil maître. Il est certain que, d'après des idées d'institution aussi strictement calquées sur nos mœurs, il devait aller loin, à moins qu'il ne fût prématurément arrêté en chemin.

LUI[225] — Oh ! ne craignez rien, me dit-il : le point important, le point difficile auquel un bon père doit surtout s'attacher, ce n'est pas de donner à son enfant des vices qui l'enrichissent, des ridicules qui le rendent précieux aux grands ; tout le monde le fait, sinon de système comme moi, mais au moins d'exemple et de leçon : mais de lui marquer la juste mesure, l'art d'esquiver à la honte, au déshonneur et aux lois ; ce sont des dissonances dans l'harmonie sociale qu'il faut savoir placer, préparer et sauver. Rien de si plat qu'une suite d'accords parfaits. Il faut quelque chose qui pique, qui sépare le faisceau, et qui en éparpille les rayons.[226]

MOI — Fort bien. Par cette comparaison, vous me ramenez des mœurs à la musique, dont je m'étais écarté malgré moi ; et je vous en remercie ; car, à ne vous rien celer, je vous aime mieux musicien que moraliste.

LUI — Je suis pourtant bien subalterne en musique, et bien supérieur en morale.

MOI — J'en doute ; mais quand cela serait, je suis un bon homme et vos principes ne sont pas les miens.

LUI — Tant pis pour vous. Ah ! si j'avais vos talents !

MOI — Laissons mes talents, et revenons aux vôtres.

LUI — Si je savais m'énoncer comme vous ! Mais j'ai un diable de ramage saugrenu, moitié des gens du monde et des lettres, moitié de la halle.

MOI — Je parle mal. Je ne sais que dire la vérité, et cela ne prend pas toujours, comme vous savez.[227]

LUI — Mais ce n'est pas pour dire la vérité ; au contraire, c'est pour bien dire le mensonge que j'ambitionne votre talent. Si je savais écrire, fagoter un livre, tourner une épître dédicatoire, bien enivrer un sot de son mérite, m'insinuer auprès des femmes !

MOI — Et tout cela vous le savez mille fois mieux que moi. Je ne serais pas même digne d'être votre écolier.

LUI — Combien de grandes qualités perdues, et dont vous ignorez le prix !

MOI — Je recueille tout celui que j'y mets.

LUI — Si cela était, vous n'auriez pas cet habit grossier, cette veste d'étamine, ces bas de laine, ces souliers épais et cette antique perruque.

MOI — D'accord. Il faut être bien maladroit quand on n'est pas riche, et que l'on se permet tout pour le devenir. Mais c'est qu'il y a des gens comme moi qui ne regardent pas la richesse comme la chose du monde la plus précieuse ; gens bizarres.

LUI — Très bizarres. On ne naît pas avec cette tournure-là. On se la donne, car elle n'est pas dans la nature.

MOI — De l'homme ?

LUI — De l'homme. Tout ce qui vit, sans l'en excepter, cherche son bien-être aux dépens de qui il appartiendra ; et je suis sûr que, si je laissais venir le petit sauvage sans lui parler de rien, il voudrait être richement vêtu, splendidement nourri, chéri des hommes, aimé des femmes, et rassembler sur lui tous les bonheurs de la vie.

MOI — Si le petit sauvage était abandonné à lui-même, qu'il conservât toute son imbécillité et qu'il réunît au peu de raison de l'enfant au berceau la violence des passions de l'homme de trente ans,[228] il tordrait le col à son père, et coucherait avec sa mère.[229]

LUI — Cela prouve la nécessité d'une bonne éducation ; et qui est-ce qui la conteste ? et qu'est-ce qu'une bonne éducation, sinon celle qui conduit à toutes sortes de jouissances, sans péril et sans inconvénient ?

MOI — Peu s'en faut que je ne sois de votre avis ; mais gardons-nous de nous expliquer.

LUI — Pourquoi ?

MOI — C'est que je crains que nous ne soyons d'accord qu'en apparence ; et que, si nous entrons une fois dans la discussion des périls et des inconvénients à éviter, nous ne nous entendions plus.

LUI — Et qu'est-ce que cela fait ?

MOI — Laissons cela, vous dis-je. Ce que je sais là-dessus, je ne vous l'apprendrais pas ; et vous m'instruirez plus aisément de ce que j'ignore et que vous savez en musique. Cher Rameau, parlons musique, et dites-moi comment il est arrivé qu'avec la facilité de sentir, de retenir et de rendre les plus beaux endroits des grands maîtres, avec l'enthousiasme qu'ils vous inspirent et que vous transmettez aux autres, vous n'ayez rien fait qui vaille.

 Au lieu de me répondre, il se mit à hocher de la tête, et, levant le doigt
au ciel, il ajouta : Et l'astre ! l'astre ! Quand la nature fit Léo,[230] Vinci,[231]
17 Pergolèse, Duni, elle sourit. Elle prit un air imposant et grave en formant le cher oncle Rameau qu'on aura appelé pendant une dizaine d'années le grand Rameau, et dont bientôt on ne parlera plus.[232] Quand elle fagota son neveu, elle fit la grimace, et puis la grimace, et puis la grimace encore. Et, en disant ces mots, il faisait toutes sortes de grimaces du visage : c'était le mépris, le dédain, l'ironie ; et il semblait pétrir entre ses doigts un morceau de pâte, le sourire aux formes ridicules qu'il lui donnait. Cela fait, il jeta la pagode hétéroclite loin de lui ; et il dit : C'est ainsi qu'elle me fit et qu'elle me jeta à côté d'autres pagodes, les unes à gros ventres ratatinés, à cols courts, à gros yeux hors de la tête, apoplectiques, d'autres à cols obliques ; il y en avait de sèches, à l'œil vif, au nez crochu ; toutes se mirent à crever de rire en me voyant ; et moi de mettre mes deux poings sur mes côtes et à crever de rire en les voyant, car les sots et les fous s'amusent les uns des autres ; ils se cherchent, ils s'attirent. Si, en arrivant là, je n'avais pas trouvé tout fait le proverbe qui dit que *l'argent des sots est le patrimoine des gens d'esprit*, on me le devrait. Je sentis que nature avait mis ma légitime dans la bourse des pagodes, et j'inventai mille moyens de m'en ressaisir.

MOI — Je sais ces moyens ; vous m'en avez parlé, et je les ai fort admirés. Mais, entre tant de ressource, pourquoi n'avoir pas tenté celle d'un bel ouvrage ?

LUI — Ce propos est celui d'un homme du monde à l'abbé Le Blanc.[233] L'abbé disait : La marquise de Pompadour[234] me prend sur la main, me porte jusque sur le seuil de l'Académie ; là elle retire sa main. Je tombe et je me casse les deux jambes... L'homme du monde lui répondait : Hé bien, l'abbé, il faut se relever et enfoncer la porte d'un coup de tête... L'abbé lui répliquait : C'est ce que j'ai tenté ; et savez-vous ce qui m'en est revenu ? une bosse au front.

Après cette historiette, mon homme se mit à marcher la tête baissée, l'air pensif et abattu ; il soupirait, pleurait, se désolait, levait les mains et les yeux, se frappait la tête du poing, à se briser le front ou les doigts, et il ajoutait : Il me semble qu'il y a pourtant là quelque chose ; mais j'ai beau frapper, secouer, il ne sort rien. Puis il recommençait à secouer sa tête et à se frapper le front de plus belle, et il disait : Ou il n'y a personne, ou l'on ne veut pas répondre.

Un instant après, il prenait un air fier, il relevait sa tête il s'appliquait la main droite sur le cœur ; il marchait et disait : Je sens, oui, je sens. Il contrefaisait l'homme qui s'irrite, qui s'indigne, qui s'attendrit, qui commande, qui supplie, et prononçait, sans préparation, des discours de colère, de commisération, de haine, d'amour ; il esquissait les caractères des passions avec une finesse et une vérité surprenantes. Puis il ajoutait : C'est cela, je crois. Voilà que cela vient ; voilà ce que c'est que de trouver un accoucheur qui sait irriter, précipiter les douleurs et faire sortir l'enfant. Seul, je prends la plume, je veux écrire. Je me ronge les ongles, je m'use le front. Serviteur. Bonsoir. Le dieu est absent ; je m'étais persuadé que j'avais du génie ; au bout de ma ligne, je lis que je suis un sot, un sot, un sot. Mais le moyen de sentir, de s'élever, de penser, de peindre fortement, en fréquentant avec des gens tels que ceux qu'il faut voir pour vivre ; au milieu des propos qu'on tient et de ceux qu'on entend, et de ce commérage : Aujourd'hui, le boulevard était charmant. Avez-vous entendu la petite marmotte ? Elle joue à ravir. Monsieur un tel avait le plus bel attelage gris pommelé qu'il soit possible d'imaginer. La belle madame celle-ci commence à passer ; est-ce qu'à l'âge de quarante-cinq ans on porte une coiffure comme celle-là ? La jeune une telle est couverte de diamants qui ne lui coûtent guère. — Vous voulez dire qui lui coûtent cher ? — Mais non. — Où l'avez-vous vue ? — À *L'Enfant d'Arlequin perdu et retrouvé*.[235] — La scène du désespoir a été jouée comme elle ne l'avait pas encore été. Le Polichinelle de la Foire a du gosier, mais point de finesse, point d'âme. Madame une telle est accouchée de deux enfants à la fois. Chaque père aura le sien... Et vous croyez que cela dit, redit et entendu tous les jours, échauffe et conduit aux grandes choses ?

MOI — Non. Il vaudrait mieux se renfermer dans son grenier, boire de l'eau, manger du pain sec, et se chercher soi-même.

LUI — Peut-être ; mais je n'en ai pas le courage ; et puis sacrifier son bonheur à un succès incertain ! Et le nom que je porte, donc ? Rameau ! s'appeler Rameau, cela est gênant. Il n'en est pas des talents comme de la noblesse qui se transmet et dont l'illustration s'accroît en passant du grand-père au père, du père au fils, du fils à son petit-fils, sans que l'aïeul impose quelque mérite à son descendant. La vieille souche se ramifie en une énorme tige de sots ; mais qu'importe ? Il n'en est pas ainsi du talent. Pour n'obtenir que la renommée de son père, il faut être plus habile que lui. Il faut avoir hérité de sa fibre. La fibre m'a manqué, mais le poignet s'est dégourdi ; l'archet marche, et le pot bout. Si ce n'est pas de la gloire, c'est du bouillon.

MOI — À votre place, je ne me le tiendrais pas pour dit ; j'essaierais.

LUI — Et vous croyez que je n'ai pas essayé ? Je n'avais pas quinze ans, lorsque je me dis pour la première fois : Qu'as-tu, Rameau ? tu rêves. Et à quoi rêves-tu ? que tu voudrais bien avoir fait ou faire quelque chose qui excitât l'admiration de l'univers. Hé oui, il n'y a qu'à souffler et remuer les doigts. Il n'y a qu'à ourler le bec, et ce sera une cane. Dans un âge plus avancé, j'ai répété le propos de mon enfance. Aujourd'hui je le répète encore, et je reste autour de la statue de Memnon.

MOI — Que voulez-vous dire avec votre statue de Memnon ?[236]

LUI — Cela s'entend, ce me semble. Autour de la statue de Memnon, il y en avait une infinité d'autres, également frappées des rayons du soleil ; mais la sienne était la seule qui résonnât. Un poète, c'est de Voltaire ; et puis qui encore ? de Voltaire ; et le troisième ? de Voltaire ; et le quatrième ? de Voltaire.

Un musicien, c'est Rinaldo da Capoua ;[237] c'est Hasse ; c'est Pergolèse ; c'est Alberti ; c'est Tartini ;[238] c'est Locatelli ;[239] c'est Terradoglias ; c'est mon oncle ; c'est ce petit Duni, qui n'a ni mine ni figure, mais qui sent, mordieu, qui a du chant et de l'expression. Le reste, autour de ce petit nombre de Memnons, autant de paires d'oreilles fichées au bout d'un bâton. Aussi sommes-nous gueux, si gueux, que c'est une bénédiction. Ah ! monsieur le philosophe, la misère est une terrible chose. Je la vois accroupie, la bouche béante pour recevoir quelques gouttes de l'eau glacée qui s'échappe du tonneau des Danaïdes.[240] Je ne sais si elle aiguise l'esprit du philosophe ; mais elle refroidit diablement la tête du poète. On ne chante pas bien sous ce tonneau. Trop heureux encore celui qui peut s'y placer ! J'y étais, et je n'ai pas su m'y tenir. J'avais déjà fait cette sottise une fois. J'ai voyagé en Bohème, en Allemagne, en Suisse, en Hollande, en Flandre ; au diable, au vert.

MOI — Sous le tonneau percé ?

LUI — Sous le tonneau percé ; c'était un juif opulent et dissipateur, qui aimait la musique et mes folies. Je musiquais comme il plaît à Dieu ; je faisais le fou ; je ne manquais de rien. Mon juif était un homme qui savait sa loi, et qui l'observait roide comme une barre, quelquefois avec l'ami, toujours avec l'étranger. Il se fit une mauvaise affaire qu'il faut que je vous raconte, car elle est plaisante. Il y avait à Utrecht[241] une courtisane charmante. Il fut tenté de la chrétienne ; il lui dépêcha un grison, avec une lettre de change assez forte. La bizarre créature rejeta son offre. Le juif en fut désespéré. Le grison lui dit : Pourquoi vous affliger ainsi ? Vous voulez coucher avec une jolie femme ; rien n'est plus aisé, et même de coucher avec une plus jolie que celle que vous poursuivez. C'est la mienne, que je vous céderai au même prix. Fait et dit. Le grison garde la lettre de change, et mon juif couche avec la femme du grison. L'échéance de la lettre de change arrive. Le juif la laisse protester et s'inscrit en faux. Procès. Le juif disait : Jamais cet homme n'osera dire à quel titre il possède ma lettre, et je ne la payerai pas. À l'audience, il interpelle le grison. — Cette lettre de change, de qui la tenez-vous ? — De vous. — Est-ce pour de l'argent prêté ? — Non. — Est-ce pour fourniture de marchandise ? — Non. — Est-ce pour services rendus ? — Non. Mais il ne s'agit point de cela ; j'en suis possesseur, vous l'avez signée, et vous l'acquitterez. — Je ne l'ai point signée. — Je suis donc un faussaire ? — Vous ou un autre dont vous êtes l'agent. — Je suis un lâche, mais vous êtes un coquin. Croyez-moi, ne me poussez pas à bout. Je dirai tout. Je me déshonorerai, mais je vous perdrai... Le juif ne tint compte de la menace, et le grison révéla toute l'affaire à la séance qui suivit. Ils furent blâmés tous les deux ; et le juif condamné à payer la lettre de change, dont la valeur fut appliquée au soulagement des pauvres. Alors je me séparai de lui. Je revins ici. Quoi faire ? car il fallait périr de misère ou faire quelque chose. Il me passa toutes sortes de projets par la tête. Un jour, je partais le lendemain pour me jeter dans une troupe de province, également bon ou mauvais pour le théâtre ou pour l'orchestre ; le lendemain, je songeais à me faire peindre un de ces tableaux attachés à une perche qu'on plante dans un carrefour, et où j'aurais crié à tue-tête : Voilà la ville où il est né ; le voilà qui prend congé de son père l'apothicaire ; le voilà qui arrive dans la capitale, cherchant la demeure de son oncle ; le voilà aux genoux de son oncle, qui le chasse ; le voilà avec un juif, et caetera, et caetera. Le jour suivant, je me levais, bien résolu de m'associer aux chanteurs des rues ; ce n'est pas ce que j'aurais fait de plus mal ; nous serions allés concerter sous les fenêtres du cher oncle qui en serait crevé de rage. Je pris un autre parti.

Là il s'arrêta, passant successivement de l'attitude d'un homme qui tient un violon, serrant des cordes à tour de bras, à celle d'un pauvre diable exténué de fatigue, à qui les forces manquent, dont les jambes flageolent, prêt à expirer, si on ne lui jette un morceau de pain ; il désignait son extrême besoin par le geste d'un doigt dirigé vers sa bouche entrouverte ; puis il ajouta : Cela s'entend. On me jetait le lopin. Nous le disputions à trois ou quatre affamés que nous étions ; et puis pensez grandement ; faites de belles choses au milieu d'une pareille détresse.

MOI — Cela est difficile.

LUI — De cascade en cascade, j'étais tombé là. J'y étais comme un coq en pâte. J'en suis sorti. Il faudra derechef scier le boyau, et revenir au geste du doigt vers la bouche béante. Rien de stable dans ce monde. Aujourd'hui au sommet ; demain au bas de la roue. De maudites circonstances nous mènent, et nous mènent fort mal.

Puis, buvant un coup qui restait au fond de la bouteille, et s'adressant à son voisin : Monsieur, par charité, une petite prise. Vous avez là une belle boîte ? Vous n'êtes pas musicien ? — Non. — Tant mieux pour vous ; car ce sont de pauvres bougres bien à plaindre. Le sort a voulu que je le fusse, moi ; tandis qu'il y a, à Montmartre peut-être, dans un moulin,[242] un meunier, un valet de meunier, qui n'entendra jamais que bruit du cliquet, et qui aurait trouvé les plus beaux chants. Rameau ! au moulin, au moulin, c'est là ta place.

MOI — À quoi que ce soit que l'homme s'applique, la Nature l'y destinait.

LUI — Elle fait d'étranges bévues. Pour moi, je ne vois pas de cette hauteur où tout se confond : l'homme qui émonde un arbre avec des ciseaux, la chenille qui en ronge la feuille, et d'où l'on ne voit que deux insectes différents, chacun à son devoir. Perchez-vous sur l'épicycle de Mercure[243] et de là distribuez, si cela vous convient, et à l'imitation de Réaumur,[244] lui la classe des mouches en couturières, arpenteuses, faucheuses, vous l'espèce des hommes en hommes menuisiers, charpentiers, couvreurs, danseurs, chanteurs, c'est votre affaire. Je ne m'en mêle pas. Je suis dans ce monde et j'y reste. Mais s'il est dans la nature d'avoir appétit, car c'est toujours à l'appétit que j'en reviens, à la sensation qui m'est toujours présente, je trouve qu'il n'est pas du bon ordre de n'avoir pas toujours de quoi manger. Que diable d'économie ! des hommes qui regorgent de tout tandis que d'autres qui ont un estomac importun comme eux, une faim renaissante comme eux, et pas de quoi mettre sous la dent. Le pis, c'est la posture contrainte où nous tient le besoin. L'homme nécessiteux ne marche pas comme un autre ; il saute, il rampe, il se tortille, il se traîne ; il passe sa vie à prendre et à exécuter des positions.

MOI — Qu'est-ce que des positions ?

LUI — Allez le demander à Noverre.[245] Le monde en offre bien plus que son art n'en peut imiter.

MOI — Et vous voilà aussi, pour me servir de votre expression, ou de celle de Montaigne, *perché sur l'épicycle de Mercure*, et considérant les différentes pantomimes de l'espèce humaine.

LUI — Non, non, vous dis-je. Je suis trop lourd pour m'élever si haut. J'abandonne aux grues le séjour des brouillards. Je vais terre à terre. Je regarde autour de moi, et je prends mes positions, ou je m'amuse des positions que je vois prendre aux autres. Je suis excellent pantomime, comme vous en allez juger.

Puis il se met à sourire, à contrefaire l'homme admirateur, l'homme suppliant, l'homme complaisant ; il a le pied droit en avant, le gauche en arrière, le dos courbé, la tête relevée, le regard comme attaché sur d'autres yeux, la bouche entrouverte, les bras portés vers quelque objet ; il attend un ordre, il le reçoit ; il part comme un trait ; il revient, il est exécuté ; il en rend compte. Il est attentif à tout ; il ramasse ce qui tombe ; il place un oreiller ou un tabouret sous des pieds ; il tient une soucoupe, il approche une chaise, il ouvre une porte ; il ferme une fenêtre ; il tire des rideaux ; il observe le maître et la maîtresse ; il est immobile, les bras pendants, les jambes parallèles ; il écoute ; il cherche à lire sur des visages ; et il ajoute : Voilà ma pantomime, à peu près la même que celle des flatteurs, des courtisans, des valets et des gueux.

Les folies de cet homme, les contes de l'abbé Galiani,[246] les extravagances de Rabelais m'ont quelquefois fait rêver profondément. Ce sont trois magasins où je me suis pourvu de masques ridicules que je place sur le visage des plus graves personnages ; et je vois Pantalon[247] dans un prélat, un satyre[248] dans un président, un pourceau dans un cénobite, une autruche dans un ministre, une oie dans son premier commis.

MOI — Mais à votre compte, dis-je à mon homme, il y a bien des gueux dans ce monde-ci ; et je ne connais personne qui ne sache quelques pas de votre danse.

LUI — Vous avez raison. Il n'y a dans tout un royaume qu'un homme qui marche, c'est le souverain. Tout le reste prend des positions.

MOI — Le souverain ? Encore y a-t-il quelque chose à dire. Et croyez-vous qu'il ne se trouve pas, de temps en temps, à côté de lui, un petit pied, un petit chignon, un petit nez qui lui fasse faire un peu de la pantomime ? Quiconque a besoin d'un autre, est indigent et prend une position. Le roi prend une position devant sa maîtresse et devant Dieu ; il fait son pas de pantomime. Le ministre fait le pas de courtisan, de flatteur, de valet ou de gueux devant son roi. La foule des ambitieux dansent vos positions, en cent manières plus viles les unes que les autres, devant le ministre. L'abbé de condition, en rabat et en manteau long,[249] au moins une fois la semaine, devant le dépositaire de la feuille des bénéfices. Ma foi, ce que vous appelez la pantomime des gueux, est le grand branle de la terre. Chacun a sa petite Hus et son Bertin.

LUI — Cela me console.

Mais tandis que je parlais, il contrefaisait à mourir de rire les positions des personnages que je nommais ; par exemple, pour le petit abbé, il tenait son chapeau sous le bras, et son bréviaire de la main gauche ; de la droite, il relevait la queue de son manteau ; il s'avançait la tête un peu penchée sur l'épaule, les yeux baissés, imitant si parfaitement l'hypocrite que je crus voir l'auteur des *Réfutations* devant l'évêque d'Orléans.[250] Aux flatteurs, aux ambitieux, il était ventre à terre. C'était Bouret au contrôle général.[251]

MOI — Cela est supérieurement exécuté, lui dis-je. Mais il y a pourtant un être dispensé de la pantomime. C'est le philosophe qui n'a rien et qui ne demande rien.

LUI — Et où est cet animal-là ? S'il n'a rien, il souffre ; s'il ne sollicite rien, il n'obtiendra rien, et il souffrira toujours.

MOI — Non. Diogène se moquait des besoins.

LUI — Mais il faut être vêtu.

MOI — Non. Il allait tout nu.

LUI — Quelquefois il faisait froid dans Athènes.

MOI — Moins qu'ici.

LUI — On y mangeait.

MOI — Sans doute.

LUI — Aux dépens de qui ?

MOI — De la nature. À qui s'adresse le sauvage ? à la terre, aux animaux, aux poissons, aux arbres, aux herbes, aux racines, aux ruisseaux.

LUI — Mauvaise table.

MOI — Elle est grande.

LUI — Mais mal servie.

MOI — C'est pourtant celle qu'on dessert pour couvrir les nôtres.[252]

LUI — Mais vous conviendrez que l'industrie de nos cuisiniers, pâtissiers, rôtisseurs, traiteurs, confiseurs y met un peu du sien. Avec la diète austère de votre Diogène, il ne devait pas avoir des organes fort indociles.

MOI — Vous vous trompez. L'habit du cynique était, autrefois, notre habit monastique avec la même vertu. Les cyniques étaient les carmes et les cordeliers d'Athènes.[253]

LUI — Je vous y prends. Diogène a donc aussi dansé la pantomime ; si ce n'est devant Périclès, du moins devant Laïs ou Phryné.[254]

MOI — Vous vous trompez encore. Les autres achetaient bien cher la courtisane qui se livrait à lui pour le plaisir.

LUI — Mais, s'il arrivait que la courtisane fût occupée, et le cynique pressé ?

MOI — Il rentrait dans son tonneau et se passait d'elle.

LUI — Et vous me conseilleriez de l'imiter ?

MOI — Je veux mourir si cela ne vaudrait mieux que de ramper, de s'avilir et se prostituer.

LUI — Mais il me faut un bon lit, une bonne table, un vêtement chaud en hiver, un vêtement frais en été ; du repos, de l'argent et beaucoup d'autres choses, que je préfère de devoir à la bienveillance, plutôt que de les acquérir par le travail.

MOI — C'est que vous êtes un fainéant, un gourmand, un lâche, une âme de boue.

LUI — Je crois vous l'avoir dit.

MOI — Les choses de la vie ont un prix sans doute ; mais vous ignorez celui du sacrifice que vous faites pour les obtenir. Vous dansez, vous avez dansé et vous continuerez de danser la vile pantomime.

LUI — Il est vrai. Mais il m'en a peu coûté, et il ne m'en coûte plus rien pour cela. Et c'est par cette raison que je ferais mal de prendre une autre allure qui me peinerait, et que je ne garderais pas. Mais je vois à ce que vous me dites là que ma pauvre petite femme était une espèce de philosophe. Elle avait du courage comme un lion. Quelquefois nous manquions de pain et nous étions sans le sou. Nous avions vendu presque toutes nos nippes. Je m'étais jeté sur les pieds de notre lit, là je me creusais à chercher quelqu'un qui me prêtât un écu que je ne lui rendrais pas. Elle, gaie comme un pinson, se mettait à son clavecin, chantait et s'accompagnait. C'était un gosier de rossignol ; je regrette que vous ne l'ayez pas entendue. Quand j'étais de quelque concert,[255] je l'emmenais avec moi. Chemin faisant, je lui disais : Allons, madame, faites-vous admirer ; déployez votre talent et vos charmes. Enlevez. Renversez. Nous arrivions ; elle chantait, elle enlevait, elle renversait.[256] Hélas ! je l'ai perdue, la pauvre petite. Outre son talent, c'est qu'elle avait une bouche à recevoir à peine le petit doigt ; des dents, une rangée de perles ; des yeux, des pieds, une peau, des joues, des tétons, des jambes de cerf, des cuisses et des fesses à modeler. Elle aurait eu, tôt ou tard, le fermier général[257] tout au moins. C'était une démarche, une croupe ! Ah ! Dieu, quelle croupe !

Puis le voilà qui se met à contrefaire la démarche de sa femme. Il allait à petits pas ; il portait sa tête au vent ; il jouait de l'éventail ; il se démenait de la croupe ; c'était la charge de nos petites coquettes la plus plaisante et la plus ridicule.

Puis reprenant la suite de son discours, il ajoutait :

Je la promenais partout, aux Tuileries,[258] au Palais-Royal, aux Boulevards. Il était impossible qu'elle me demeurât. Quand elle traversait la rue, le matin, en cheveux, et en pet-en-l'air, vous vous seriez arrêté pour la voir, et vous l'auriez embrassée entre quatre doigts, sans la serrer. Ceux qui la suivaient, qui la regardaient trotter avec ses petits pieds, et qui mesuraient cette large croupe dont ses jupons légers dessinaient la forme, doublaient le pas ; elle les laissait arriver ; puis elle détournait prestement sur eux ses deux grands yeux noirs et brillants qui les arrêtaient tout court. C'est que l'endroit de la médaille ne déparait pas le revers. Mais, hélas ! je l'ai perdue ; et mes espérances de fortune se sont toutes évanouies avec elle. Je ne l'avais prise que pour cela, je lui avais confié mes projets ; et elle avait trop de sagacité pour n'en pas concevoir la certitude, et trop de jugement pour ne les pas approuver.

Et puis le voilà qui sanglote et qui pleure, en disant : Non, non, je ne m'en consolerai jamais. Depuis, j'ai pris le rabat et la calotte.

MOI — De douleur ?

LUI — Si vous voulez. Mais le vrai, pour avoir mon écuelle sur ma tête...[259] Mais voyez un peu l'heure qu'il est, car il faut que j'aille à l'Opéra.

MOI — Qu'est-ce qu'on donne ?

LUI — Le Dauvergne.[260] Il y a d'assez belles choses dans sa musique ; c'est dommage qu'il ne les ait pas dites le premier. Parmi ces morts, il y en a toujours quelques-uns qui désolent les vivants. Que voulez-vous ? *Quisque suos patimur manes.*[261] Mais il est cinq heures et demie, j'entends la cloche qui sonne les vêpres de l'abbé de Canaye,[262] et les miennes. Adieu, monsieur le philosophe, n'est-il pas vrai que je suis toujours le même ?

MOI — Hélas ! oui, malheureusement.

LUI — Que j'aie ce malheur-là seulement encore une quarantaine d'années. Rira bien qui rira le dernier.

Notes

1. Diderot's spelling of Satyre with a 'y' brings out libidinous associations with the mythical 'Satyr'. His *Satire première* has as its full title *Satire I sur les caractères et les mots de caractère, de profession etc* [*Satire on Characters and on the Language Peculiar to Them and to Professions*] and is subtitled *A mon ami M. Naigeon, sur un passage de la première satire du second livre d'Horace* [*To my friend M. Naigeon on a passage from the first satire in the second book of Horace's Satires*]. The expansion of the main title is however in fact owed to Jacques-André Naigeon (1738–1810), Diderot's acolyte and the dedicatee of this satire; nevertheless, it has relevance to the *Satyre seconde* as well as to *Satire I* in that Rameau's Nephew is also interested in the various ways of grouping men (character, trades) and contains a large number of lists, as if partially to enumerate them.

2. Tr. Niall Rudd, *Horace, Satires and Epistles; Persius, Satires*, 1973 (rev. 2005). London: Penguin Classics, p. 67. Vertumnus is the god of change and transfer, of weather and of money. Diderot's epigraph for his *Satire seconde* is taken from the seventh satire by Horace in the second book, the same as for *Satire I*. Its subtitle since antiquity is 'only the wise are free', from a Stoic paradox, that only the philosopher/the wise man is free (see translations in the Loeb edition by H. Rushton Fairclough).

3. The Palais Royal was built in the 1630s and was given to the crown by Cardinal Richelieu at his death. It became the residence of the Orléans family, after the title of Louis XIV's younger brother. Its famous gardens were open to the public.

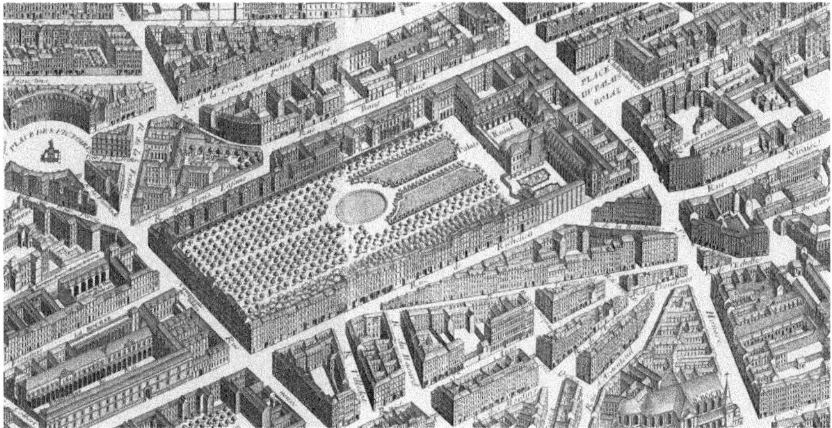

Fig. 3 The Palais Royal, detail from the *Plan de Turgot* (1734–39), by Michel-Étienne Turgot.

 http://dx.doi.org/10.11647/OBP.0044.03

Fig. 4 *Galerie et Jardins du Palais Royal* (late 18th century), artist unknown.

4. Marc-Pierre de Voyer de Paulmy comte d'Argenson (1696–1764), head of the Parisian police (lieutenant général de police) 1720 and 1722, then Secretary of State for War 1742–57. The d'Argenson bench was on the d'Argenson walk, on the east side of the garden, opposite the Foy walk, which was presumably named after the café keeper of that name.

5. François Antoine de Le Gall (1702–92), said to be the first professional chess player (i.e. playing for money). A game of his is described at http://www.chessgames.com/perl/chessplayer?pid=77039 (all links cited in this volume were active on 23 June 2014).

6. An acquaintance of Diderot, François-André Danican Philidor (1726–95) is said to have been one of the greatest chess players ever, of truly international fame. A nephew of Rameau, almost certainly not 'our' Nephew, but a child of Rameau's brother's second marriage, placed the chess pieces for a game Philidor played blindfolded in London in 1793 (see *The Sporting Magazine*, II, no. 1, April 1793, p. 8). Philidor was also an important composer. He is buried in St. James, Piccadilly.

Fig. 5 Frontespiece from A.D. Philidor, *Analyse du jeu des échecs* (1803; 1st edition, 1748).

François-André Danican Philidor, *L'Art de la modulation* [*The art of modulation*], extract:
Sixth Suite: Sinfonia (Adagio — Allegro ma non troppo)

To listen to this piece online scan the QR code
or follow this link: http://dx.doi.org/10.11647/OBP.0044.04

The sixth suite is made up of an adagio, an allegro and a minuet. The play on the modulations as a principle of composition is quite remarkable in these pieces. The adagio movement, which stresses the key of D major by long ascending scales, played in alternation with two groups of two instruments, moves away from this key, taking on those of A major and E major, with an intervening B flat which, in spite of the major key of the piece, gives a sense of melancholy to the whole of the adagio. The allegro, on the contrary, with its repeated staccato notes, its trills and appoggiatura, never forsakes the spirit of joy it began in. With its sonata form, the piece offers a development through careful modulation and numerous harmonic sequences.

7. Fabre suggests, after Isambert in his edition of 1883, that Foubert may have been a surgeon from the rue de la Monnaie. Mayot has not been traced.

8. Diderot contrasts a monastic order famed for austerity (Trappist) with one possessing great wealth (Bernardin).

9. The Champs-Elysées were a kind of park at this point in time.

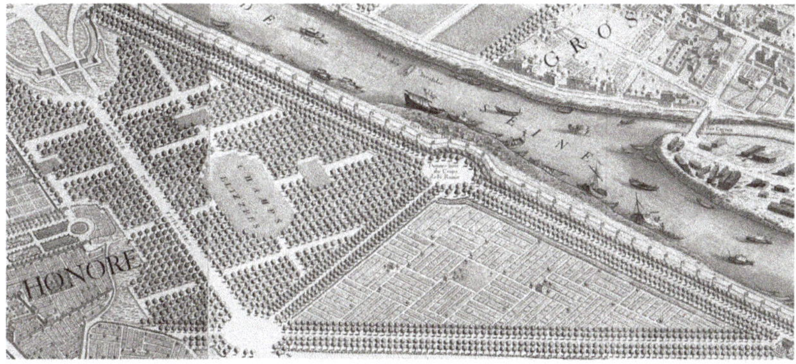

Fig. 6 The Champs-Elysées, detail from the *Plan de Turgot* (1734–39), by Michel-Étienne Turgot.

10. I.e. Jean-Philippe Rameau (1683–1764). See the French edition associated with this one, *Satyre Seconde: Le Neveu de Rameau*, ed. Marian Hobson, 2013. Droz: Geneva (hereafter referred to as the French edition), for an extended discussion of the role of music in this dialogue. Rameau the uncle was an important theorist of the acoustical basis of harmony (see Thomas Christensen, *Rameau and Musical Thought in the Enlightenment*, 1993. Cambridge: Cambridge University Press).

Fig. 7 Jean-Philippe Rameau (c.1728), attributed to Jacques-André-Joseph Aved.

11. Jean-Baptiste Lulli (1632–87), born in Florence, Lulli was the major composer of Louis XIV's reign, in particular of operas and opera-ballets (see fig. 8).

Fig. 8 Jean-Baptiste Lulli (early 18th century), by Henri Bonnart (1642–1711).

12. Diderot here is mocking the formulaic vocabulary employed in French opera seria.

13. Pierre Carlet de Chamblain de Marivaux (1688–1763), playwright, journalist and important novelist (see fig. 9).

14. Claude-Prosper Jolyot de Crébillon (1701–77), novelist and journalist (see fig. 10).

Fig. 9 Pierre Carlet de Chamblain de Marivaux (1743), by Louis-Michel van Loo.

15. Claude de Thiard de Bissy (1721–1810), soldier, author, member of the Académie française at 29, on a rather slim output which included at least one work of doubtful orthodoxy. He would repay further investigation; see the French edition, p. 11.

16. Stage name (1723–1803) (see figs. 11 and 12). A famous actress and a supporter of the *philosophes*. What is said of Mademoiselle Clairon here is close to the account given of her acting in Diderot's dialogue, *Paradoxe sur le comédien* [*Paradox on the Actor*], which he probably worked on at about the same time as *Rameau's Nephew*, c.1772–c.1773. See the French edition, pp. 228–32, for further details of her as a huge star in Paris.

Fig. 10 Claude-Prosper Jolyot de Crébillon, by Jean-Baptiste André Gautier-Dagoty (1740–86).

Fig. 11 *Mlle Clairon en Médée*, detail (1760), by Charles-André van Loo.

Fig. 12 *Mlle Clairon dans 'L'Orphelin de la Chine'* [n.d.], by J.B. Le Prince.

17. Diogenes of Sinope (c.412–c.323 BC), a Greek philosopher and one of the founding fathers of Cynic philosophy.

Fig. 13 Diogenes (18th century), by Maurice Quentin de La Tour (1704–88).

18. Phryne, a famous prostitute in 4th century BC Greece. Diogenes and Phryne reappear in the dialogue just before the end — an indication of careful construction not always accepted by Diderot's critics.

19. Silenus, a fat and bald follower of Dionysus, the god of wine and sometimes wine-inspired frenzy.

Fig. 14 *Drunken Silenus supported by Satyrs* (c.1620), attributed to Anthony van Dyck.

20. A reference to the acoustical basis given to harmony by Rameau, most clearly in his *Génération harmonique*, 1737.

21. Le Duc de Choiseul was an enemy of the *philosophes* because the political and military enemy of the French, Frederick II of Prussia, called 'the Great', supported intellectuals who were in difficulties in France owing to their unorthodox thinking. Frederick gathered a group of such around him, and used them for political ends. Diderot, unlike Voltaire, did not have contact with this particular enlightened despot, and refused to visit Berlin on his way back from Russia in 1774.

Fig. 15 Etienne-François de Choiseul (1763), by Louis-Michel van Loo.

22. A principle for Diderot throughout his life. See his final bitter denunciation (in private, on paper) of his 'friend' Baron von Grimm, for his criticism of the Abbé Raynal and his *Histoire des deux Indes* [*A History of the Two Indies*], 1770, a major attack on European colonization. Grimm thought Raynal's work incautious and upsetting to the great (Lewinter, vol. XIII, p. 67; all references to works of Diderot are to this edition, *Œuvres complètes*, ed. Roger Lewinter, 15 vols. 1973. Paris: Club français du livre).

23. Throughout the dialogue, Diderot amuses himself at Voltaire's membership of the nobility by inserting his 'particule', incorrectly for cultivated usage. Voltaire (see fig. 16) used the 'particule' from time to time well before he acquired a firm right to do so, on being made *gentilhomme ordinaire du Roi* in 1746.

24. Antoine-Claude Briasson (1700–75), one of the publishers of Diderot's and d'Alembert's *Encyclopédie*.

Fig. 16 Voltaire (18th century), by de La Tour (1704–88).

25. A draper dealing in luxury fabrics, according to Jean Fabre, and earlier Maurice Tourneux, in their editions.

26. Diderot throughout his life struggled with a version of what could be called 'the problem of evil'. He was unwilling to see any action as irremediable, any situation as unchangeable. This is why a tragic vision is quite simply missing from his work, unlike his former friend Rousseau. Behind this difference in viewpoint is a radical difference in their experience of time and of causality. See M. Hobson, '"Nexus effectivus" and "nexus finalis": Causality in Rousseau's *Discours sur l'inégalité* and the *Essai sur l'origine des langues*', in M. Hobson, ed. and trans. Kate Tunstall and Caroline Warman, *Diderot and Rousseau: Networks of Enlightenment*, 2011. Oxford: Voltaire Foundation, pp. 165–99.

Fig. 17 Charles Pinot Duclos (first half of the 18th century), by de La Tour (1704–88).

27. Charles Pinot Duclos (1704–72), journalist and moralist (see fig. 17). He managed to remain friends with Rousseau.

28. Nicolas Charles Trublet (1697–1770), essayist, journalist and object of Voltaire's satirical attentions; he eventually became a member of the Académie française (see fig. 18).

Fig. 18 Nicolas Charles Trublet (late 18th century), artist unknown.

29. Pierre-Joseph Thoulier d'Olivet (1683–1768), head of the religious party at the Académie française and famously intolerant. His works on poetics and prosody are still of interest.

Fig. 19 Pierre-Joseph Thoulier d'Olivet [n.d.], after Charles-André van Loo.

30. Jean Baptiste Greuze (1725–85), painter especially known for introducing new, more ordinary subjects, see his painting *L'Accordée de village* [*The Village Bride*] (fig. 21). Diderot appreciated this style of painting, which one may think attempts to do in paint something like what Diderot tried to accomplish in his plays, *Le Fils naturel* [*The Natural Son*], 1757, and *Le Père de famille* [*The Family Man*], 1758. He was also famous for his vanity.

Fig. 20 Jean-Baptiste Greuze, *Self-portrait* (before 1785).

Fig. 21 *L'Accordée de Village* (1761), by Greuze.

31. *Mérope*, 1743, tragedy by Voltaire, an imitation of the Italian Scipione Maffei's tragedy of the same name. Voltaire's contemporaries experienced the play as extremely moving.

32. 'Good' is thus only a comparative term, and only has meaning if there is also evil in the world.

33. Diderot here puts forward what is sometimes his own view: that there is a strict net of causality enveloping the world, so that actual freedom (as opposed to the subjective experience of action as free) is an illusion. It is when he envisages a more statistical view of causality that this necessitarianism is countered — see his novel *Jacques le fataliste*.

Fig. 22 René-Augustin de Maupeou (18th century), by Pierre Lacour (1745–1814).

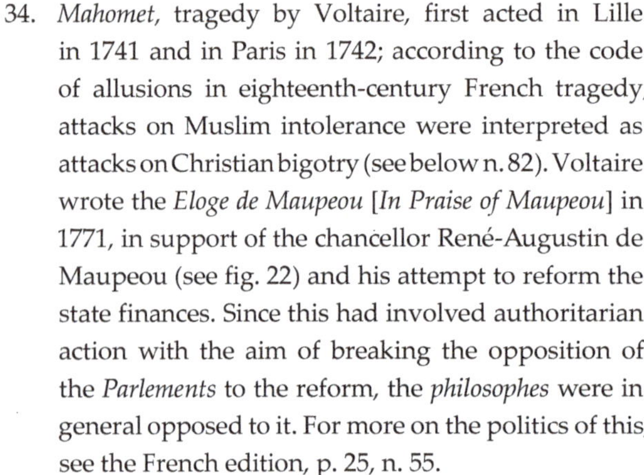

34. *Mahomet*, tragedy by Voltaire, first acted in Lille in 1741 and in Paris in 1742; according to the code of allusions in eighteenth-century French tragedy, attacks on Muslim intolerance were interpreted as attacks on Christian bigotry (see below n. 82). Voltaire wrote the *Eloge de Maupeou* [*In Praise of Maupeou*] in 1771, in support of the chancellor René-Augustin de Maupeou (see fig. 22) and his attempt to reform the state finances. Since this had involved authoritarian action with the aim of breaking the opposition of the *Parlements* to the reform, the *philosophes* were in general opposed to it. For more on the politics of this, see the French edition, p. 25, n. 55.

Fig. 23 Charles Palissot de Montenoy, *Oeuvres de M. Palissot* (1788).

35. *Les Indes galantes*, 1735, an opéra-ballet by Rameau. See http://www.youtube.com/watch?v=3zegtH-acXE.

36. From *Le Temple de la gloire*, an opera by Rameau, with libretto by Voltaire, written to celebrate the victory of the French army over the British, Dutch and Hanoverian armies at Fontenoy in 1745. See http://www.youtube.com/watch?v=we6vxXQ9hwo.

Fig. 24 Antoine Alexandre Henri Poinsinet, *Oeuvres de Poinsinet* (1784).

37. Charles Palissot de Montenoy (1730–1814), enemy of the *philosophes*, flatterer of Voltaire, journalist, playwright, satirist (see fig. 23). Of pretty scabrous morality. See the French edition, pp. 205–11, especially p. 207, for the treatment of his sister.

38. Antoine Alexandre Henri Poinsinet (1735–69), known as 'little Poinsinet' (see fig. 24). He collaborated with Diderot on the libretto of the first version of Philidor's opera, *Ernelinde*, 1767, the first French 'reform' opera.

Fig. 25 Elie-Cathérine Fréron (1771), Ch.E. Gaucher, after Ch.-N. Cochin.

39. Elie-Cathérine Fréron (1718–76), journalist, enemy of the *philosophes*, most especially of Diderot and Voltaire (see fig. 25). His son, Stanislas Fréron (1754–1802), was one of the organisers of the bloody repression of the insurrections against the Revolution at Toulon in 1793, which involved large-scale summary executions (see fig. 26).

Fig. 26 L.-M.S. Fréron, *Album du Centenaire* (1889), by H. Rousseau and E. Thomas.

40. Joseph de La Porte (1713–79), journalist, gossip, an acquaintance of Diderot. It was he who related to Diderot the story of the split between Hus and Bertin (see Diderot's letter to Sophie Volland of 12 September 1761 and French edition, p. 218). For Louis Carrogis de Carmontelle's portrait of La Porte see www.wikigallery.org/wiki/painting_92775/Louis-(Carrogis)-de-Carmontelle/The-Abbe-de-La-Porte-and-the-Marquis-de-Saint-Chamans,-c.1766.html

41. *Les trois siècles de la littérature française* [*Three Centuries of French Literature*], 1772–74, by Sabatier de Castres, opponent of the *philosophes*, after having failed to gain their approval.

42. The Rameau family was from Dijon, in Burgundy.

43. The Hôtel de Soubise, Paris, now houses the Archives nationales; it had the largest stables in Paris, now the reading room (see fig. 27).

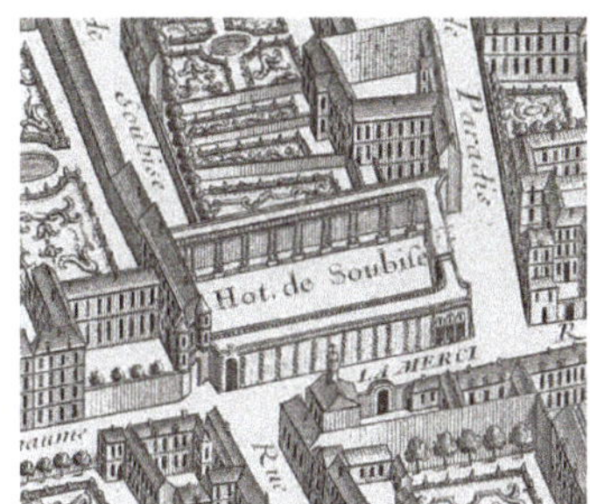

Fig. 27 The Hôtel de Soubise, detail from the *Plan de Turgot* (1734–39), by Michel-Étienne Turgot.

44. Robbé de Beauveset (1712–92), a satiric and erotic poet, known to Diderot, who liked Robbé's enthusiastic method of declaiming his verses, see Diderot, *Essais sur la peinture* [*Essays on Painting*], 1766 (Lewinter, vol. VI, p. 292).

Fig. 28 Robbé de Beauveset (1765), by Jean Baptiste II Lemoyne.

45. Mlle Adélaïde-Louise-Pauline Hus (1734?-1805), a mediocre actress of the Comédie française. She was the lover of the 'hero' of the text, Louis-Auguste Bertin de Blagny (1725–88). From 1742 Blagny occupied the office of Treasurer of the king's private funds for 'les parties casuelles', that is, the sale of public offices when they became vacant ('the casual parts' of his title). Legal and standard procedure, it was of course a major source of income for Bertin, and for the throne. He was also co-author of the libretto of the opéra comique *L'Île des fous* (see n. 192).

Fig. 29 Mlle Hus, *Galerie historique des portraits des comédiens* (1861).

46. Monsieur Viellard, lover of Mlle Hus.

47. The *Fêtes de Polymnie* is an opéra-ballet in three acts (or '*entrées*') by Jean-Philippe Rameau. The air *A la beauté tout cède sur la terre* occurs at the end of the first *entrée*, entitled *La Fable* [*Fable*], to which respond *L'Histoire* [*History* — second *entrée*] and *La Féérie* [*Fairyland* — third *entrée*].

Jean-Philippe Rameau, *Fêtes de Polymnie* [*The Festivals of Polyhymnia*], extract: Air: 'A la beauté tout cède sur la terre' [Everything on earth gives way to beauty]

To listen to this piece online scan the QR code or follow this link: http://dx.doi.org/10.11647/OBP.0044.05

Three stories and three distinct moods to celebrate the French victory at Fontenoy in the War of Austrian Succession. In this air, the music is subordinate to the text, brilliant in order to evoke the triumph of beauty, stormy in order to evoke the 'terrible God of thunder'. The piece is a rondeau in three parts. The opening is a triumphal march, in three sections separated by a kind of attack from the voice with high-pitched notes and *a cappella*, starting off a second part with more movement and resolving in a final section with strongly marked cadences.

Jean-Philippe Rameau, *Fêtes de Polymnie* [*The Festivals of Polyhymnia*], extract: Air: 'Au vain plaisir de charmer...' [To the empty pleasure of charming...]

To listen to this piece online scan the QR code or follow this link: http://dx.doi.org/10.11647/OBP.0044.06

This air occurs in the third *entrée* of the opera, *La Féérie*. It appears as a march in triple time in the key of A minor. It is made up of two parts which contrast in their key, but are in a stable tempo. The second part begins in the related key of C major, bringing a kind of luminosity to the term 'victory' before returning to A minor, with a close in cadence emphasized by a very lyrical leap of a major seventh, which projects the voice into a high register before returning to the tonic.

Jean-Philippe Rameau, *Fêtes de Polymnie* [*The Festivals of Polyhymnia*], extract: Air en rondeau: 'Hélas, est-ce assez pour charmer...' [Alas, in order to charm, is it enough...]

To listen to this piece online scan the QR code or follow this link: http://dx.doi.org/10.11647/OBP.0044.07

This air from the beginning of *La Féérie* is characterized by its vocal writing, which is very free and natural, over an accompaniment showing great stability, with many held notes; the melody is emphasized by the appoggiatura which unfolds into a short *da capo* aria, culminating on a high A sharp at the end of the middle section.

48. A similar portrait of Rameau was drawn by Charles-Germain de Saint-Aubin.

Fig. 30 *Avez vous Jamais vü le Celebre Rameau?* (c.1740–c.1775), by Charles-Germain de Saint-Aubin.

49. Mme de La Marck (1719–93, a natural death, not the guillotine), was a supporter of the opera (see David Charlton, *Opera in the Age of Rousseau*, 2012. Cambridge: Cambridge University Press). Her relation to Diderot and his friend Grimm is not well understood; she would repay further investigation (see French edition, pp. 179–80). Bergier: there were two brothers, Claude and Nicolas Sylvestre, the latter an enemy of the *philosophes*. It is probably the latter (1719–90) who is being referred to here (see fig. 31): he was author of such works as *Le Déisme réfuté par lui-même* [*Deism Disproved from its Own Arguments*], 1766, and *La Certitude des preuves du Christianisme* [*The Certainty of the Proofs of Christianity*], 1767, and attacked Diderot's friend, d'Holbach, despite frequenting his salon.

Fig. 31 Abbé Nicolas-Sylvestre Bergier (18th century), by Jacques-André-Joseph Aved (1702–66).

50. Polish-style dresses, which first came into fashion in the 1770s, had a close-fitting bodice and a large skirt which was gathered up at the back to reveal the petticoat below.

Fig. 32 A Polish-style dress (c.1777), Carl Gottlieb Guttenberg, after Jean-Michel Moreau.

51. As yet, this song is unlocated.

52.

Fig. 33 *Lulli's Opera* Armide, *performed at the Palais Royal* (1761), by Gabriel de Saint-Aubin.

53. A quotation from Virgil's *Georgics* and a joke attributed to d'Alembert when at stool (he suffered from hæmorrhoids), see French edition, p. 40, n. 88.

Fig. 34 Samuel Bernard (1729), by Pierre Imbert Drevet.

54. Samuel Bernard (1651–1739), an immensely rich financier who lent money to Louis XIV and Louis XV for their wars; he had been born a Protestant but converted when the toleration of Protestants was abolished in 1685.

55. Choir boys from orphanages in two different areas of Paris — the red boys from the Marais in the third arrondissement (see http://www.evous.fr/Histoire-du-Marche-des-Enfants,1118276.html) and the blue boys from the rue Saint-Denis in the second arrondissement (see fig. 35 and http://www.paris-pittoresque.com/rues/190.htm).

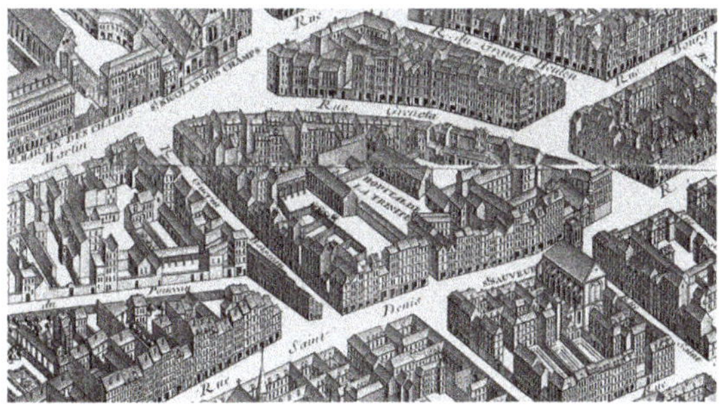

Fig. 35 Les Enfants Bleus, detail from the *Plan de Turgot* (1734–39), by Michel-Étienne Turgot.

Fig. 36 Pietro Locatelli (1733), by Cornelis Troost.

56. Pietro Antonio Locatelli (1695–1764), born in Bergamo, but established in Amsterdam (see fig. 36). Said by Grove's *Dictionary of Music and Musicians* to be the founder of modern virtuoso violin playing. See Daniel Heartz, 'Locatelli and the Pantomime of the Violinist in *Le Neveu de Rameau*', *Diderot Studies*, XXVII, 1998, pp. 115–27.

Pietro Locatelli, Sonata op. VI no. 5, extract: Aria (Vivace)

To listen to this piece online scan the QR code
or follow this link: http://dx.doi.org/10.11647/OBP.0044.08

This aria is taken from the fifth of the twelve sonatas for solo violin and chamber basso continuo dating from 1746, which make up opus VI by Pietro Antonio Locatelli. This movement follows the andante and allegro movements, and constitutes a set of four variations on the same air, made up of two musical phrases. The basso continuo remains the same throughout the air, and the solo violin offers four different versions of it, with ever increasing embellishments, first by the arrival of more rapid rhythms, then by the expanding of the range, and lastly through the intervention of a second voice which doubles the main melody at the interval of a third. This movement constitutes the final of the sonata and seems to foreshadow the classical rondeau which will take up the idea of variations on a theme.

57. *Concert spirituel*, a concert series set up in 1725 to provide music in Lent, when theatres and the Opéra were closed.

58. The name of Alberti is associated with the transition between the baroque and the classical styles, and in particular with that invention of a bass line which would become typical for the classical style.

Domenico Alberti, Sonata for the fortepiano op. I n° 5, extract: Andante — Allegro

To listen to this piece online scan the QR code or follow this link: http://dx.doi.org/10.11647/OBP.0044.09

This, known as 'Alberti bass', is found everywhere in Mozart and his contemporaries. It departs from the baroque principle of the 'continuous bass', in that it is a line of broken arpeggios. This 'Alberti bass' makes up the greater part of the accompaniment in the second movement of this sonata, and allows one single voice to accompany the melodic line, thus making possible a great freedom of development. So the second movement is written right through for two voices only, and the bass line on its own represents the combination of two or three voices, making up a single line, a feature that is highly idiomatic in music for a keyboard instrument.

Like the writing, the form of this sonata is characteristic of the pre-classical period in which Alberti was working. The first movement is made up of an exposition leading from the main key (A major) to the dominant (E major); there is then a development that leads to a restatement bringing back the main key. This movement has the main characteristics of a sonata. In his early years, Mozart had studied the scores of Alberti. He then extended these principles of composition and made them the driving force of the developments in his music, which was built on a larger scale. The second movement of this sonata, more virtuoso in style, is likewise based on the same tension in the keys, but in a simpler binary form allowing a coming and going between the tonic and the dominant (section A), and then from the dominant to the tonic (section B).

59. Baldassare Galuppi (1706–85), a Venetian composer, especially of comic opera; he collaborated with Carlo Goldoni (1707–93), a Venetian playwright who moved to Paris in 1761 to work at the Comédie italienne. Galuppi travelled widely, working in England, Russia, and for a while in Vienna; see for instance http://www.youtube.com/watch?v=fxFR_r_Wb0I.

Fig. 37 Baldassare Galuppi (1751), artist unknown.

60. See Thomas Christensen, *Rameau and Musical Thought*, pp. 200–05. Rameau's enharmonic modulatory progressions were so difficult that they were originally not singable by everyone in the cast of *Hippolyte et Aricie* at the Opéra (p. 205).

61. Van Loo's portrait of Diderot, painted in 1767, shows him as a well-dressed and apparently well-off gentleman.

Fig. 38 Denis Diderot (1767), by Louis-Michel van Loo.

62. 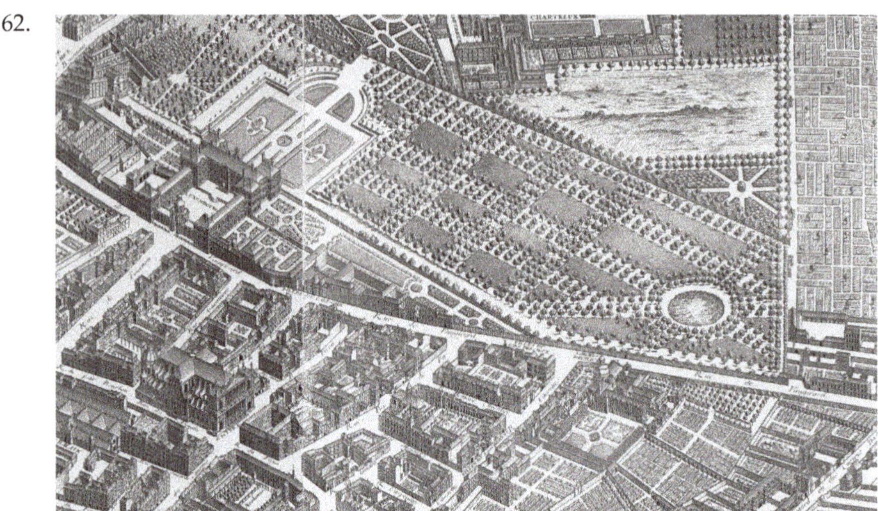

Fig. 39 The Luxembourg Gardens, detail from the *Plan de Turgot* (1734–39), by Michel-Étienne Turgot.

63. Angélique Diderot (1753–1824), sole surviving child of Diderot and his wife, Toinette Champion, and much loved.

64. Luckily, the teenage Angélique did in fact dance at balls, see her letters conserved at the Institut et musée Voltaire, Geneva. She actually went to a ball held by one of the butts of this text's satire, Bertin. Diderot, moreover, took a great deal of trouble over her musical education. This sort of discrepancy suggests we should be careful not to align 'ME' and Diderot.

65. Jean Le Rond de D'Alembert (1717–83), major mathematician (among many other important contributions to mathematics, he formulated what is now known as 'd'Alembert's principle'), co-editor of the *Encyclopédie*, littérateur, hero of Diderot's dialogue *Le Rêve de d'Alembert* [*D'Alembert's Dream*], illegitimate son of the novelist and former nun Mme de Tencin, left on the steps of the church of Saint-Jean-le-Rond (hence his name), cared for by his father, who however died young, though his family contributed to his son's upkeep; adopted by his wet-nurse, the wife of a window-maker. After he became famous, very young, his real mother is said to have made overtures, which he refused: he regarded Mme Rousseau, the woman who had adopted him, as his mother. See http://www-groups.dcs.st-and.ac.uk/history/Biographies/D%27Alembert.html.

Fig. 40 Jean Le Rond de D'Alembert (1753), by de La Tour.

66. Marie-Jeanne Lemierre (1733–86), singer at the French Opéra (Académie royale de musique) and at the *Concert spirituel*. Through marriage to the singer Henri Larrivée, she is also referred to as Mme Larrivée.

67. Sophie Arnould (1740–1802), actress, opera singer, and courtesan. Famous for her liaison with the comte de Lauraguais ('the little count').

Fig. 41 Sophie Arnould (c.1770), after Jean-Baptiste Greuze.

68. M. de Montami (1702–65), maître d'hôtel of the duc d'Orléans, who presumably lived in the Palais Royal, owned by the Orléans family. He was an industrial chemist. Diderot published his book for him posthumously: *Traité des couleurs pour la peinture en émail et sur la porcelaine* [*Treatise on Colours for Enamel Painting and on Porcelain*], 1765. Paris: G. Cavelier. A letter to Diderot's lover, Sophie Volland, recounts a visit to Montami after having failed to find her at their rendez-vous in the allée d'Argenson (letter of 12 October 1759).

Fig. 42 Pierre Louis Dubus Préville, attributed to Jean-Baptiste Massé (1687–1767).

69. Pierre-Louis Dubus Préville (1721–99) was allied with the anti-*philosophe* group at the Comédie française. He starred in a restaging of the play, *Le Mercure galant*, by Edme Boursault (1638–1701) in 1763 (source: Bibliothèque nationale de France, catalogue).

70. Mlle Dumesnil (1713–1803), actress at the Comédie française; see Virginia Scott, *Women on the Stage in Early Modern France*, 2010. Cambridge: Cambridge University Press, for an interesting account of her career. The journal *Mémoires secrets*, a kind of eighteenth-century 'celebrity mag' suggests why she doesn't know what she's doing — she was an alcoholic (see French edition, p. 229).

Fig. 43 Mlle Dumesnil: Phèdre (1770–88).

Fig. 44 Mlle Dumesnil: Agrippine (1754).

71. Jean-Baptiste Javillier came from a famous Parisian line of dancing masters; for instance he taught the comte de Cheverny, see *Mémoires sur les règnes de Louis XV et Louis XVI et sur la Révolution par J.N. Dufort, comte de Cheverny, publiés avec une introduction et des notes par Robert de Grèvecœur*, 1886.

Fig. 45 *A Rake's Progress: 2. The Levee* (1732–33), by William Hogarth.

72. C. Ernest Baron de Bagge (1718–91) — Diderot is spelling by ear — was a music lover originally from Latvia. See Georges Cucuel, *Un mélomane du XVIIIe siècle: Le Baron de Bagge et son temps (1718–1791)*, 1911. Paris: F. Alcan. Bagge was famous for the concerts given in his private house.

Fig. 46 C. Ernest Baron de Bagge (1781), by Charles-Nicolas Cochin the Younger.

73. French: *idiotisme*, which until relatively recently (1835) only referred to specific turns of phrase proper to a dialect or language, see *Encyclopédie*: 'article IDIOTISME, [...] c'est une façon de parler éloignée des usages ordinaires, ou des lois générales du langage, adaptée au génie propre d'une langue particuliere. R. ἴδιος, *peculiaris, propre, particulier*' [a way of talking removed from ordinary usage or the general laws of language, adapted to the genius proper to a particular language].

74. Bernard le Bovier de Fontenelle (1667–1767 — he died one month short of his 100th birthday), popularizer of science, writer of light verse, secretary in perpetuity of the Académie des Sciences until 1737, a head of the *modernes* in the long-running quarrel between the partisans of classical literature and those who preferred the moderns.

Fig. 47 Bernard le Bovier de Fontenelle [n.d.], by Nicolas de Largillière (1656–1746).

75. Marie-Madeleine Guimard (1743–1816), a famous ballerina and courtesan, even more famous for the luxury of her dwelling houses — one on the Chaussée d'Antin was designed by the great architect Claude Nicolas Ledoux. Diderot seems to have known her, see French edition, p. 57, n. 125, for his letter to Sophie Volland of 22 November 1768.

Fig. 48 Marie-Madeleine Guimard [n.d.], artist unknown.

76. According to Jean Fabre in his great edition (*Le neveu de Rameau*, 1950. Geneva: Droz, p. 177), Anne Marie Pagès, called la Deschamps (1730–75?), courtesan, dancer and a famous spendthrift; Fabre refers to Diderot's letter of 26 October 1760: 'la Deschamps, who is barely thirty years old and who boasts that she has already spent her way through two millions' (Lewinter, vol. IV, p. 937). Lewinter points out that the sale of her furniture (9 April 1760) to pay her debts caused so much interest that there was nearly a riot.

Fig. 49 *Casseuse de Porcelaine, chez le Fermier Général de Vilm... (1753?1764?)* [*The Smasher of China at the house of the tax farmer de Vilm[orien]?... or la Deschamps, a famous courtesan (1753?-1764?)*], by Charles-Germain de Saint-Aubin.

77. Philippe Charles Le Gendre de Villemorien (1717–89), son-in-law of the financier Bouret. It was Villemorien's wife who in 1753 helped Diderot, by means of bribery, to keep an office connected with the distribution of tobacco in the family of his future son-in-law (see French edition, p. 203).

78. Georges Louis Leclerc, comte de Buffon (1707–88), important naturalist, became superintendant of the Jardin Royal (still to be visited in Paris as the Jardin des plantes). His work as a naturalist was more important because of the collections he assembled for the king, and because of his publication of the *Histoire naturelle*, 1749–1804, a work of synthesis written with collaborators, than for his own discoveries. The exception to this is his first article, on mathematical probability. He was famous in his lifetime for his style, and was already criticized for being too ponderous. Ironically enough, he is today principally famous, among a non-specialist French public, for his 'Discourse on Style'.

Fig. 50 Georges Louis Leclerc, comte de Buffon (1753), by François-Hubert Drouais.

79. Charles-Louis de Secondat, baron de la Brède et de Montesquieu (1689–1755), author of *De l'esprit des lois* [*On the Spirit of the Laws*], 1748. Diderot was the only man of letters to follow Montesquieu's coffin at his funeral in 1755, according to Rousseau, who himself was ill at the time. Montesquieu and Voltaire, both distinguished elders, in that they belonged to the preceding generation, contributed to the *Encyclopédie*, mostly on the relatively neutral subject of aesthetics, and probably as a sign of support.

Fig. 51 Montesquieu (1728), artist unknown.

80. An urge felt by Diderot on occasions: see his letter to Sophie Volland, 31 August 1760.

81. Diderot is parodying the Old Testament here, *Ecclesiastes*, I, v.2.

82. *Mahomet*, by Voltaire is a plea for toleration, under cover of an attack on fanaticism. In the play, the fanaticism is Mahomet's; Voltaire made it clear elsewhere, however, that it is any fanaticism that is at stake, and at the time, this meant Christian fanaticism. France was after all a Christian country, and intolerance shown there was Catholic intolerance. Contemporary readers were

quite used to reading 'Christian' where the text said 'Muslim', and had little doubt that it was the institution of Christianity that Voltaire was attacking.

83. Jean Calas, a Protestant, was tortured to death by order of the Parlement of Toulouse in 1763, in order to extract a confession to the murder of his son. This confession was not forthcoming, and the case against Calas collapsed. Voltaire had begun by believing him guilty, and had inveighed against Protestant bigotry. However when he met Calas's family, who had fled, he became convinced of his innocence. He conducted a Europe-wide campaign to clear Calas's name, and succeeded. Calas was rehabilitated in 1765. Voltaire wrote an influential *Traité de la tolérance* on the basis of the case.

Fig. 52 *Les adieux de Calas à sa famille* [n.d.], by Daniel Chodowiecki (1726–1801).

84. Probably to become a merchant in Cartagena, in what is now Colombia.

85. Jacques Rochette, chevalier de La Morlière (1719–85), a novelist who is still sometimes in print (*Angola, histoire indienne,* 1746); contemporary accounts are very like the description Diderot gives through the mouth of 'HIM' (for further information, see French edition, p. 67, n. 142).

86. A famous pornographic novel, published in 1741. The author is not known with certainty, but it is often attributed to Jean-Charles Gervaise de La Touche (1715–82).

Fig. 53 Frontispiece from Jacques Rochette de La Morlière, *Contes du chevalier de la Morlière — Angola* (1879).

87. *I Modi*, 1524, by Pietro Aretino, a pornographic classic written to accompany paintings by Julio Romano, engraved by Raimondi, then by Agostino Carracci.

88. The two Catos, 'the censor' and 'the younger' were famed for their austere morals.

89. The whole question of freedom here, of finding a kind of freedom to be abject, asserted against social circumstances which insist on abjection, is one of the elements which fascinated Hegel, see G.W.F. Hegel, *The Phenomenology of Spirit*, trans. A.V. Miller, with analysis of the text and foreword by J.N. Findlay, 1977. Oxford: Oxford University Press. The paragraph numbers cited below refer to this translation.

90. Father Noël, a Benedictine monk, in favour with Louis XV because of the optical lenses he fashioned. See French edition, p. 70, n. 50.

91. French: *Pagode*. The Nephew refers here to a porcelain figure, known as a 'pagoda', which was popular in the eighteenth century (see fig. 54).

Fig. 54 Seated figure (c.1715), Meissen Porcelain.

Fig. 55 Mme Bouvillon (early 18th century), by Jean-Baptiste Pater (1695–1736).

92. Madame Bouvillon (see fig. 55), a personage from Scarron's novel, the *Roman comique* (1651–57).

93. One of the key ideas in Diderot's materialism of the 1770s.

94. François Thomas Marie Baculard d'Arnaud (1718–1805), an acquaintance of Diderot from the early 1740s, when they both inhabited Grub Street. See French edition, pp. 221–22.

95. Stentor, a herald of the Greek army in the Trojan War. A classical reference in a low-market context — a typical satirical procedure.

96. The Nephew discusses his performance as parasite as belonging to one of the fine arts, see Lucian, 2nd century AD satirist: 'On Parasites' and especially 'On salaried posts in great houses, or the dependent scholar'. See *The Works of Lucian of Samosata: Complete with Exceptions Specified in the Preface*, trans. H.W. Fowler and F.G. Fowler, 1905. Oxford: Clarendon Press. It is from this that the 'in Praise of flattery' is sometimes said to come.

97. Etienne Michel Bouret (1709–77), the son of a *laquais*, he was a tax farmer (see n. 257) from 1741, and for much of his life immensely rich, lending money to the king, famous in the popular press for his talent for flattery. Diderot owed him favours. See French edition pp. 202–04.

98. French: *Garde des Sceaux*. The names of the holders of the office in this period were: Berryer (1761–62), secretary of state for the navy and lieutenant of police, Diderot knew him; Feydeau de Brou (1763–68); Maupeou (1768–74) who united the office of Keeper of the Seals with that of Chancellor, before being replaced by Miromesnil in both offices. With thanks to Dr Michael Sonnenscher, King's College, Cambridge.

99. In Lacour's portrait, Maupeou is depicted wearing the costume of the Keeper of the Seals (see fig. 56).

100. French: *la gimblette*, the name of a little ring-shaped biscuit. In one version of Fragonard's painting, *la gimblette* obviously refers to the girl's vagina as well as to the biscuit she is offering her dog (see fig. 57).

Fig. 56 Maupeou in the costume of the Keeper of the Seals (18th century), by Pierre Lacour.

Fig. 57 *La Gimblette* (1770–75), by Jean-Honoré Fragonard.

Fig. 58 A French nobleman wearing the Cross of Saint-Louis (1756), by Jean-Marc Nattier.

101. A military decoration founded by Louis XIV in 1693, the first that could be awarded to non-nobles (see fig. 58).

102. Turenne (1611–75), marshal of France, perhaps the most famous (and talented) French general before Napoleon (see fig. 59). He took part in the Fronde (a small-scale civil war between 1648 and 1653), first on the side of the insurrectionary nobles then on the side of the King.

103. Sébastien Le Prestre de Vauban, general and marshal of France, like Turenne, fighting on both sides in the Fronde (see fig. 60). He is principally known for his system of constructing near-impregnable fortresses. Also for his attempt to relieve the poor, among whom he had lived as an orphaned child. He formulated a method of reforming the French tax system, *Projet d'une dixième royale* [*Project for the Royal Tax of a Tenth*], 1707.

Fig. 59 Turenne (1837), by Charles-Philippe Larivière.

Fig. 60 Sébastien Le Prestre de Vauban (after 1703), by Hyacinthe Rigaud (1649–1743).

104. The Marquise de Tencin (1682–1749) (natural mother of d'Alembert, and a successful novelist), her brother the Cardinal and his secretary, the Abbé Trublet (for whom see above n. 28). A descent into bathos, from great generals to a secretary and cleric, who was an object of scornful fun.

Fig. 61 Claudine Guérin de Tencin [n.d.], artist unknown.

105. Mlle Anne-Marie Botot Dangeville (1714–96), a famous comic actress of the Comédie française (see fig. 62).

106. An accurate account of their relative popularity, it seems — the Comédie française was always full if Clairon was acting that night, see French edition, p. 231.

107. Persius, prologue to his *Satires* (*Choliambes*, tr. Rudd, in *Horace, Saitres and Epistles; Persius, Satires*). The line has been completed here.

Fig. 62 Mlle Dangeville (18th century), by de La Tour (1704–88).

108. Palissot's first tragedy, taken on at the Comédie française in 1751 through influence, and a failure. The name is mangled, no doubt deliberately: it should be *Zarès*.

109. Antoine Bret (1718–1805), like Baculard, was an acquaintance from Diderot's past, all three formerly the recipients of police attention.

110. Monsauge and Villemorien, the sons-in-law of Bertin, both held highly lucrative offices, the first a *Maître des postes*, the second also a tax farmer (see n. 257). Monsauge's name appears as a member of the *surintendance des Postes*, the group of notables at the top of the system of renting horses for travel and for the letter post. He was responsible for the east of France. The tax farm or *ferme* included others, among them his brother-in-law, Legendre de Villemorien, and Bouret.

111. Jean-Jacques Rousseau (1712–78), important philosopher, writer and composer; formerly, a close friend of Diderot's — they quarrel definitively in 1757.

Fig. 63 Jean-Jacques Rousseau (third quarter of the 18th century), by de La Tour.

112. A pastiche of a line from Molière, *Les Femmes savantes* [*The Learned Ladies*], Act III, sc. 2: 'Nul n'aura de l'esprit, hors nous et nos amis' [None shall have wit, save us and our friends].

113. The satirical play by Palissot, *Les Philosophes*, may have been the first impetus for Diderot's dialogue. Palissot is said to have been given permission in 1760 for it to be represented at the Comédie française as a reward for writing a pamphlet against France's enemy, Frederick II of Prussia (see fig. 64). A fellow, and much better, playwright, Charles Collé (1709–83), thought that it had actually been ordered by the government. It was acted at the Comédie française in spite of Mlle Clairon's opposition. In it, Rousseau, that defender of natural man, was shown coming on on all fours, munching a lettuce, and Diderot was presented as a confidence trickster. The actress playing the part meant to indicate Mme Geoffrin, a patron of the *philosophes*, actually dressed like her. It was extremely successful in its first run, but even then, the treatment of the *philosophe* Helvétius shocked, because everyone knew the latter had helped Palissot pay his doctor's bills. Its plot is a reworking of Molière's *Les Femmes savantes*.

Fig. 64 Frederick II of Prussia (1781), by Anton Graff.

114. *La Théologie en quenouille* [*Theology in Petticoats*], a play by le père Guillaume-Hyacinthe Bougeant (1690–1743), printed in 1731 but never acted, which attacked the Jansenists.

115. Abbé Jean-Bernard Leblanc (1707–81), a protégé of Madame de Pompadour, who, with the engraver Cochin, accompanied her brother the Marquis de Marigny on the tour of Italy which was to prepare him for his duties as Director of the King's Buildings. She couldn't get Leblanc into the Académie française, but she did obtain for him the post of Historiographer of the King's Buildings. See the story told later by 'HIM'.

Fig. 65 Abbé Jean-Bernard Leblanc (18th century), by de La Tour (1704–88).

116. Abbé Charles Batteux (1713–80). Diderot had already attacked Batteux, in his *Lettre sur les sourds et muets* [*Letter on the Deaf and Dumb*], 1751, for his *Les beaux-arts réduits à un meme principe* [*The Fine Arts Reduced to a Single Principle*], 1746, which is indeed much inferior to his later *Cours de belles lettres* [*Lessons on Literature*], 1765. Batteux is somewhat mysterious: in his relation to Diderot, who seems to have known him, and in his choice of classical texts for translation and commentary.

117. Alexis Piron (1688–1773), poet and playwright. His play *La métromanie* [*Mad about Metre*], 1738, was one of the best comedies of the century.

Fig. 66 Alexis Piron (1775), by Augustin de Saint-Aubin.

118. The Convulsionaries, a group of Jansenists who opposed the papal bull *Unigenitus*, which clamped down on the sect; some of them went into trances in the churchyard of Saint-Médard, in a poor area of Paris. Diderot must have witnessed these, since he lived fairly close by, in the rue de la vieille Estrapade. The Jansenists also claimed miraculous cures. Neither Church nor different governments liked this mixture of poverty and inspired, unorthodox religion, which seemed too close to an insurrectional ideology.

Fig. 67 Claude-Henri de Fusée de Voisenon (1760), by Louis Carrogis de Carmontelle.

119. Usually, and plausibly, identified as the Abbé de Voisenon (1708–75). See French edition p. 86, n. 189.

120. Corbi and Moette followed Monnet as directors of the theatres at the Fairs. The Fair theatres were among the principal sites of the development of native French comic opera, see Charlton, *Opera in the Age of Rousseau*.

121. *L'Avant-Coureur* (1760–73), a weekly journal; its first editor Meusnier de Querlon was also a writer of salacious novels.

122. *Les Petites Affiches*, a journal consisting mostly of announcements about the theatre and spectacles.

123. *L'Année littéraire* (1754–76), a journal begun by Elie Fréron, continuing *Lettres sur quelques écrits de ce temps* (1749–54), and continued by his son, Stanislas. Fréron the elder was imprisoned several times for publishing matter which the government didn't wish put about.

124. *L'Observateur littéraire* (1758–61), editor abbé Joseph de La Porte, an acquaintance of Diderot. La Porte defended Diderot's play *Le Fils naturel*, 1757, the subject of much ridicule from the groups around Palissot.

125. *Le Censeur hebdomadaire* (1759–62), started by d'Acquin and Abraham Chaumeix, it was originally anti-*philosophe*; it toned down its later numbers.

126. Abbé de La Porte.

127. Moreau illustrated a lavish dinner of the sort described here in his painting of the inaugural feast held on the 2 September 1771 at Louveciennes [the house of Madame Du Barry, reigning mistress of Louis XV] in the presence of the King.

Fig. 68 Feast given at Louveciennes (1771), by Jean-Michel Moreau.

128. Claude-Joseph Dorat (1734–80), dramatist, poet of 'elegant nothings', producing magnificent editions of his own poems at his own expense on royal occasions; he seems to have plagiarized Diderot. See Manuel Couvreur, 'Diderot et Philidor: le philosophe au chevet d'*Ernelinde*', *Recherches sur Diderot et sur l'Encyclopédie*, XI, 1991, p. 85.

129. 'I am always sitting like a mighty cock between two balls'.

130. French: *Messer Gaster*, a reference to a character in Rabelais's *Quart Livre* [*Fourth Book*], 1552.

Fig. 69 Claude-Joseph Dorat (left) (1764), by Charles Eisen.

131. Allusion to Homer's *Iliad*, Book 1.

132. The emblem of Melancholy is sometimes portrayed in a similar way.

Fig. 70 *Melancholia I* (c.1514), by Albrecht Dürer.

133. French: *pacte*, one can wonder whether Diderot isn't referring surreptitiously to Rousseau's *Contrat social*, where the word appears first as the title of Chapter VI.

134. Brun is not identified with certainty. He is possibly the poetaster nicknamed 'Le Brun-Pindare', who certainly was acquainted with Palissot, see his *Lettre de M. Le Brun à l'auteur de la Dunciade* [*Letter from M. Le Brun to the Author of the 'Dunciade'*] [i.e. Palissot], which was published in *La Dunciade, poème en dix chants* [*The Dunciade, A Poem in Ten Cantos*], 2 vols. 1771. London.

135. Abbé Rey is not identified with certainty. He is possibly the author of *Considérations philosophiques sur le christianisme*, 1785.

136. Michel-Antoine David, one of the editors in the group who published the *Encyclopédie*. He was a guarantor at the marriage of Diderot's daughter in 1772.

137. See above n. 113.

138. Palissot had indeed persuaded the naïve Poinsinet that the King of Prussia would nominate him as governor of his children, if he converted to Protestantism. Poinsinet did so in a ceremony invented and performed by Fréron and Palissot. He seems to have been the butt of a deliberate campaign of practical jokes, both cruel and mocking. He wrote libretti for comic operas, the genre which is one of the main thematic threads of *Rameau's Nephew*.

139. In his play *L'Homme dangereux* [*The Dangerous Man*], 1770; he added the word to the title in 1778: *Le satirique ou l'homme dangereux* [*The Satirist, or the Dangerous Man*].

140. The comtesse de la Marck, see n. 49.

141. The French is *espèce*, species. It is the word that caught the attention of Hegel, in his *Phenomenology of Spirit*, no doubt because Goethe had left it in French in his translation into German. Rightly, because one of the unthematized but powerful threads in *Rameau's Nephew* seems to be the question of groups, social or natural. Again and again lists in the dialogue seem to create groups, of characteristics, of trades, even of actions.

142. Rameau's Nephew has turned his patrons into a kind of latinized animal specimen by joining up their names (see fig. 71).

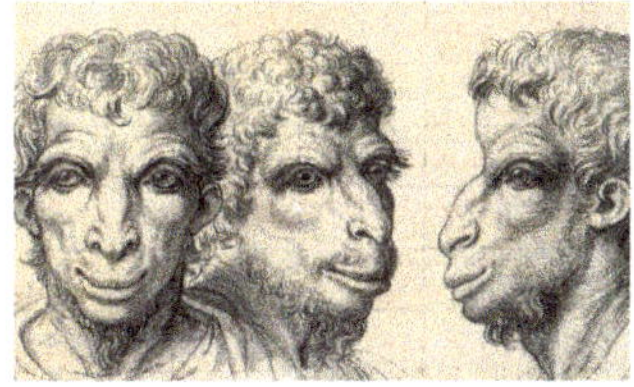

Fig. 71 *Physiognomic heads inspired by a camel* (c.1670), by Charles Le Brun.

143. The Nephew has appointed himself and his like to be the punishment in this

world of Bertin and his like; the Nephew, like Doctor Bordeu in the third part of *Le Rêve de d'Alembert*, and like a fragment from a manuscript (cited by the Diderot scholar Pierre Hermand, †1916), proposes a kind of naturalistic moral order: if not the law, then nature will punish wrong-doing or excess. The Nephew gives the likes of 'ME' the task of punishing those who have taken advantage of and thus punished the stupidity of the likes of Bertinhus. For 'ME' and his like will paint this chain of predator and predated as they are.

144. 'HIM', like Diderot at various other points in his writings, breaks apart the assimilation between the good and the beautiful. Some philosophers in the eighteenth century, and in many ways the general public, were inclined to treat them as equivalent.

145. See Morris Wachs, 'The identity of the "Renégat d'Avignon" in the *Neveu de Rameau*', *Studies on Voltaire and the Eighteenth Century*, 90, 1972, pp. 1747–56. Avignon was in fact a place of relative safety for Jews in eighteenth-century France; the events of this story seem rather to have occurred in Lisbon.

146. Diderot makes a similar claim in *Le Rêve de d'Alembert*, see *Rameau's Nephew and D'Alembert's Dream*, trans. Leonard Tancock, 1966. London: Penguin, pp. 212–13.

147. Here, as in his writing on the art of the actor, Diderot is interested in the relation between acting and exaggerating. See *Paradoxe sur le comédien*, probably completed in c.1772–c.1773.

148. 'Sanbenito', a sort of yellow-coloured tunic favoured by the Inquisition.

Fig. 72 *The Inquisition Trial* (1812–19), by Francisco Goya.

149. French: *Auto-da-fé*; literally 'act of faith'. The execution of heretics by burning was so called, apparently without irony. The last one at Lisbon seems to have taken place in 1739. See the ferocious denunciation by Montesquieu, *De l'esprit*

des lois, book XXV, ch. 13, 'Very humble remonstration to the inquisitors of Spain and Portugal', which begins: 'A Jewess aged eighteen, burned at Lisbon in the last auto-da-fé', and ends with a condemnation and furious warning 'if someone at future times ever dares say that the European peoples were civilized in the century we are living in, you will be cited to prove that they were barbarous'.

150. Hegel, using Goethe's translation into German of 1805 (see Preface), refers closely in his *Phenomenology of Spirit* to the dialogue from this point on. The extended nature of Hegel's commentary has not been generally recognized — it goes well beyond the passages from Diderot's dialogue that Hegel actually quotes.

151. Egidio Duni (1708–75), was personally known to Diderot, indeed he introduced Goldoni to him, at Goldoni's request. He had been recruited while in Parma to provide an opéra comique, on words by Anseaume, *Le Peintre amoureux de son modèle* [*The Painter in Love with his Model*]. Duni came to Paris for its première at the Saint-Laurent Fair in 1757, and as a result of its success stayed to work on other opéras comiques. Like many Italian composers of opéras comiques Duni had been trained at Naples.

Fig. 73 Egidio Duni (c.1760), by Louis Carrogis de Carmontelle.

152. Daniel Heartz, who has done so much to give context and interpretation to *Rameau's Nephew*, uses this phrase to underline the swing to a new kind of opera being developed in Paris (see D. Heartz, *Music in European Capitals: The Galant Style 1720–1780*, 2003. New York and London: W.W. Norton and Company; ed. John Rice, *From Garrick to Gluck: Essays on Opera in the Age of Enlightenment*, 2004. New York: Pendragon Press (Opera series no. 1)).

153. Throughout his life, Diderot was interested in the relation between the word and the sense we give it — see, for instance, *Lettre sur les sourds et muets.*

154. There is a real problem of interpretation here. It was precisely Diderot, in *Lettre sur les sourds et muets*, who among European critics insisted most clearly that the arts cannot be aligned, though they can be compared. His work attracted the sustained attention of Gotthold Ephraim Lessing (1729–81) (see *Laocoon, Essay on the Limits of Painting and Poetry*, 1766) and also of Johann Georg

Hamann (1730–88). But one cannot say Diderot's work has received the study it deserves. This also poses the problem: What does this mean for *Rameau's Nephew*? Had Diderot changed his mind? Does it mean that we are no more to follow Rameau's Nephew in his ideas on music, than we are in morals?

155. The Nephew is puzzling here: he seems to refer to Hogarth's 'serpentine line' (Diderot knew *The Analysis of Beauty. Written with a View of Fixing the Fluctuating Ideas of Taste,* 1753). And yet Diderot has altered the sense from the logo on the title page, and from Hogarth's actual words. He makes of it a kind of mathematical figure, of a serpentine line approximating but never equal to a straight line.

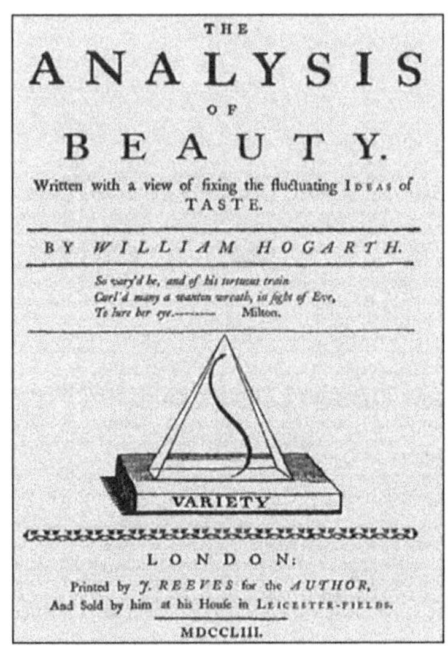

THE
ANALYSIS
OF
BEAUTY.
Written with a view of fixing the fluctuating Ideas of TASTE.

BY WILLIAM HOGARTH.

So vary'd he, and of his tortuous train
Curl'd many a wanton wreath, in sight of Eve,
To lure her eye.—— Milton.

VARIETY

LONDON:
Printed by J. REEVES for the AUTHOR,
And Sold by him at his House in LEICESTER-FIELDS.
MDCCLIII.

Fig. 74 Frontispiece of William Hogarth, *The Analysis of Beauty* (1753).

156. *O terre, reçois mon trésor*: it is possible that Diderot is citing Bertin here. He, together with Anseaume and Marcouville was the author of this *comédie mêlée d'ariettes* (an 'ariette' is a light air which breaks off the thread of the plot to give a character the possibility of expressing a feeling — see n. 193 below). What is more to the purpose is that the libretto is a 'parodie', that is, words written to an already existing score.

157. *Le Maréchal-ferrant,* an opéra comique with libretto by Quétant, performed at the Saint-Laurent Fair in 1761. For excerpts from this work, see: https://www.youtube.com/watch?v=ROQhqBo8_EA (*Oui, je suis expert*), https://www.youtube.com/watch?v=L9wuqFTtbyM (*Brillant dans mon emploi*), https://www.youtube.com/watch?v=50B98nuThfc (*Trio des ânes*). The implication is that art and reality cannot be distinguished. This is something against which Diderot argues in a much more subtle way in his dialogue *Le Paradoxe sur le comédien,* which was probably written at more or less the same time, so that once more the question arises of how much faith to put in 'HIS' aesthetics.

158. Pierre-Jean-Baptiste Nougaret, *Art du théâtre, où il est parlé des différents genres de spectacles et de la musique adaptée au théâtre* [*The Art of the Theatre, Where are Discussed Different Kinds of Spectacle, and the Music Which is Adapted for the Theatre*], 2 vols. 1769. Paris: Cailleau, satirically and backhandedly praises the opéra comique for its treatment of the ordinary, especially ordinary trades and professions. The irony in the work has not always been recognized by modern critics. The Nephew appears to be taking quite another approach.

159. 'HIM' could have read the same phrase in Diderot's writings, given that the latter quotes the same phrase in the major piece of art criticism, *The Salon of 1767*, in Lewinter, vol. VII, p. 170, but also in a magnificent letter to Grimm about language and the sound of language: 'The quantity of words is limited; that of accents is infinite. Thus it is that each person has his own individual language, and speaks as he feels; it is him, and is only him', Lewinter, vol. VII, p. 799.

160. According to Charles Burney, who knew Diderot, recitative is free of the time signature when the accompanist merely gives the chord for the song; when the recitative is accompanied, it must have a regular tempo (see the article 'Récitatif' in Michel Noiray, *Vocabulaire de la musique de l'Epoque classique*, 2005. Paris: Minerve).

161. The rules of the Académie royale de musique provided that if a modern opera should fail, it should be replaced by one of Lulli's.

162. André Campra (1660–1744), especially known for *Europe galante*, 1679, an opéra-ballet.

163. Philippe Néricault-Destouches (1680–1754, libretto) and Jean-Joseph Mouret (1682–1738, music), collaborated on *Les Amours de Ragonde* [*The Loves of Ragonde*], a comédie-ballet. See https://www.youtube.com/watch?v=IjhD0hURdOY.

164. The Nephew is imitating the foundational notes in Rameau's chordal harmony.

165. Giovanni Battista Pergolesi (1710–36), his music made a huge impression in Paris (see fig. 75). His *Stabat Mater* was first sung at the *Concert spirituel* in 1753, and remained in the repertory for a long time.

Giovanni Battista Pergolesi, *Stabat Mater*, extract, transcribed for solo violin by Johan Helmich Roman.

To listen to this piece online scan the QR code or follow this link: http://dx.doi.org/10.11647/OBP.0044.10

More than any other age, transcription played a hugely important role in the eighteenth century, allowing interpreters to make the repertoire their own. Johan Helmich Roman, a descendant of a family of musicians attached to the royal house of Sweden, came to court in 1711, at the age of 17, as a violinist and oboist. He divided his time between his Court duties — he became Deputy Master for the Swedish Royal Chapel in 1721 — and his several journeys in Europe, and strove to make the foreign repertoire known in his native country.

As well as the original works which he wrote down and translated tirelessly in order to make them accessible to his fellow countrymen, he also did a great deal of transcription. Technically very difficult, his reworking of Pergolesi's famous *Stabat Master* for the solo violin is remarkable proof of his skill in transcription and also of his mastery of the violin.

Fig. 75 Giovanni Battista Pergolesi [n.d.], artist unknown.

166. Pergolesi's *Serva padrona* played a major part in the success enjoyed by the Italian troupe, or *Buffoni,* whose visit to Paris in 1752–53 sparked off a furious public quarrel, the *Querelle des Bouffons,* around the respective value of Italian and French music. See https://www.youtube.com/watch?v=NsUeywPFEgQ. The *Buffoni* were interpreted as threatening the hegemony of French opera seria. To compare serious and comic opera was to compare the incomparable; however, the Italian works used a music which was indeed very different from the French musical tradition associated with the Académie royale de musique. It emphasized melody and supple musical transitions, whereas French opera seria tended, in the case of Rameau at any rate, towards bold harmonic constructions. This quarrel indicates a real swing in public taste, for in fact this was not the first visit of such a troupe — one had visited in 1746, creating nothing like the storm that erupted in 1752. Rousseau added fuel to the flames by publishing his *Lettre sur la musique française* [*Letter on French Music*] whose last phrase reads: 'the French have no music and are unable to have one; or, if they should ever have one, that's just too bad for them'. Rousseau claimed that this social crisis around opera staved off a political crisis: see Rousseau, 'Confessions', *Œuvres complètes,* vol. I, pp. 384–85. For an assessment of this rather self-regarding claim, see Heartz, ed. Rice, *From Garrick to Gluck,* p. 223.

167. For *Tracollo* see http://www.youtube.com/watch?v=u9VpiCjiSSU.

168. *Tancrède,* 1702, *tragédie en musique* by André Campra (1660–1744). See http://www.youtube.com/watch?v=qukSyIvBmUU (Overture).

169. *Issé,* 1697, pastorale héroïque by André Cardinal-Destouches. See http://www.youtube.com/watch?v=8D6zoQ2poHM.

170. *Europe galante,* 1697, opéra-ballet by Campra. See http://www.youtube.com/watch?v=B58U3fu2oO4&list=PLC61043D2097E3FDE (entrée *La Turquie*).

171. *Les Indes* [*galantes*], 1735, ballet héroïque by Rameau. See http://www.youtube.com/watch?v=3zegtH-acXE.

172. *Castor* [*et Pollux*], 1737, tragédie lyrique by Rameau. See http://www.youtube.com/watch?v=rSKe5WTVR0g&index=10&list=PL2TaO4x8VJQxc4srbA-XHIexb03lAcmWa.

173. *Les Talents lyriques ou les fêtes de Hébé*, 1739, opéra-ballet by Rameau. See http://www.youtube.com/watch?v=w32WVmyzs8U.

174. *Armide*, 1686, tragédie en musique by Lulli. See http://www.youtube.com/watch?v=HWIaanFmhYY (Overture).

175. Rebel and Francœur, known as the 'petits violons' [little violins], directed the Opéra. Heartz says that they were 'lacklustre' as directors (ed. Rice, *From Garrick to Gluck*); David Charlton (*Opera in the Age of Rousseau*) makes a case for their work being more innovative. The music by François Rebel is difficult to separate from that of his colleague, François Francœur (1698–1787) with whom he was constantly associated; we have recorded work by Rebel père (Jean-Féry Rebel, 1666–1747), whose music has been more influential, inasmuch as musicians still remember and sometimes record one or two other pieces, especially 'Les Éléments' and the 'Caractères de la danse', but would perhaps not do the same for François (though he did issue two sets of sonatas).

Jean-Féry Rebel, Pieces for the violin, divided into suites by keys, extracts: First suite in G-sol-ré: Allemande

To listen to this piece online scan the QR code
or follow this link: http://dx.doi.org/10.11647/OBP.0044.11

Jean-Féry Rebel, Pieces for the violin, divided into suites by keys, extracts: First suite in G-sol-ré: Prelude

To listen to this piece online scan the QR code
or follow this link: http://dx.doi.org/10.11647/OBP.0044.12

The first of these pieces for the violin by Rebel is a French suite. In a very classical manner it is made up of a prelude, allemande, courante, sarabande, gig in the form of a rondeau, chaconne and a bourrée, also in the form of a rondeau. The suite is written for violin and basso and following the principle of the collection, explores a tonal universe, that of the neighbouring keys of G and D major. The function of the prelude is to introduce this tonal universe, stressing it from the very first bars by the chords of G and D major. The first phrase is then picked up in the key of D major before returning to the principal key after a short development of the principal melodic and rhythmic figures from the prelude. The allemande is a dance in two with moderate tempo, but one that permits great virtuosity in the playing of the violin over a simple basso continuo; composed of two sections with repeats, it is well balanced between the keys of G and D major.

176.

Fig. 76 Performance of *Athalie* at the Opéra Royal de Versailles (1770), by Jean-Michel Moreau.

177. Duni's opera, staged in 1757 at the Saint-Laurent Fair, was a huge success. For a recreation of the pantomime see http://www.dailymotion.com/video/x10l840_acte-pantomime-tire-du-peintre-amoureux-de-son-modele-ballet-pantomime-de-m-ferrere-1782_creation.

178. The Opéra was at the end of a cul-de-sac at the north end of the Palais Royal.

179. See Collé, *Journal et mémoires*, ed. H. Bonhomme, nouvelle édition, 3 vols. 1868. Paris: Firmin Didot, vol. II, p. 33, for July 1755. Collé complains that a comic opera by André Cardinal Destouches and de La Motte has no success when revived because 'Rameau's music, Italian music have changed people's ears'. This was one of the spurs to Hegel's reflection on cultural change in this part of *Rameau's Nephew* — for Diderot clearly discusses the way in which an artistic past is carried over into a different artistic present, and Hegel by his very

choice of quotations shows he recognizes the relation of this understanding of cultural change to music.

180. As discussed in n. 166 above, the *Querelle des Bouffons*, 1752, was followed almost immediately by Rousseau's attack on French music for its lack of musicality, owing to its relation to a language, French, naturally unmusical when spoken. Diderot here is more interested in the relation between a nation's music and the sound of its language than in the quality of the sound involved.

181. Other commentators on music make a similar point, see M. Hobson, *The Object of Art*, 1982, 2009. Cambridge: Cambridge University Press, Part V. But Diderot's awareness of cycles of historical change here is somewhat different, in that they are put forward as successive not as repetitive. They develop out of a process of opposition. One can see why Hegel was interested — his quotations, with one exception, all come from this section of the dialogue.

182. A satire on the limited number and type of words, which return again and again in the libretti of Rameau's operas. Diderot had already criticized the stereotyped nature of libretti of French opera in *Entretiens sur 'le Fils naturel'*, [*Conversations on 'The Natural Son'*], 1757.

183. The phrase seems to have been a common refrain in a variety of popular poems. It probably derives ultimately from a popular song or songs.

184. 

Jean-Joseph Mouret, *Les Amours de Ragonde, ou la soirée de village* [*The Loves of Ragonde*, subtitled *An Evening in the Village*], extract: Bourrées I-II

To listen to this piece online scan the QR code
or follow this link: http://dx.doi.org/10.11647/OBP.0044.13

Les Amours de Ragonde is an opera by Jean-Joseph Mouret. This work, which dates from 1714, was rediscovered by Rousseau and Rameau at the beginning of the 1740s. It is a comic opera, written in the manner of a pastiche of the great operas of Lulli, and parodying the music and the manner of speech of peasants. This scene is a concentration of the spirit of the opera: the bourrée, a peasant dance par excellence, is defined both by its catchy rhythm and by its somewhat heavy bass — this last is the village lads' dance, as they come on stage. This dance is composed of two parts, each divided into two phrases, in the manner of a popular song. Each phrase is played a first time by the oboe, and is then taken up by the violins, creating an effect typical of popular music, where one theme is stated first by an instrument or by a voice before being picked up by the ensemble. The writing of this piece is characteristic of the first years of the eighteenth century, notably in its use of a long sequence at the beginning of the second bourrée, derived from more sophisticated music and sticking out from the rest of the piece, which otherwise stays in a decidedly peasant style.

Jean-Joseph Mouret, *Les Amours de Ragonde, ou la soirée de village* [*The Loves of Ragonde,* subtitled *An Evening in the Village*], extract:
Air: 'Accourez, jeunes garçons' [Come running, young men]

To listen to this piece online scan the QR code
or follow this link: http://dx.doi.org/10.11647/OBP.0044.14

In fact this extract, from the same opera by Mouret, comes just before the bourrée. In this air, Mathurine calls on the young men to come and 'frolic and laugh'. 'Come running, young men, join in our songs. Come and frolic, come and laugh; let pleasure be your guide and your leader, follow no other lessons, the simple goods we enjoy must suffice for our desires'. The words indicate the tone of the air, simple and playful. The structure of the air is twofold. After a brief introduction emphasizing the key of E major, the first part of the air, which is played twice over, is completed by a second, slower part, starting in the key of A major but coming back to the main key. In the cycle of fifths, the passage from E major to A major provokes the sense of descent, which itself in turn emphasizes the more restrained character of these bars, and permits a more striking return to the original key.

185. *Platée,* a ballet bouffon with music by Rameau, produced as part of the Dauphin's wedding festivities at court in 1745. The opera tells the story of the belief nourished by the queen of the frogs, Platée, that Jupiter the king of the gods is in love with her. See https://www.youtube.com/watch?v=xbHsmr2YoBI (production by the Opéra National de Paris, in two parts). The story is thought to refer to the arrival and marriage at court of the Spanish Infanta, who was found to be ugly. If so, one hopes she didn't understand the undercurrent of public mockery in the entertainment created for her wedding to the Dauphin. The Dauphine died soon after her marriage, in childbirth; however, she eventually had the last laugh — the Dauphin became devoted to her and when he died twenty years later, although remarried and with children by his second wife, he asked to be buried beside her.

186. This is the substance of Rousseau's attack on French music: the language is simply unmusical, and has affected even instrumental music.

187. An attack on the plots and the form of French opera seria.

188. However, elsewhere the Nephew, like Diderot in other works, understands the beauty of evil, and they have broken the alignment, common in the eighteenth century, of ethics and aesthetics. Which suggests that 'the true', 'the good' and 'the beautiful' are already stripped of ethical meaning in this passage, and that the Nephew is supplying them as three near-synonyms, to bring in an undercurrent of deliberately off-key religious language (see Jean Fabre's reaction to it, who asks 'if this "trinity" so dear to Diderot is anything other than scholastic verbiage refreshed by a parody in doubtful taste', ed. Fabre, *Le Neveu de Rameau*, p. 222, n. 268). This analogy of cultural and religious change gains purchase a few lines later as a metaphor for how musical styles succeed each other.

189. Hegel quotes this passage (§332) describing cultural change which is both long-prepared and sudden in its effect, like a snake casting its skin.

190. This passage, not quoted by Hegel, seems to point to the structure the German philosopher gives to the development of human culture as a process of opposition and incorporation.

191. Henri Louis Duhamel du Monceau (1700–82), referred to by Diderot as 'le grand', farmer, agronomist, author of *Art du charbonnier*, 1760. He is cited in the *Encyclopédie*. Later (c.1771, i.e. around the time *Rameau's Nephew* was put together) he was involved in a mild dispute with Diderot's friend, Galiani and his brother, about plagiarism (see French edition, p. 118).

Fig. 77 Henri Louis Duhamel du Monceau [n.d.], by Ambroise Tardieu after François-Hubert Drouais (1727–75).

192. *L'Île des fous*, an *opéra mêlé d'ariettes* by Duni; ironically enough, Bertin was involved with Anseaume and Marcouville in creating the libretto.

See French edition, p. 111, n. 233 for further details, and for a relation with Goldoni which deserves investigation. See excerpts at http://www.youtube.com/watch?v=2LYVuIPgOkU.

193. Egidio Duni, *Le Peintre amoureux de son modèle* [*The Painter in Love with his Model*], extract: Arietta: 'Dans le badinage, l'Amour se plait' [Love is pleased with playfulness]

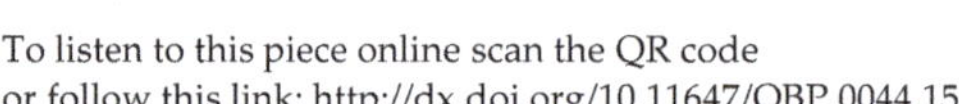

To listen to this piece online scan the QR code or follow this link: http://dx.doi.org/10.11647/OBP.0044.15

Duni's *Le Peintre amoureux de son modèle,* a comic opera in two acts from 1757, parodies an Italian opera. The painter Alberti and his student Zerbin are both in love with a young girl, Laurette, who loves Zerbin but repels the overtures of Alberti. The arietta *Dans le badinage, l'Amour se plait* occurs at the beginning of Act II, when Laurette has learned that she is loved by both men, and thus that she may choose between them. 'In playfulness, Love enjoys himself like the child he is. If he ever wins over me, it will be with gaiety. I want to find all the enjoyment of liberty in my enslavement'.
An *arietta* is a light air which breaks off the thread of the plot to give a character the possibility of expressing a feeling. Its very lightness entails great simplicity in form: here, we have a structure: A A', the second part being identical to the first and written around exactly the same text but in a more virtuoso fashion, with more ornamentation. Unlike an aria, there is no further element which might create a contrast with these two parts.

194. *La Plaideuse, ou le procès*, an *opéra comique mêle d'ariettes,* libretto by Favart, music by Duni, first performed 19 May 1762.

195. More airs from the *Île des fous.* See http://www.youtube.com/watch?v=pHVtS8hVRc0.

196. Airs from Pergolesi's *La Serva padrona.* See http://www.youtube.com/watch?v=xfbhdeSSbPo.

197. Hegel picks these sentences out for quotation. But he is using the Goethe translation, which is not of the same manuscript, the autograph manuscript that we now use. The manuscript used by Goethe has disappeared. I should like here very tentatively to fly the following kite: that the manuscript Goethe

used might just have been supplied not from the group deposited by his daughter in St. Petersburg at his death, as a gift to Catherine the Great, as is usually thought, but by the Princess Golitsyn, who certainly tampered with the trunk in which Diderot's manuscripts had been left for safe keeping with her and her husband in The Hague, while he was in Russia (winter 1773–74). Goethe was certainly in contact with her at various times.

198. French: *Les Petites Maisons,* an asylum founded in 1557 and located in the 6th arrondissement of Paris. The French equivalent of the Bethlem Royal Hospital (Bedlam) in London.

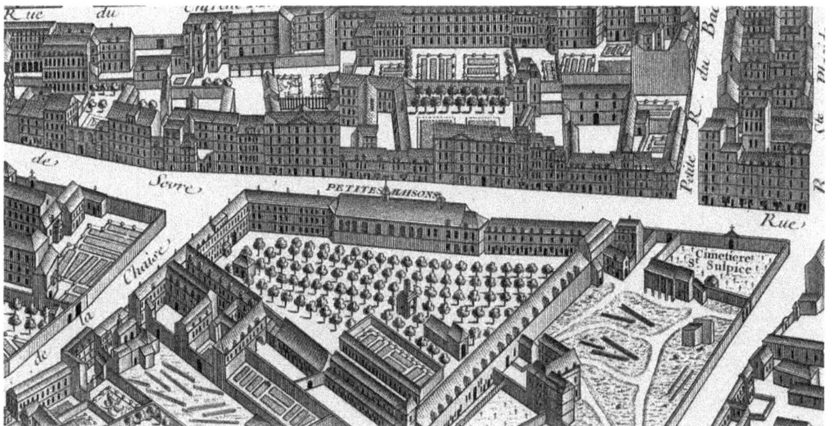

Fig. 78 Les Petites Maisons, detail from the *Plan de Turgot* (1734–39), by Michel-Étienne Turgot.

199. See http://www.youtube.com/watch?v=s5hHwuOISu8 for a beautiful and disturbing excerpt.

200. A translation of *Récitatif obligé,* itself a translation of 'recitativo obbligato'. 'The actor is agitated and transported by a passion which does not allow him to say everything; he interrupts himself, stops, holds back, during which time the orchestra speaks for him', Rousseau, *'Récitatif obligé'*, in his *Dictionnaire de musique.* Michel Noiray defines it thus: 'it is marked off from a formal air essentially because it allows the music to penetrate deeply into the thought of a character' and makes the telling point that Mozart's Don Giovanni never sings such recitative. (*'Récitatif'*, in his *Vocabulaire de la musique*).

201. The last lines of this paragraph are quoted by Hegel while bringing out the kind of mad mixing which, he says, is 'the universal deception of itself and others: and the shamelessness which gives utterance to this deception is just for that reason the greatest truth' (§522).

202. This is close to a passage in Rousseau's *Essai sur l'origine des langues* [*Essay on the Origin of Languages*], where he argues that music can 'paint' everything, even silence: Rousseau, *Œuvres complètes,* vol. V, p. 421. There is no definite date of composition for the *Essai,* although it is certainly connected with the work Rousseau did around his *Discours sur l'origine et les fondements de l'inégalité* [*Discourse on the Origin and Foundations of Inequality*], 1755.

203. *Roland,* 1685, tragédie en musique, music by Lulli, libretto by Quinault, 1685; Act IV, sc. 2.

204. *Castor et Pollux,* 1737, by Rameau, Act II, sc. 2. Diderot has misquoted — the libretto reads 'day'. For the aria see http://www.youtube.com/watch?v=rSKe5WTVR0g.

205. *Le Temple de la gloire,* 1745, by Rameau.

206. Diderot seems here to suggest that grandiose Church music has been left behind in the past, like the setting to music of religious texts. New ones are needed. Diderot had shown an interest in reforming libretti since at least his *Entretiens sur 'Le Fils naturel',* 1757. Rousseau, in his *Lettre sur la musique française,* spoke against large scale Church music and almost immediately mentioned meeting Terradellas in Venice, who criticized large-scale polyphonic music (Rousseau, *Œuvres complètes,* vol. V, p. 308). Diderot, likewise, has the Nephew mention Terradellas only a few lines later.

207. Johann Adolf Hasse, nicknamed 'The Saxon' (1699–1783), born near Hamburg, but worked in Dresden, Vienna, and Venice. His movement between the north and south of the Alps meant that he was a conduit between Italian and German styles. His very numerous operas are largely neglected now, unjustly for many. Several are online in excerpted form, see for example http://www.youtube.com/watch?v=YIz_guxlPdU.

Fig. 79 Johann Adolf Hasse (1740), by Balthasar Denner.

Johann Adolf Hasse, *Cléofide,* extract:
Air: 'Vuoi saper se tu mi piaci?' [Do you want to know if I like you?]

To listen to this piece online scan the QR code or follow this link: http://dx.doi.org/10.11647/OBP.0044.16

Cleofide is an opera seria in three acts, first performed at Dresden in 1731. The libretto, taken from Metastasio, centres on the conflicts between the rulers of the Indies after the conquest by Alexander the Great in 325 BC. A *da capo* aria is typical of eighteenth-century opera or oratorio. It has three sections, the second contrasting in key or mood with the first; the third repeats the first, on which the performer is expected to improvise embellishments as he or she plays. This *da capo* aria in D minor has a middle section in F major which is striking for its concerto-like features, made up of a play of questions and answers between voice and orchestra, and by its use of ritornello. In spite of the basso continuo, the discourse is occasionally suddenly interrupted by long silences, to which the characteristic figure of the ritornello responds, namely the ascending three related notes of an anacrusis which regularly punctuate the air. Anacrusis (or upbeat) is the term for an unstressed note or group of notes at the beginning of a phrase of music preparing for the first downbeat of the first bar.

208. Domenech Terradellas (1713–51). A Catalan, he studied music in Naples. He worked in London for a while. His opera *Sesostri* was a considerable success and has been recorded.

Fig. 80 Domenech Terradellas, *L'Avens* (1884), artist unknown.

209. Tommaseo Traetta (1727–79), trained in Naples like many of the Italian composers mentioned in *Rameau's Nephew*. His music may be being rediscovered — a recording of his magnificent, *Antigona*, 1772, is available, and excerpts can be found at http://www.youtube.com/watch?v=Ae0-dxtyykc. Traetta seems to have been in St. Petersburg at the time of Diderot's visit, since his name, misspelled, is an addition in the margin of the autograph manuscript (see ed. Fabre, *Le neveu de Rameau*, p. 86). One can wonder if they met, or if Diderot heard Traetta's music there.

Fig. 81 Tommaso Traetta [n.d.], artist unknown.

210. 

Nicola Antonio Porpora, *Polyphemus*, extract:
Act III, sc. 5: Aria: 'Alto Giove' [Jove on high]

To listen to this piece online scan the QR code or follow this link: http://dx.doi.org/10.11647/OBP.0044.17

Polyphemus is an opera seria composed for the famous castrato singer Farinelli around the figure of the Cyclops, Polyphemus, son of Poseidon and the nymph

Toosa. *Alto Giove* is one of the composer's most famous arias. This air to the glory of Jupiter takes the form of a *da capo* aria with an air in E minor, a middle section in G major, and reprise of the air without transition, the possible embellishments improvised by the soloist. This aria's accompaniment rests on a writing in repeated notes, the four parts opening out towards the deeper tones, in a depressive movement, before starting out on an ascending movement which leads to a progression of cadences. This motif of accompanying takes on the role of a ritornello and punctuates the first and last parts of the air. The middle section, in a major key, is in contrast through its character and its tempo, andantino.

Nicola Antonio Porpora, *Polyphemus*, extract:
Act III, sc. 5: Recitativo and Aria: 'Senti il fato' [Feel the hand of destiny]

To listen to this piece online scan the QR code
or follow this link: http://dx.doi.org/10.11647/OBP.0044.18

This air, preceded by its recitative, follows the same structure as the preceding. This recitative, by using many modulations, introduces in a very free and natural manner the key of C flat major. This is stressed right from the first bars of the aria by the recurrent motif which is constructed round the two notes which are the poles of this key: E flat and C flat. This allegro is based on a contrast and alternation between these first solemn bars and a rapid and virtuoso movement. Besides the speed of execution of the semiquavers, even demisemiquavers, on the strings, the virtuosity of this air is revealed in the constant utilisation of melisma (several notes, sometimes a good many, on one single syllable), big leaps (sevenths, sometimes even twelfths), with a range of two octaves.

211. Metastasio (pseudonym of Pietro Antonio Domenico Trapassi) (1698–1782), the most important librettist of the eighteenth century, was born in Rome, but spent the most successful part of his career in Vienna. His dramas were set several times over by different composers, including Mozart. He was also considered an excellent poet by his contemporaries.

Fig. 82 Metastasio (19th century), artist unknown.

212. Once more, Diderot's concern with libretti as vectors for the fusing of language and music is clear.

213. Since the work of Daniel Heartz, this 'new style' of music has been identified with the music of the opéra comique, Italian and also French.

214. Rameau claimed to be able to set anything, even the *Gazette d'Hollande,* to music, to Collé's disgust — Collé himself was an excellent comic writer and librettist: Collé, *Journal,* vol. II, pp. 211–12.

215. It has often been remarked that these cut-about phrases resemble bits and pieces of Racine's *Phèdre*. But, and there is a but, Racine's verse is never so disjointed.

216. Diderot has the Nephew wonder here about the relation between the phonic qualities of a language and the sound-scape of the associated music, the point of Rousseau's *Lettre sur la musique française*. The Nephew dates the development of the opéra comique from the arrival of Egidio Duni in 1757; but this seems to have been at the invitation of Anseaume the librettist. That Parma, from where Duni was poached, had a French princess, is probably relevant to understanding his move to Paris. French was *the* diplomatic language at the time; until 1768, Etienne Bonnot de Condillac (1714–80) was tutor to Louis XV's grandchilden in Parma. Duni collaborated with Anseaume, Favart, and later with Diderot's friend, Sedaine. As already mentioned, n. 151, he knew Diderot personally.

217. *Armide,* music by Lulli, libretto by Quinault, Act I, sc. 2.

218. *Les Indes galantes,* Act II, sc. 3. Both this quotation and the preceding are invitations to marriage. Omitting the connection is one of Diderot the writer's most telling characteristics.

219. The Nephew here connects the split between the beautiful and the good to physiology which, for him, is the foundation of character. In this passage, the relation between the Nephew's point of view and a particularly hard, perhaps slightly cynical materialism becomes apparent — a thread that runs through the core of Diderot's sensibility, from the notes to the *Essai sur le mérite et la vertu* [*Essay on Merit and Virtue*], 1745, to *Rameau's Nephew.*

220. French: *espèce,* this is the term picked out by Hegel in §488–89, and left in French in his extended commentary in the section 'Culture and its Realm of Actuality'. He has, it seems to me, almost seized on this word because it offers

two advantages, one possibly social, one intellectual. First, Diderot's work has been honoured by a translation by Germany's foremost poet and intellectual, Goethe. Second, *espèce* as a term of logic, *species*, fits in very well with one of the structures of argument he had inscribed in his *Phenomenology of Spirit*. This is that of the '*besondere*', the particular or special, which in traditional logic mediated between the general, applicable to everything, and the individual, applicable to only one thing.

221. Possibly between Diderot himself and a music master, Bemetzrieder, whom he employed to give music lessons to his talented daughter. Diderot is thought to have had a hand, or more than a hand, in the work by Bemetzrieder, *Leçons de clavecin et principes d'harmonie* [*Lessons for the Clavichord and Principles of Harmony*], 1771, which is usually treated as a work by Diderot.

222. Samuel von Puffendorf (1583–1645) and Hugo Grotius (1632–94), theorists of Natural Law (see figs. 83 and 84). Diderot is thought to have studied for the law, briefly; he certainly studied mathematics, on his own.

Fig. 83 Samuel von Pufendorf (17th century), by Joachim von Sandrart (1606–88).

223. Another of Diderot's dialogues, entitled *Lui et Moi* [*Him and Me*], is very brief, but seems to end with a mention of parricide. The attribution to Diderot has been contested; however, the autograph manuscript is in the Fondation Martin Bodmer, Geneva.

Fig. 84 Hugo Grotius (1631), by Michiel Jansz. van Mierevelt.

224. One can wonder whether this remark is not a satirical side-swipe at Rousseau and his *Emile ou de l'éducation*, 1762.

225. 'HIM' is answering something that 'ME' has not expressed in the actual word-flow of the conversation. Does this point to a careless stitching together of different pre-existing elements of text (see Preface)? Or on the contrary is it deliberate, pointing to the fact that the subjectivities behind the speakers 'HIM' and 'ME' are unstable sometimes, and most strikingly at this point? There are related problems in the text of Diderot's novel, *La Religieuse* [*The Nun*].

226. 'HIM' seems to move here from acoustics to optics (see Diderot's *Leçons de clavecin*, 1771). This passage needs more investigation: by the time he put together *Rameau's Nephew*, Diderot had a long track record of discussing the relation between sound and sight, most notably in *Lettre sur les sourds et muets*.

227. Diderot later wrote a play, *Est-il bon, est-il méchant?* [*Is He Good, Is He Bad?*], based on actual events in his own life. These involve doing good turns, actual ones, by means which approximate to lies. The comedy (which develops *La pièce et le prologue*, distributed in the manuscript journal *La Correspondance littéraire* in 1777) was written over the remaining years of Diderot's life.

228. Diderot, in the *Encyclopédie* article 'Hobbisme', quotes Hobbes, *De Cive*, 1642, preface, while referring to Rousseau's political thought. Another sign that in this part of the dialogue, anyway, there is a kind of reflexion on and writing over of Rousseau's thought.

229. Freud noticed this passage, for obvious reasons (see *Standard Edition of the Complete Psychological Works of Sigmund Freud*, XXI, 1931), quoting it in his expert evidence in the trial of Dr Philippe Halsmann, the 'Austrian Dreyfus' case. Halsmann was tried for the murder of his father. Freud used the universality of the complex in his criticism of the prosecutor's case (which had cited Freud but was so evidently anti-Semitic that the verdict was quashed in 1930).

230. Leonardo Leo (1694–1744), studied in Naples. He created an opera *La 'mpeca scoperta* (1723) in Neapolitan dialect. Unlike other composers of the Neapolitan school, he does not seem to have travelled. He wrote serious operas, including *Demofoonte*, 1735, but his comic operas were more successful. For an excerpt from his opera *Le nozze di Ercole et Iole*, see http://www.youtube.com/watch?v=pfGFtqgypuU.

Fig. 85 Leonardo Leo [n.d.], artist unknown.

Fig. 86 Leonardo Vinci [n.d.], by Vincenzo Volpe (1855–1929).

231. Leonardo Vinci (1690–1730), like Leo, he wrote comic operas in Neapolitan dialect (see fig. 86). In total he is thought to have written about forty operas.

Leonardo Vinci, Twelve solos for a German flute or violin with a thorough bass for the harpsichord or cello, extract: Sonata II: Sicilienne and Allegro

To listen to this piece online scan the QR code or follow this link: http://dx.doi.org/10.11647/OBP.0044.19

Leonardo Vinci succeeded Alessandro Scarlatti at the Naples Royal Chapel. He was a typical representative of the new generation of Italian composers of opera seria, and had great influence on the generations that succeeded him. He was admired for the tender and sorrowful expression of his compositions. Besides a large number of lyric works, he also left some instrumental pieces, published in 1748 in an anthology entitled *Twelve solos by Vinci and other Italian authors*. This sonata exhibits all the simplicity of melody and the flexibility of rhythm which characterized his opera airs, that song which, so Marmontel said, presents the ear with something like a thought completely rendered in music, and thus reveals the deep mystery of melody.

Leonardo Vinci, *Elpidia*, extract:
Air: 'Barbara, mi schernisci' [Cruel woman, you scorn me]

To listen to this piece online scan the QR code
or follow this link: http://dx.doi.org/10.11647/OBP.0044.20

This air, originally written for a castrato singer, offers several characteristics of the opera seria genre: its sombre tonality constrasts with the comic operas from which some of our earlier extracts were taken. This feature is accentuated by the slow tempo and the dotted rhythms; likewise, its form is that of a *da capo* aria, with an air composed out of a theme, a modulating development and a long cadence, succeeded by a part which is in contrast through its key and the use of chromaticism, and which precedes a reprise of the air, this last staying identical though it can be freely ornamented by the interpreter. As was usual in this genre of opera, the air was created specifically for the castrato singer who was to interpret the role at its first performance in 1725.

232. It seems true that Rameau's reputation suffered a much longer and more complete eclipse than other later composers. Yet the *Correspondance littéraire* of October 1778 says of a performance of *Castor and Pollux*: 'people hardly clap; yet everyone rushes to go and the sixteenth performance is as crowded as the first', ed. Maurice Tourneux, vol. XII, p. 173.

233. See above n. 115.

Fig. 87 Mme de Pompadour (1756), by François Boucher.

234. Madame de Pompadour (1721–64), the official mistress of Louis XV from 1745; she was intelligent, educated and for a long time very powerful. The nature of her connection to the *philosophes* is not clear — she is portrayed, for instance, in one portrait by Boucher, with a large volume of the *Encyclopédie* beside her;

there are allusions in Diderot's writings of the 1740s which suggest some kind of perhaps only imaginary acquaintance.

235. *L'Enfant d'Arlequin perdu et retrouvé*, possibly identical with a play by Goldoni, performed at the Comédie italienne in 1761. Mentioned in the *Dictionnaire dramatique contenant l'histoire des théâtres…* by the Abbé de La Porte, vol. I, p. 431 (see https://archive.org/details/dictionnairedram01lapo).

236. The statue of Memnon, so called by early Greek tourists to Egypt, one of a pair to the honour of the Pharoah Amenophis III. After an earthquake in 27 BC one of the statues began to emit strange sounds; the Emperor Septimius Severus most unromantically had the damage repaired in 199 AD. See http://www.victorianweb.org/authors/carlyle/signs/memnon.html.

Fig. 88 The Colossi of Memnon (2011), by Marc Ryckaert.

237. Rinaldo da Capua (1705?-1780?), who is now obscure, despite receiving the approbation of Charles Burney. His *La Zingara* was performed during the *Querelle des Bouffons* by Bambini's company (19 June 1753), and reworked with a libretto by Favart for the Italians and then the Saint-Laurent Fair (source: Bibliothèque nationale de France, catalogue). His work may have recycled others' music, and certainly his was rekitted with different libretti.

238. Giuseppe Tartini (1692–1770), a famous virtuoso who is said to have established the modern style of bowing. He wrote sonatas, including the famous 'Devil's trill'. He mainly lived in Padua, but did work in Prague for a couple of years. See http://www.youtube.com/watch?v=DkFI5mwbAqQ.

Fig. 89 Giuseppe Tartini [n.d.], artist unknown.

239. 

Pietro Locatelli, Six sonatas for three parts, two violins, or two flutes, and bass with a harpsichord, extract:
Sonata op. V no. 2: 1st Movement: Largo-Andante

To listen to this piece online scan the QR code or follow this link: http://dx.doi.org/10.11647/OBP.0044.21

These six sonatas for three parts, which constitute Locatelli's opus V, date from 1746. This extract from the second sonata makes up the first movement, in the key of E minor. It is preceded by an introduction marked largo, and characterized by slowly repeated chords, followed by heavy silences. The whole exposition of the sonata, where the flute and the violin parts supersede each other and then play together over a basso continuo, leads from the key of E minor to the related key of G major, in a movement completely typical of the original sonata form. Then comes a development that leads to a restatement of the theme in the key of E minor. What is particular to this sonata is its writing as a trio with two principal instruments (here a flute and a violin, the composer leaving the choice of which instruments to the interpreters) and a basso continuo — a group that allows a great variety in the combination of different voices, which sometimes respond to each other, sometimes double each other, for example at the interval of a third, and sometimes accompany each other.

240. In Greek mythology, the Danaides, daughters of the King Danaeus were condemned to fill a leaking tub, as punishment for the murder of their husbands.

241. It seems likely that Diderot heard this story from an acquaintance, Isaac de Pinto, whom he had met in Paris, and whom he saw again in Holland. Lewinter implies that the story is told about Pinto, of whom Diderot certainly relates that he had been fined two hundred ducats for 'libertinage vague des hommes mariés' [vague promiscuity of married men], Lewinter, vol. XI, p. 388. Pinto himself was an economist of considerable importance (his work has been more sympathetically studied recently). See *Traité de la circulation et du crédit* [*Treatise on the Circulation of Money and on Credit*], 1771. Amsterdam: Marc-Michel Rey. There is a manuscript in the University of London library. He may have

influenced Diderot in his understanding of probability: 'Lettre à M.D. sur le jeu des cartes' [Letter to Mr D. on Playing Card Games].

242. Lulli was the son of a Florentine miller.

243. An allusion to Montaigne, *Essays*, Book II, chapter 17, 'De la présomption' [On Presumption].

244. René Antoine Ferchault de Réaumur (1683–1757), a scientist, important for his study of the measurement of temperature (the 'Réaumur' scale) and of insects: *Mémoires pour servir à l'histoire des insectes*, 6 vols., with 267 plates, 1734–42. Amsterdam: P. Mortier. It is this work that Diderot is referring to, and the reference drives home one of the inexplicit themes of Diderot's text, that of classification. Réaumur and Diderot were enemies from the beginning of Diderot's career.

Fig. 90 René Antoine Ferchault de Réaumur [n.d.], artist unknown.

245. Jean-Georges Noverre (1727–1810), in many ways the founder of modern European ballet. He was influenced by Diderot's ideas on pantomime, and developed ballets around Diderot's two published plays, insisting in his *Lettres sur la danse et sur les ballets* [*Letters on Dancing and on Ballets*], 1760, that ballets needed content. But Diderot is at this point in the dialogue once more interested in classification, here of movement, the 'positions'.

Fig. 91 Jean-Georges Noverre (18th century), by Barthélémy Joseph Fulcran Roger after Jean Urbain Guérin (1760–1836).

246. Ferdinando Galiani (1728–87), a Neapolitan economist who between 1759 and 1769 was secretary to the Neapolitan embassy in Paris. His most important economic work for the period was his *Dialogues sur le commerce des blés* [*Dialogues on the Commerce in Wheat*].

Fig. 92 Ferdinando Galiani (18th century), artist unknown.

247. One of the most important characters in *commedia dell'arte*, Pantalone is a metaphorical representation of money (see fig. 93).

Fig. 93 Pantalone (1550), artist unknown.

248. In Greek mythology the satyrs were the companions of Pan and Dionysus, and were usually depicted with goat-like features (see fig. 94).

Fig. 94 Attic red-figure plate featuring a Satyr (520–500 BC), by Epiktetos.

249. Nicolas Bonnart's late-seventeenth century drawing illustrates the type of robes that Diderot refers to here.

Fig. 95 *Abbé en Sotane*, from *Recueil des modes de la cour* (c.1678–c.1693).

250. Abbé Gauchat, *Analyse et réfutation de divers écrits modernes contre la religion* [*Analysis and Refutation of Different Modern Writings against Religion*], 19 vols. 1756–63. Paris: Claude Herissant. The Bishop of Orléans seems to have been a key dispenser of Church patronage (see ed. Henri Coulet, *Diderot: le Neveu de Rameau*, 1989. Vol. XII of *Œuvres complètes*, ed. Dieckmann, Proust, Varloot. Paris: Hermann).

251. French: *Contrôleur general,* the office was, according to Marcel Marion, more or less equivalent to that of prime minister, given the condition of the state's finances under the last three Bourbon kings (*Dictionnaire des institutions de la France au XVIIe et XVIIIe siècles,* 1923. Paris: Auguste Picard). Bertin held this office from 1759–63 (i.e. through much of the Seven Years War). Bouret went bankrupt for the last time in 1777, the day before his death (a suicide was rumoured). For their careers and characters see the French edition.

252. See Diderot: 'I [Diderot] don't like acorns or animal lairs or hollow oak trees [he is thinking of the picture of the life of early man that Rousseau has given]. I would like a carriage, a comfortable apartment, fine linen, a perfumed prostitute, and I would put up easily with all the rest of the curses of our civilized state', to l'Abbé Le Monnier, on about 15 September 1755, in *Rousseau: Correspondance complète,* ed. R.A. Leigh, vol. III, letter 322.

253. The figure of Diogenes the cynic bears a complex role among the *philosophes,* see the French edition, pp. 154–55. He also appears at the beginning of Diderot's dialogue, suggesting a more careful construction of the dialogue than is often admitted.

254. Pericles, 5th century BC, was a general and statesman. Lais and Phryne were Greek courtesans. Phryne, fabulously wealthy, made the wonderful offer to the Thebans of rebuilding their city walls, if they would inscribe on them: 'destroyed by Alexander, restored by Phryne the courtesan' (*Encyclopædia Britannica*).

Fig. 96 Bust of Pericles (c.430 BC), artist unknown.

255.

Fig. 97 *The Concert* (1774), by Antoine Jean Duclos.

256. This well known illustration of an afternoon concert is believed to show the child prodigy that was Mozart being exhibited at a social gathering. HIM is proposing a sexually orientated showing off of his wife's talents during a concert he will be giving at a party no doubt later in the day and less sedate. See note 72 for a famous holder of private concerts in his salon.

Fig. 98 *Le Thé à l'anglaise* (1764), by Michel Barthélemy Ollivier.

257. In 1726, after the financial crisis of the 'Law System', named after the Scot John Law — who founded a national bank in France using paper money, which collapsed, ruining many — a more stable monetary system allowing the collection of taxes by a system of 'farming', was set up for the rest of the Ancien Régime.

Every six years the lease of the collection of taxes was passed, or rather sold, to a group of financiers, known as 'Fermiers généraux', or 'La Ferme'. They were 40 in number, and they acquired their positions as tax collectors not only from the group itself, but also from the group financing the whole, and backing it with the huge sums of money needed to buy the position. The interest paid them for this was known as the 'croupe', that is, the 'backside'; in Diderot's text, it seems clear that there is some connection here, perhaps merely a pun. Louis XV was himself a 'croupier'. See 'Croupe', in Marion, *Dictionnaire des institutions de la France*, n. 234.

258.

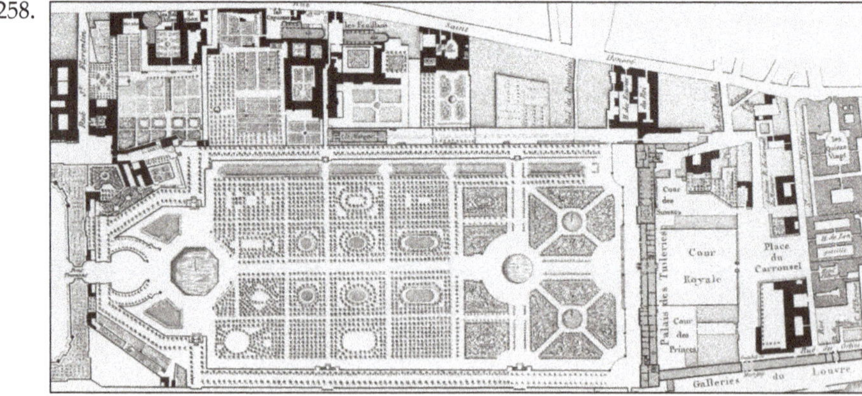

Fig. 99 *Jardin et Palais de Tuileries* (1770).

259. Pierre Chartier, in his edition of the *Neveu de Rameau*, 2002. Paris: Livre de Poche, has explained this joke: the dog's bowl upside-down has the shape of a clerical cap, *la calotte*.

260. Antoine Dauvergne (1713–97), a composer of opera seria — though it isn't clear which one might be referred to here; but also of *Les Troqueurs* [*The Wife Swappers*], often called the first French opéra comique, and performed with huge success at the Saint-Laurent Fair in July 1753. It is interesting that no mention of it is made in Diderot's text. Rousseau disliked it because, one suspects, it successfully brought together Italian-type music and a French libretto by Jean Joseph Vadé (1720–57), an important deviser of libretti for opéras comiques and a writer of one act comedies, some in the *genre poissard*, that is using the dialect of the lowest classes in Paris). This contradicted his theory about the relation of a national language to a national music. Diderot, like Rousseau in his *Lettre sur la musique française*, ends with a reference to Dauvergne, but to his opera seria.

Fig. 100 Mlle Lionnois in Dauvergne's *Polyxène* (1763), by Louis René Boquet.

261. 'We put up with our forebears, each one of us', with this Latin quotation from Virgil (*Æneid*, VI, 743), Diderot brings up the 'anxiety of influence' that seems to run lightly throughout the text. When he quotes it elsewhere, in his *Salon of 1767*, he adds 'says the madman Rameau', Lewinter, vol. VII, p. 205.

262. Etienne de Canaye (1694–1782), celebrated for his learning and his impish sense of humour. Diderot in his *Satire première* (Lewinter, vol. X, pp. 273–86) recounts an evening at the Opéra in the company of Canaye, and Fougeret de Monbron (?-1761), a care-for-nothing and writer of cynical works (*Le cosmopolite ou le citoyen du monde* [*The Cosmopolitan or the Citizen of the World*], 1750) and mildly licentious novels (*Le canapé couleur de feu* [*The Flame-Coloured Sofa*], 1741; *Margot la ravaudeuse* [*Margot the Mender*], 1750).

List of Illustrations

Contributors

Pascal Duc began his career in music working in the Direction régionale for Cultural Affairs in the Paris basin (the Île de France) and as administrator of the Festival of the Île de France. He met Philippe Herreweghe at a moment when the rediscovery of ancient music was taking off in France; this led to a collaboration round the Chapelle Royale with the Orchestre des Champs-Elysées. Pascal then became musical advisor to William Christie and *Les Arts florissants*. He still holds this post while being the Head of the Department of Early Music at the Conservatoire national supérieur de musique et de danse de Paris. Pascal has prepared a great number of working scores for *Les Arts florissants,* among which may be mentioned: Monteverdi's *Madrigals,* Books 1 to 7 (8 and 9 are in preparation); Handel's *Belshazzar* and *Te Deum* HWV 208; Fauré and Messager's *Mass for the Association of the Fishermen of Villerville,* a version for choir, organ, and violin; Purcell's Incidental Music for *The Virtuous Wife*; and for *Distress'd Innocence.*

Marian Hobson is Professorial Research Fellow at Queen Mary, University of London. She is a CBE and a Fellow of the British Academy. Prior to her post at Queen Mary, she was the first woman Fellow of Trinity College, Cambridge, and earlier taught at the University of Geneva. Her main interest is in the form and language in which philosophical writing is couched: her work in two areas, on Denis Diderot and on Jacques Derrida, both develop that interest (cf. *Jacques Derrida, Opening Lines* (1998), and a number of recent articles). She has published widely on eighteenth-century philosophy, in particular a study on illusion and aesthetics in relation to Diderot: *The Object of Art* (1982, 2008; 2007 in French). *Rousseau and Diderot: Networks of Enlightenment* is a selection and translation of some of her articles, made by Caroline Warman and Kate Tunstall (2011). She has edited French editions of three texts by Diderot, *Lettre sur les aveugles, Lettre sur les sourds et muets* (2000), and *Le Neveu de Rameau* (2013).

Kate E. Tunstall is Lecturer in French at the University of Oxford and a Fellow of Worcester College. She is the author of *Blindness and Enlightenment* (2011), which includes new translations of Diderot's *Letter on the Blind* and of La Mothe Le Vayer's *Of a Blind Man*. She has published on a broad range of subjects in French literature and culture from Diderot to Zola, and from Chardin to Racine and silent cinema. She has recently edited the volume of the Oxford Amnesty Lectures, entitled *Self-Evident Truths? Human Rights and the Enlightenment* (2012), and co-edited a special issue of *Romance Studies* on questions of naming and renaming in early-modern Europe, to which she and Caroline Warman both contributed articles.

Caroline Warman is Lecturer in French at the University of Oxford and a Fellow of Jesus College. She is the author of *Sade: From Materialism to Pornography* (2002) and has written widely on eighteenth and nineteenth century intellectual history. She is currently preparing a book on Diderot's late text, the *Eléments de physiologie*. She is also the translator of Isabelle de Charrière's *The Nobleman and Other Romances* (2012). She coordinated the translation by 102 Oxford students and tutors of the anthology *Tolerance: The Beacon of the Enlightenment* (2016), also published by Open Book. She and Kate Tunstall both have essays in the periodical *Europe*'s 2013 celebratory Diderot issue. In 2010, together they wrote and presented a series of BBC Radio programmes on Diderot.

Acknowledgements

Grateful thanks to The Leverhulme Trust for its enabling support of this project. Thanks to Alessandra Tosi, Catherine Heygate, and Bianca Gualandi of Open Book Publishers for their help and encouragement. The music was researched and recorded by the staff and students of the Conservatoire national supérieur de musique et de danse de Paris (Director: Bruno Mantovani), and we should particularly like to thank students from the Department for Training Sound Engineers (Head of Department: Denis Vautrin); the class specialising in recording, artistic direction of recording and post-production techniques (Professor: François Eckert): Guillaume Defer, Raphaël Faverjon, Mathilde Genas, Gaëtan Juge; students from the Department of Musicology and Musical Analysis (Head of Department: Corinne Schneider), in particular the class for the professions associated with musical culture (Professor: Lucie Kayas); students from the Department of Vocal Training (Head of Department: Jean-Marc Demeuré); and students from the Department of Early Music (Head of Department: Pascal Duc). Jean Baptiste Fournier prepared the Notes on the composers and the musical works mentioned. Claude Maury selected the musical extracts and prepared the students. Martin Gester, musical director of the Parlement de Musique (Strasbourg), conducted pieces 13 and 14. Kate Tunstall and Caroline Warman would like to thank Sarah Gracie for her critical and creative reading of the translation, and David Charlton and Tili Boon Cuillé for their constructive suggestions about the first edition of this translation, which we have tweaked in response. Marian Hobson gratefully acknowledges the advice of John Easterling, Trinity College, Cambridge; Mark Darlow, University of Cambridge; Michel Noiray, CRNS; Graham Sadler, University of Hull; Catherine Walser and François Jacob (Director), Institut et musée Voltaire, Bibliothèque de Genève, Geneva. She would like to thank William St. Clair for having suggested the Open Access format, and for making the online publication possible in the first instance; Nicole Vérat-Pant for her long-term support and advice; and most especially, the interest and skill of Max Engammare, CEO of Droz, the publisher of the 2013 paper edition in French (Denis Diderot, *Satyre Seconde Le Neveu de Rameau*, ed. Marian Hobson) which this translation uses. Radu Suciu, Research Associate for Digital Humanities, University of Geneva, has been a constant source of advice and suggestions.

This book need not end here...

At Open Book Publishers, we are changing the nature of the traditional academic book. The title you have just read will not be left on a library shelf, but will be accessed online by hundreds of readers each month across the globe. OBP publishes only the best academic work: each title passes through a rigorous peer-review process. We make all our books free to read online so that students, researchers and members of the public who can't afford a printed edition will have access to the same ideas.

This book and additional content is available at:
http://www.openbookpublishers.com/9781909254909

Customise

Personalise your copy of this book or design new books using OBP and third-party material. Take chapters or whole books from our published list and make a special edition, a new anthology or an illuminating coursepack. Each customised edition will be produced as a paperback and a downloadable PDF. Find out more at:

http://www.openbookpublishers.com/section/59/1

Donate

If you enjoyed this book, and feel that research like this should be available to all readers, regardless of their income, please think about donating to us. We do not operate for profit and all donations, as with all other revenue we generate, will be used to finance new Open Access publications.

http://www.openbookpublishers.com/section/13/1/support-us

You may also be interested in:

Tolerance: The Beacon of the Enlightenment
Translated by Caroline Warman, et al.

https://www.openbookpublishers.com/product/418

A Musicology of Performance: Theory and Method Based on Bach's Solos for Violin
By Dorottya Fabian

https://www.openbookpublishers.com/product/346

The Classic Short Story, 1870–1925
Theory of a Genre
By Florence Goyet

https://www.openbookpublishers.com/product/199